EGOs
EARTH • GALACTIC • OPERATIVES

VOLUME 1
QUINTESSENCE

Created by
STUART MOORE
&
GUS STORMS

image

IMAGE COMICS, INC.
Robert Kirkman – Chief Operating Officer
Erik Larsen – Chief Financial Officer
Todd McFarlane – President
Marc Silvestri – Chief Executive Officer
Jim Valentino – Vice-President

Eric Stephenson – Publisher
Ron Richards – Director of Business Development
Jennifer de Guzman – Director of Trade Book Sales
Kat Salazar – Director of PR & Marketing
Jeremy Sullivan – Director of Digital Sales
Emilio Bautista – Sales Assistant
Branwyn Bigglestone – Senior Accounts Manager
Emily Miller – Accounts Manager
Jessica Ambriz – Administrative Assistant
Tyler Shainline – Events Coordinator
David Brothers – Content Manager
Jonathan Chan – Production Manager
Drew Gill – Art Director
Meredith Wallace – Print Manager
Monica Garcia – Senior Production Artist
Jenna Savage – Production Artist
Addison Duke – Production Artist
Tricia Ramos – Production Assistant
IMAGECOMICS.COM

Originally published as EGOs #1-4
EGOs #0 originally presented via Twitter

Lettering: Rob Steen
Logo/Book Design: Brett Evans
Co-Editor/Production: Marie Javins

ISBN: 978-1-63215-103-2

For international rights inquiries, contact: foreignlicensing@imagecomics.com

EARTH • GALACTIC • OPERATIVES

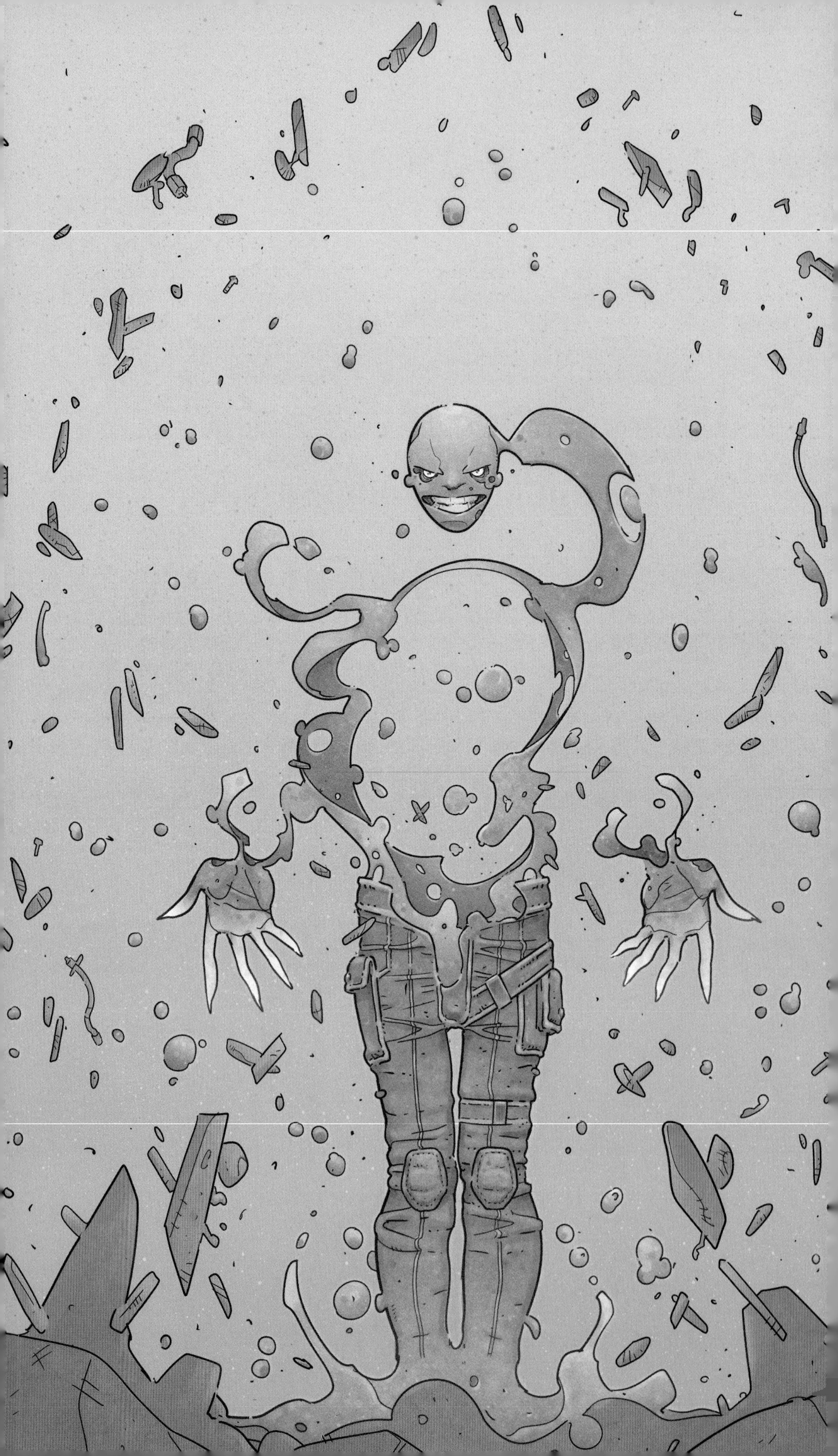

A Word from the Writer/Editor
by Stuart Moore

hen I started work on **EGOs**, I knew what I wanted to do. I wanted to combine the colorful comics tradition of ulti-character hero teams with a more sophisticated, HBO-influenced style of characterization. I wanted to see how uch story and character I could pack into each page without confusing the reader. I wanted a sharp twist at the nd of issue (chapter) one. And most of all, I wanted to write a book that combined a lot of things I loved about genre tion into a tight, explosive package.

lso knew the credit I wanted on the book: Writer/Editor.

hen I got into reading comics, a lot of titles bore that credit—and many of them were among the best books on the ands. Roy Thomas's CONAN and STAR WARS. Marv Wolfman's SPIDER-MAN and, later, NEW TEEN TITANS. Len ein's GREEN LANTERN. Steve Gerber's HOWARD THE DUCK. Gerry Conway's FURY OF FIRESTORM.

nd, of course, everything Stan Lee wrote in the '60s.

here have been Artist/Editors in comics, too, but not as many. Joe Kubert comes to mind, and George Perez shared ditorial duties with Marv Wolfman for a while on TITANS. But for the most part, it's a different skill set.)

ver the years, mainstream comics universes became more complicated and harder to manage. First Marvel and en DC discontinued the Writer/Editor position, preferring the jobs to be handled by different people. This is com-etely understandable; certainly there's an argument that the two roles represent a conflict of interest, especially thin a large corporation.

ut still. CONAN. NEW TITANS. HOWARD THE DUCK.

hen we released these issues of EGOs as singles, only one reviewer noticed the credit. He took exception to it—not om a corporate point of view, but from a creative one. He believed, as many people do, that no writer should try to dit herself. That an editor is necessary because the writer is, by nature, too close to the material; he can't always erceive glaring holes in the story, or how his words will come across to a reader.

m sympathetic to this. As an editor, I've worked with writers who thought they'd written something perfectly clear nd obvious—but while the information was all in their heads, it sure wasn't on the page. And I'm writing a prose oject right now that I could not have pulled off without my smart and helpful editor. It's too complex, has too many quirements, and needs a lot of fine-tuning for all the pieces to fall into place.

GOs, though, is quite literally a different story. I created it, and from the start, I knew how I wanted it to come across. lso had complete control over the story, so I could change details at will if necessary: powers, history, future tech.

nat's not to diminish the contribution of Gus Storms in any way. When he joined the project, he became co-creator nd co-owner. The look of the book is entirely his, and his visuals have influenced the story in countless, fruitful ways. e's also a voracious reader and follower of modern science and science fiction, as you'll see in the dialogue between s that's reproduced at the end of this book. In particular, Gus made a significant contribution to the motivation of asse, the Living Galaxy.

nd, of course, I'm not stupid enough to send out a book without *someone* looking it over. Gus backstops me in that gard, and so does Marie Javins, whose contribution to this book is both vast and easy to overlook. Image Comics as been incredibly supportive; they leave us alone to work, but let us know when something's wrong. You couldn't sk for more.

o sometimes, yes, we all need an editor. But other times—and this really is true—we don't.

nd so, gentle reader, I give you EGOs. As editor, I hope you enjoy the story you're about to read. And as writer, I just ant to say one thing: If you ***don't*** like anything, blame the editor. That's what I always do.

INTRODUCTION

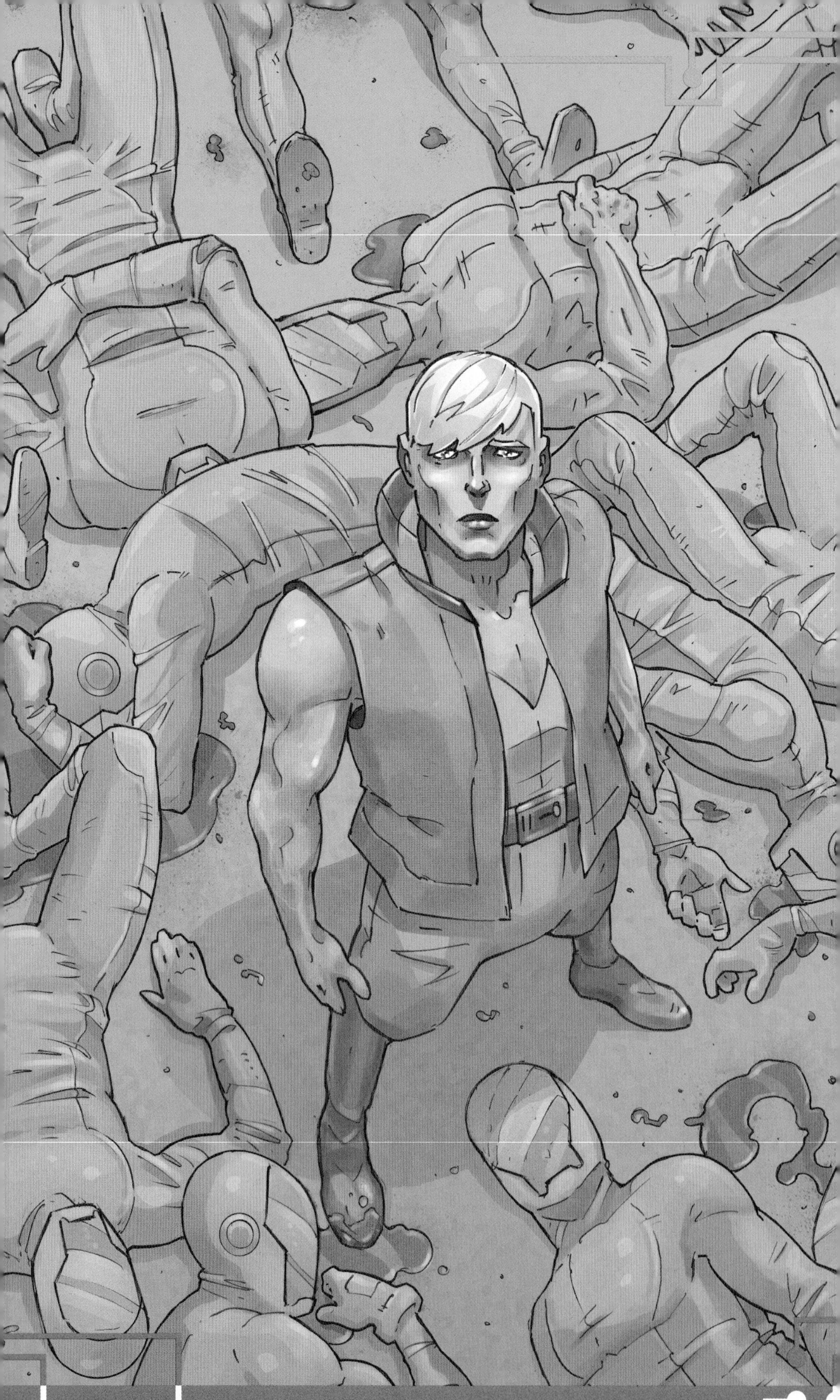

1 DEAD WORLDS

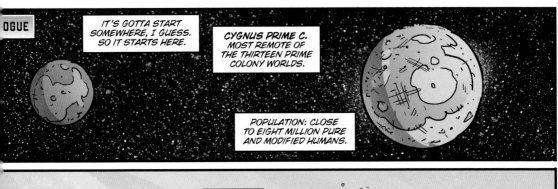

IT'S GOTTA START SOMEWHERE, I GUESS. SO IT STARTS HERE.

CYGNUS PRIME C. MOST REMOTE OF THE THIRTEEN PRIME COLONY WORLDS.

POPULATION: CLOSE TO EIGHT MILLION PURE AND MODIFIED HUMANS.

WHOOPS.

THAT WAS YESTERDAY.

THIS DUDE IS VIGGO RASCH. Y CALL HIM THE PLANETARIAN.

YOU'VE HEARD OF PROFILERS, GUYS WHO CAN TRACK A KILLER BY STARING AT A CRIME SCENE? BEEN AROUND FOR CENTURIES?

VIGGO DOES IT WITH WORLDS.

UNNATURALLY ND PATTERN OF BLAST CRATER.

THE BURN MARKS ON A POWER PLANT, QUINTESSENCE PARTICLES MIXED WITH THE LINGERING SMOKE.

STRANGE BURNED-OZONE SCENT, VERY FAINT ON THE BREEZE.

THE PLANETARIAN TAKES IT ALL IN.

THAT'S HIS POWER.

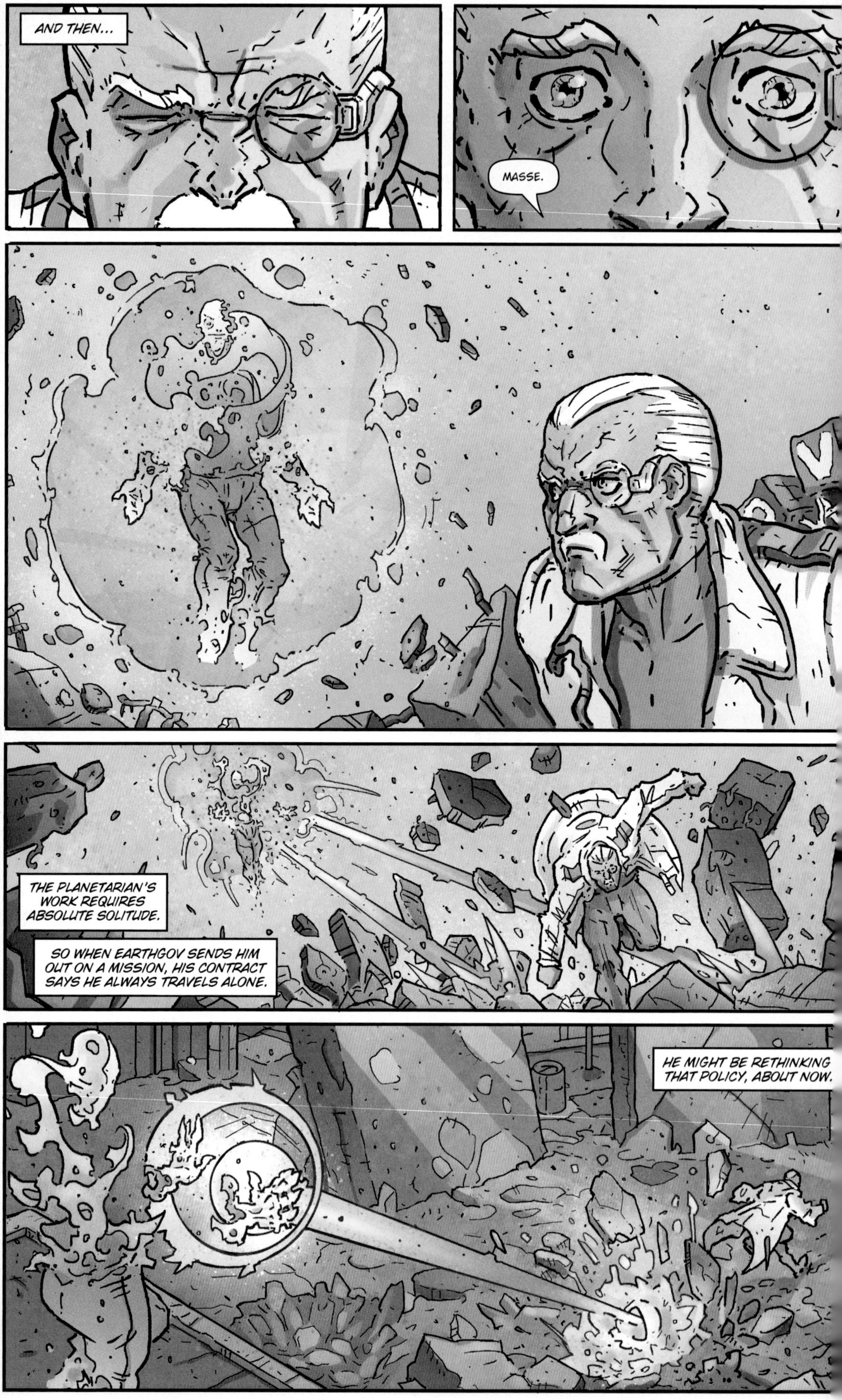
AND THEN...
MASSE.
THE PLANETARIAN'S WORK REQUIRES ABSOLUTE SOLITUDE.
SO WHEN EARTHGOV SENDS HIM OUT ON A MISSION, HIS CONTRACT SAYS HE ALWAYS TRAVELS ALONE.
HE MIGHT BE RETHINKING THAT POLICY, ABOUT NOW.

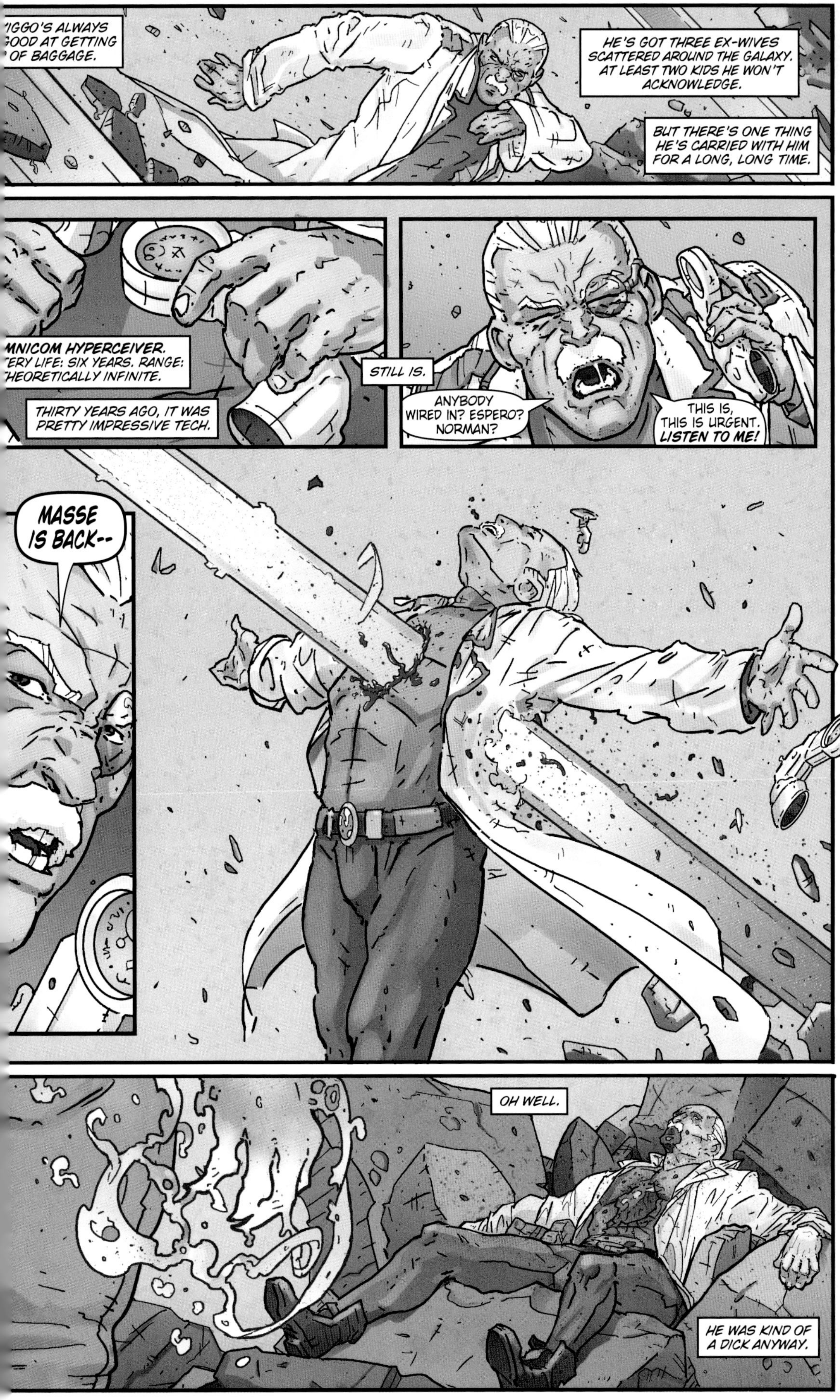

IGGO'S ALWAYS
GOOD AT GETTING
OF BAGGAGE.
HE'S GOT THREE EX-WIVES SCATTERED AROUND THE GALAXY. AT LEAST TWO KIDS HE WON'T ACKNOWLEDGE.
BUT THERE'S ONE THING HE'S CARRIED WITH HIM FOR A LONG, LONG TIME.
MNICOM HYPERCEIVER.
TERY LIFE: SIX YEARS. RANGE:
THEORETICALLY INFINITE.
THIRTY YEARS AGO, IT WAS PRETTY IMPRESSIVE TECH.
STILL IS.
ANYBODY WIRED IN? ESPERO? NORMAN?
THIS IS, THIS IS URGENT. LISTEN TO ME!
MASSE IS BACK--
OH WELL.
HE WAS KIND OF A DICK ANYWAY.

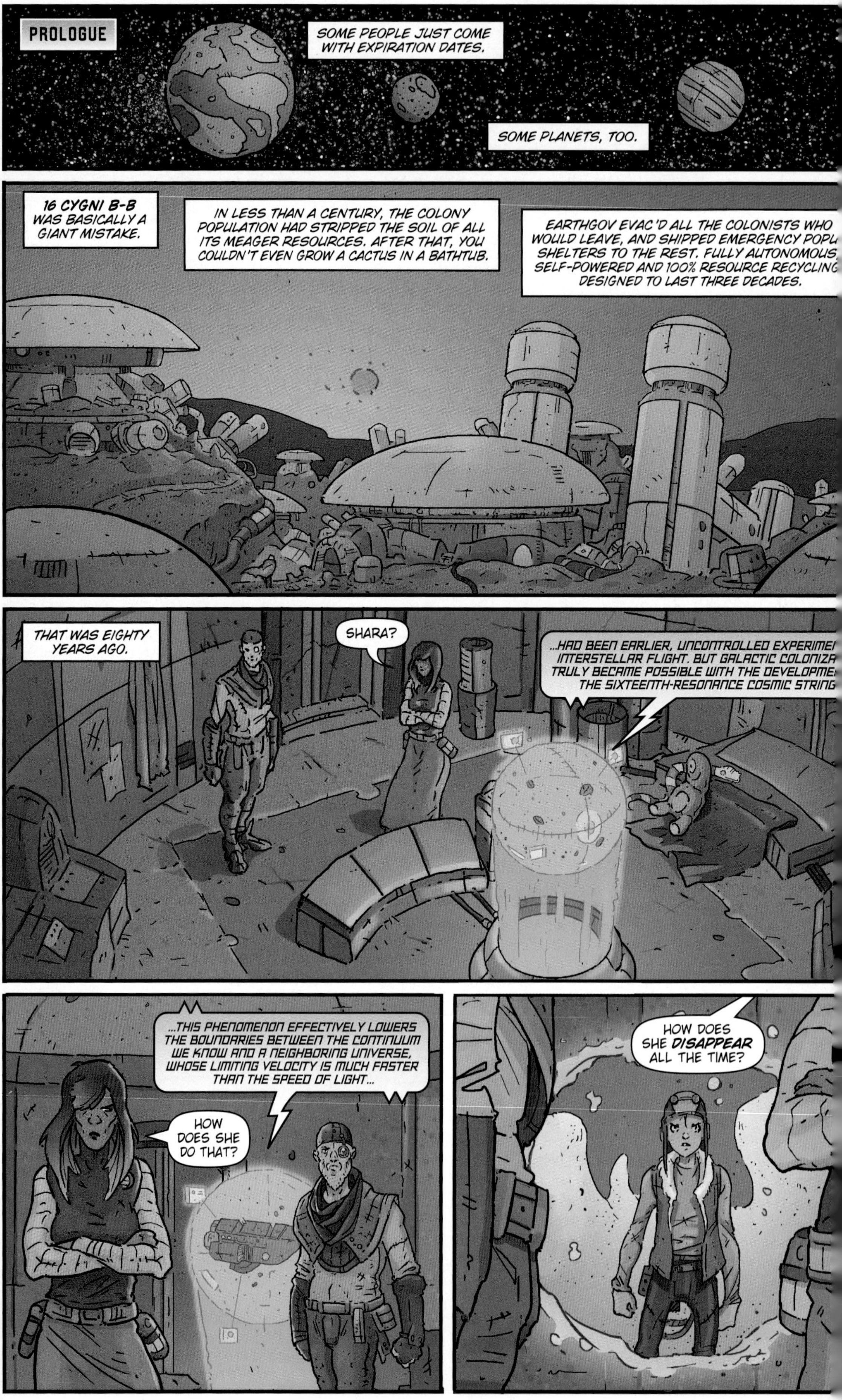
PROLOGUE
SOME PEOPLE JUST COME WITH EXPIRATION DATES.
SOME PLANETS, TOO.
16 CYGNI B-B WAS BASICALLY A GIANT MISTAKE.
IN LESS THAN A CENTURY, THE COLONY POPULATION HAD STRIPPED THE SOIL OF ALL ITS MEAGER RESOURCES. AFTER THAT, YOU COULDN'T EVEN GROW A CACTUS IN A BATHTUB.
EARTHGOV EVAC'D ALL THE COLONISTS WHO WOULD LEAVE, AND SHIPPED EMERGENCY POPU SHELTERS TO THE REST. FULLY AUTONOMOUS, SELF-POWERED AND 100% RESOURCE RECYCLING DESIGNED TO LAST THREE DECADES.
THAT WAS EIGHTY YEARS AGO.
SHARA?
...HAD BEEN EARLIER, UNCONTROLLED EXPERIME INTERSTELLAR FLIGHT. BUT GALACTIC COLONIZA TRULY BECAME POSSIBLE WITH THE DEVELOPME THE SIXTEENTH-RESONANCE COSMIC STRING
...THIS PHENOMENON EFFECTIVELY LOWERS THE BOUNDARIES BETWEEN THE CONTINUUM WE KNOW AND A NEIGHBORING UNIVERSE, WHOSE LIMITING VELOCITY IS MUCH FASTER THAN THE SPEED OF LIGHT...
HOW DOES SHE DO THAT?
HOW DOES SHE DISAPPEAR ALL THE TIME?

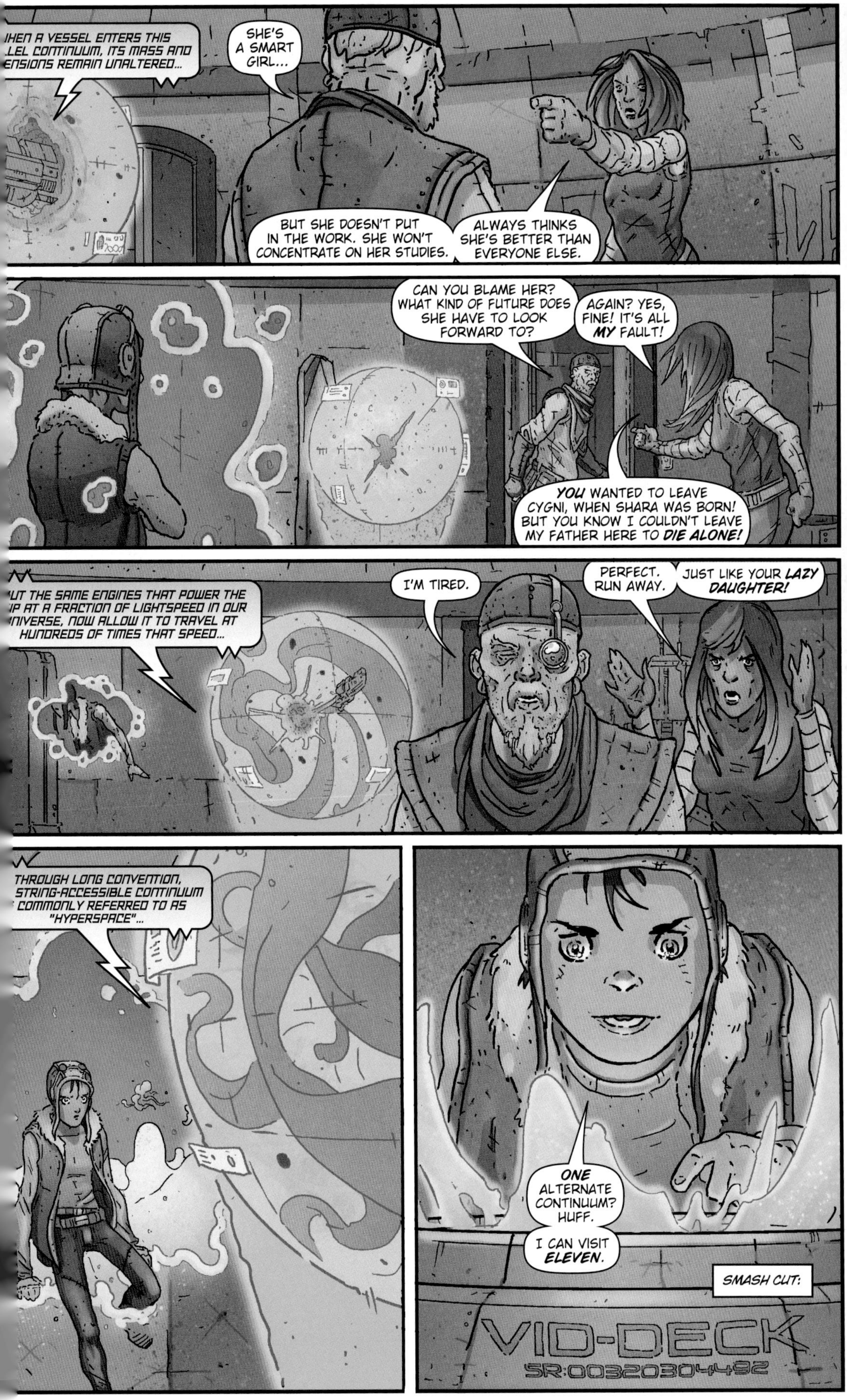
HEN A VESSEL ENTERS THIS LLEL CONTINUUM, ITS MASS AND ENSIONS REMAIN UNALTERED...
SHE'S A SMART GIRL...
BUT SHE DOESN'T PUT IN THE WORK. SHE WON'T CONCENTRATE ON HER STUDIES.
ALWAYS THINKS SHE'S BETTER THAN EVERYONE ELSE.
CAN YOU BLAME HER? WHAT KIND OF FUTURE DOES SHE HAVE TO LOOK FORWARD TO?
AGAIN? YES, FINE! IT'S ALL **MY** FAULT!
YOU WANTED TO LEAVE CYGNI, WHEN SHARA WAS BORN! BUT YOU KNOW I COULDN'T LEAVE MY FATHER HERE TO ***DIE ALONE!***
UT THE SAME ENGINES THAT POWER THE IP AT A FRACTION OF LIGHTSPEED IN OUR NIVERSE, NOW ALLOW IT TO TRAVEL AT HUNDREDS OF TIMES THAT SPEED...
I'M TIRED.
PERFECT. RUN AWAY.
JUST LIKE YOUR ***LAZY DAUGHTER!***
THROUGH LONG CONVENTION, STRING-ACCESSIBLE CONTINUUM COMMONLY REFERRED TO AS "HYPERSPACE"...
ONE ALTERNATE CONTINUUM? HUFF.
I CAN VISIT ***ELEVEN.***
SMASH CUT:
VID-DECK
SR:00320304492

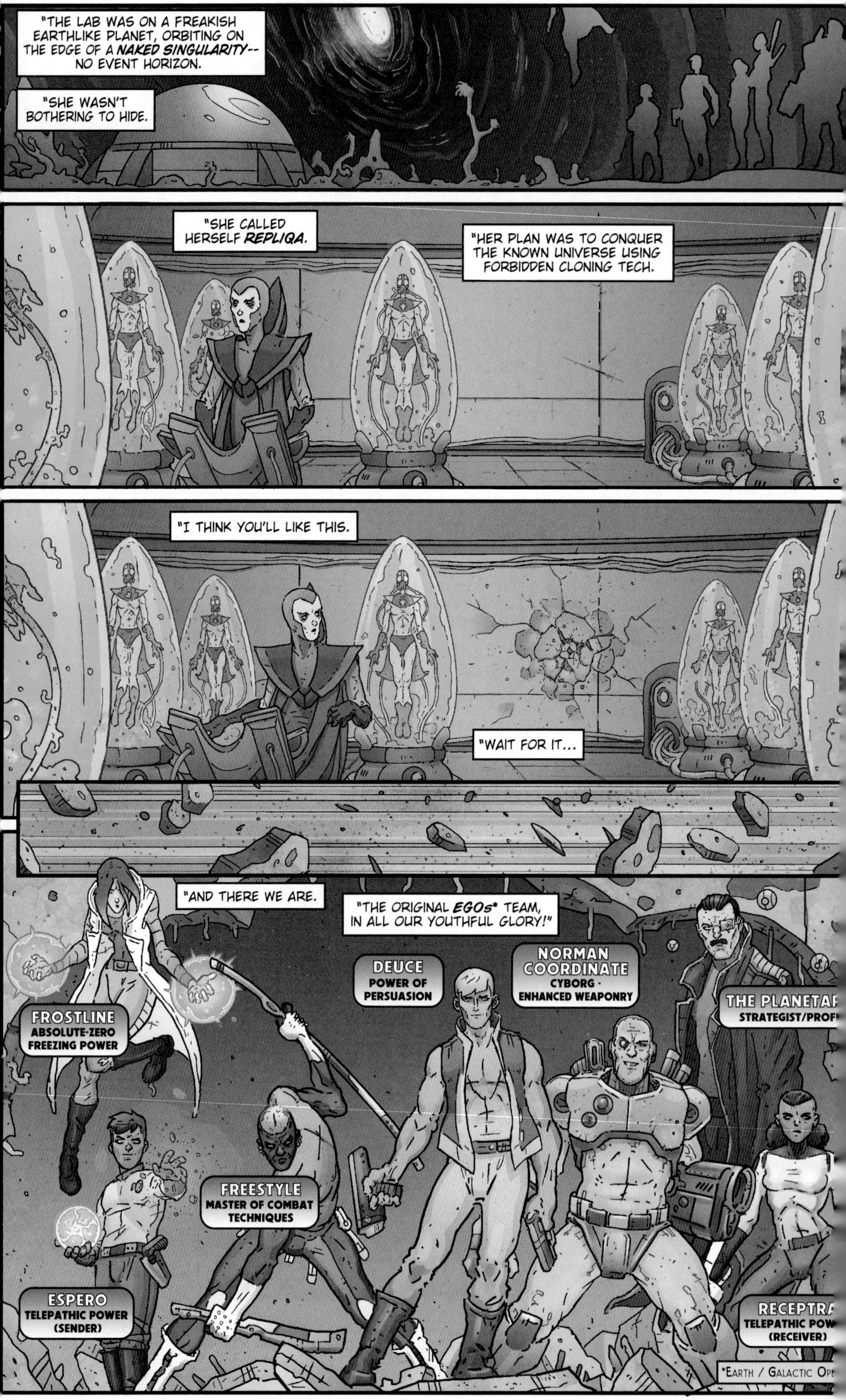
"THE LAB WAS ON A FREAKISH EARTHLIKE PLANET, ORBITING ON THE EDGE OF A NAKED SINGULARITY-- NO EVENT HORIZON.
"SHE WASN'T BOTHERING TO HIDE.
"SHE CALLED HERSELF REPLIQA.
"HER PLAN WAS TO CONQUER THE KNOWN UNIVERSE USING FORBIDDEN CLONING TECH.
"I THINK YOU'LL LIKE THIS.
"WAIT FOR IT...
"AND THERE WE ARE.
"THE ORIGINAL EGOs* TEAM, IN ALL OUR YOUTHFUL GLORY!"
DEUCE POWER OF PERSUASION
NORMAN COORDINATE CYBORG - ENHANCED WEAPONRY
THE PLANETAR STRATEGIST/PROF
FROSTLINE ABSOLUTE-ZERO FREEZING POWER
FREESTYLE MASTER OF COMBAT TECHNIQUES
ESPERO TELEPATHIC POWER (SENDER)
RECEPTRA TELEPATHIC POW (RECEIVER)
*EARTH / GALACTIC OP

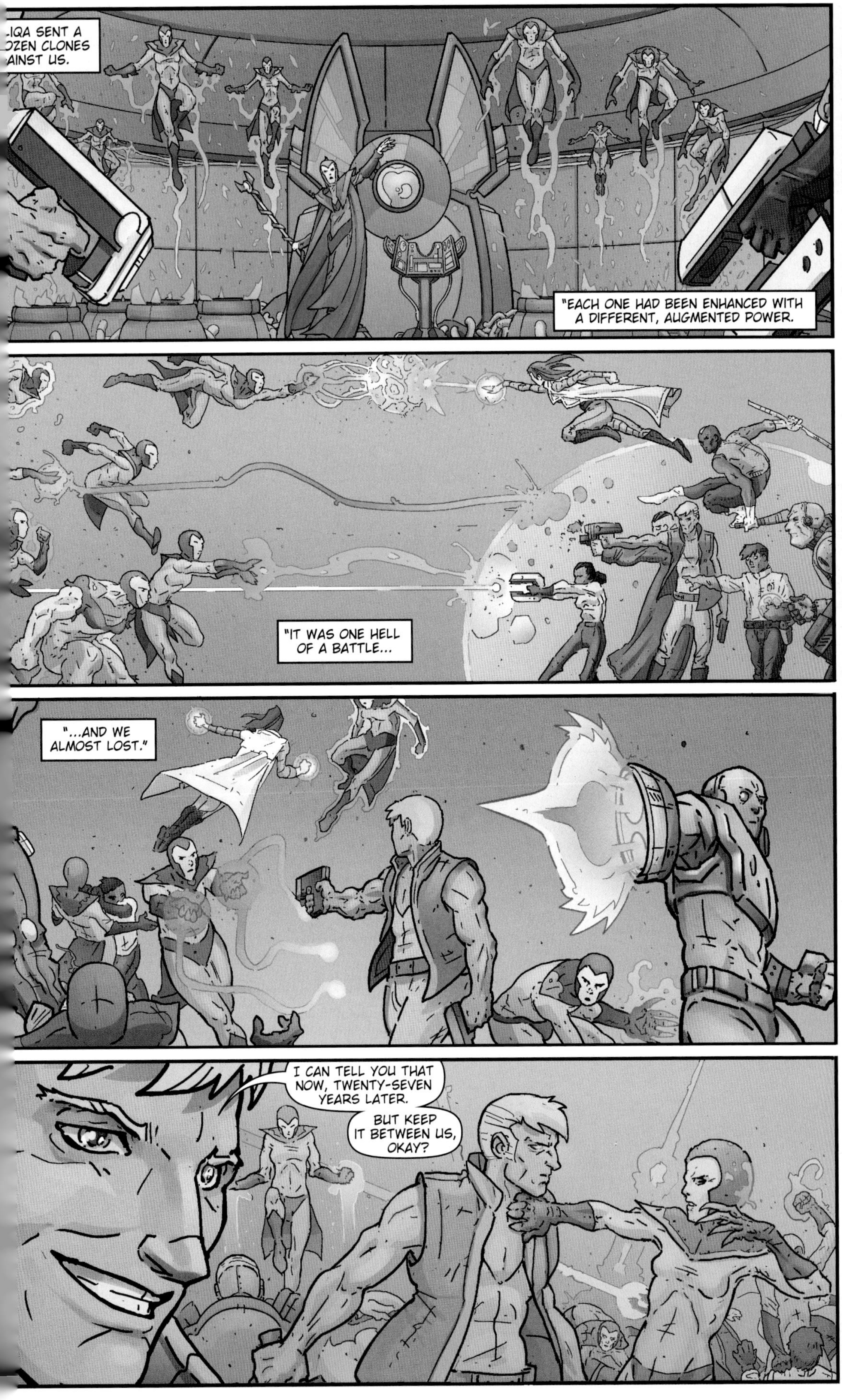

LIQA SENT A DOZEN CLONES AGAINST US.
"EACH ONE HAD BEEN ENHANCED WITH A DIFFERENT, AUGMENTED POWER.
"IT WAS ONE HELL OF A BATTLE...
"...AND WE ALMOST LOST."
I CAN TELL YOU THAT NOW, TWENTY-SEVEN YEARS LATER.
BUT KEEP IT BETWEEN US, OKAY?

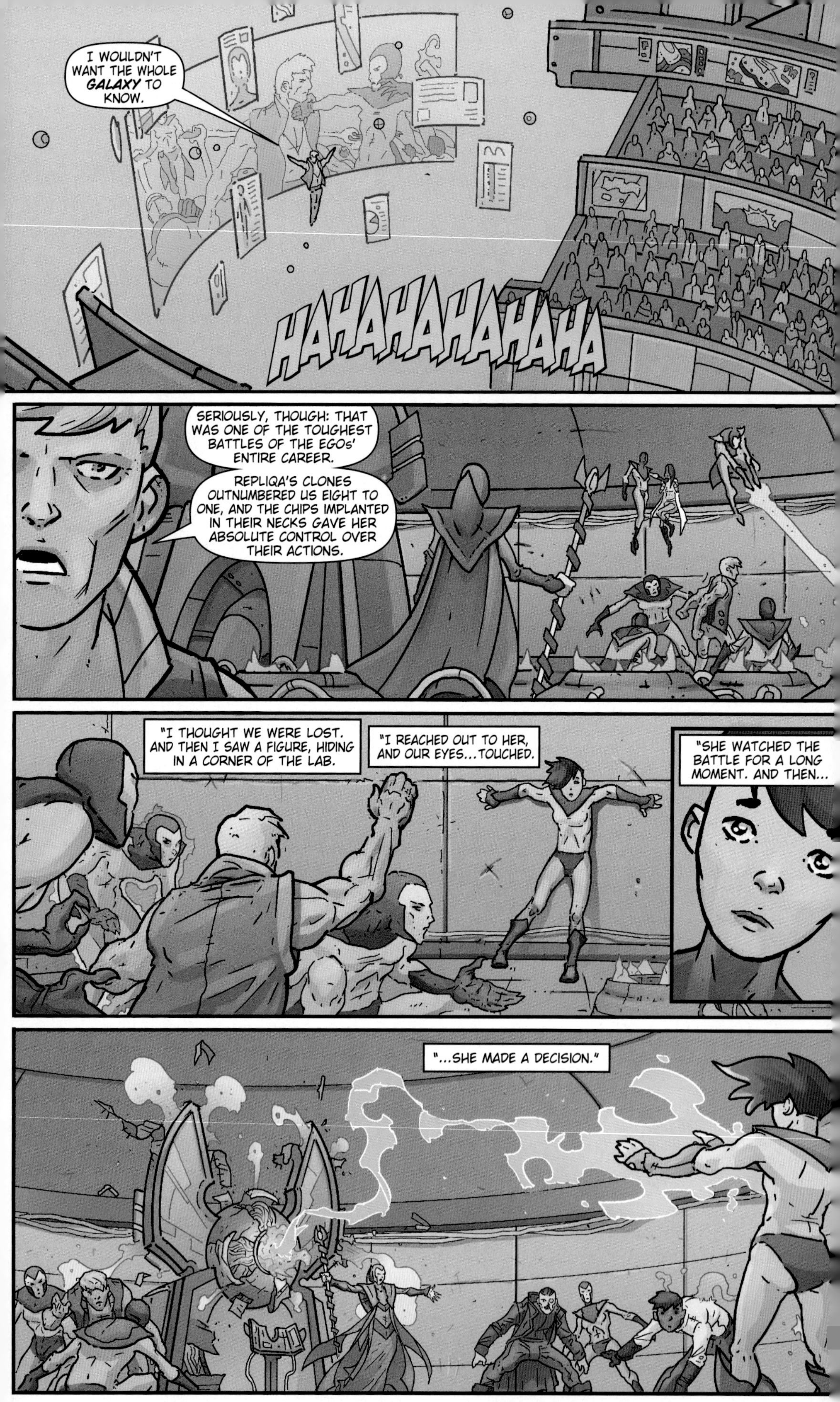
I WOULDN'T WANT THE WHOLE **GALAXY** TO KNOW.
HAHAHAHAHAHAHA
SERIOUSLY, THOUGH: THAT WAS ONE OF THE TOUGHEST BATTLES OF THE EGOs' ENTIRE CAREER.
REPLIQA'S CLONES OUTNUMBERED US EIGHT TO ONE, AND THE CHIPS IMPLANTED IN THEIR NECKS GAVE HER ABSOLUTE CONTROL OVER THEIR ACTIONS.
"I THOUGHT WE WERE LOST. AND THEN I SAW A FIGURE, HIDING IN A CORNER OF THE LAB.
"I REACHED OUT TO HER, AND OUR EYES...TOUCHED.
"SHE WATCHED THE BATTLE FOR A LONG MOMENT. AND THEN...
"...SHE MADE A DECISION."

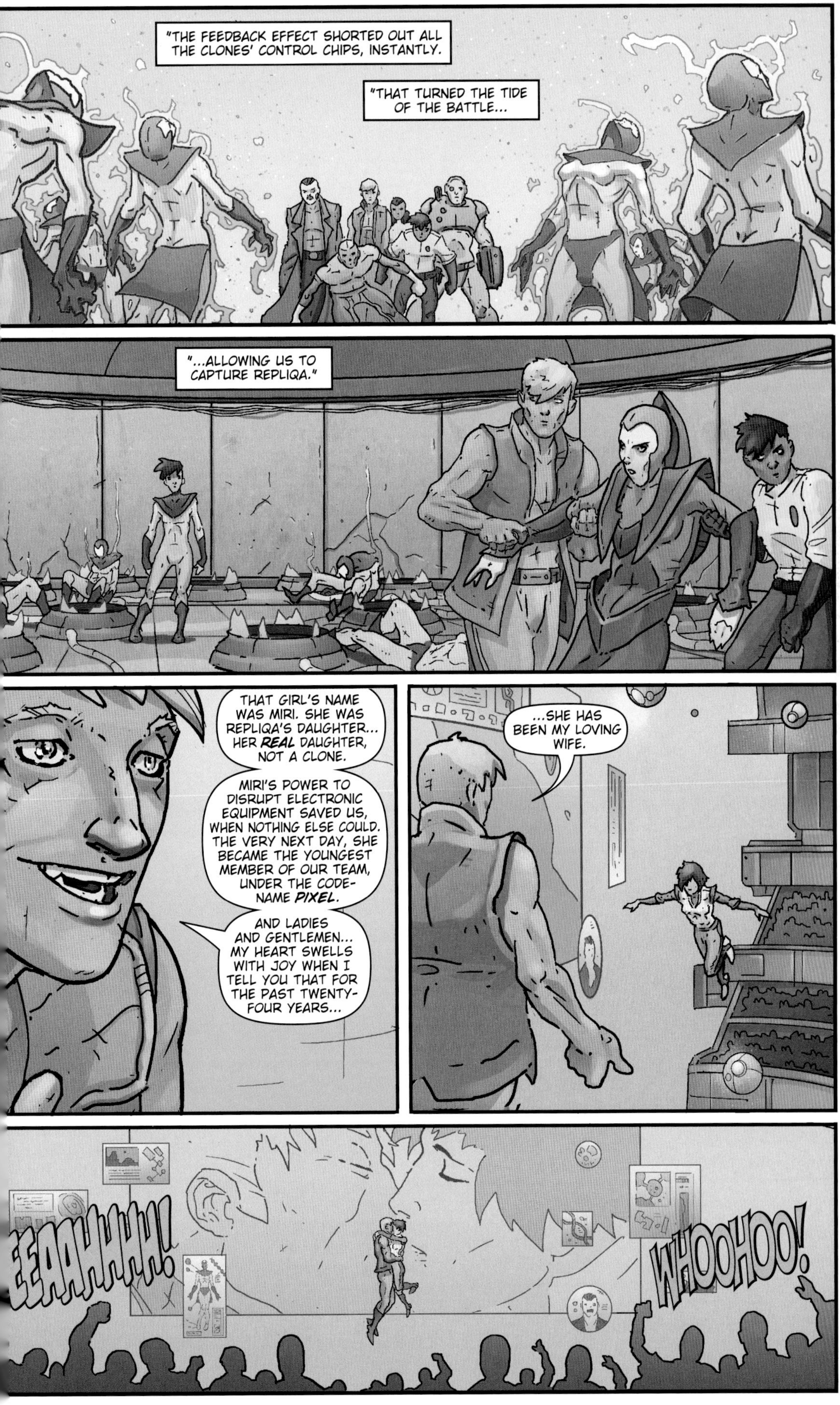
"THE FEEDBACK EFFECT SHORTED OUT ALL THE CLONES' CONTROL CHIPS, INSTANTLY.
"THAT TURNED THE TIDE OF THE BATTLE...
"...ALLOWING US TO CAPTURE REPLIQA."
THAT GIRL'S NAME WAS MIRI. SHE WAS REPLIQA'S DAUGHTER... HER **REAL** DAUGHTER, NOT A CLONE.
MIRI'S POWER TO DISRUPT ELECTRONIC EQUIPMENT SAVED US, WHEN NOTHING ELSE COULD. THE VERY NEXT DAY, SHE BECAME THE YOUNGEST MEMBER OF OUR TEAM, UNDER THE CODE-NAME ***PIXEL***.
AND LADIES AND GENTLEMEN... MY HEART SWELLS WITH JOY WHEN I TELL YOU THAT FOR THE PAST TWENTY-FOUR YEARS...
...SHE HAS BEEN MY LOVING WIFE.
EEAAHHHH!
WHOOHOO!

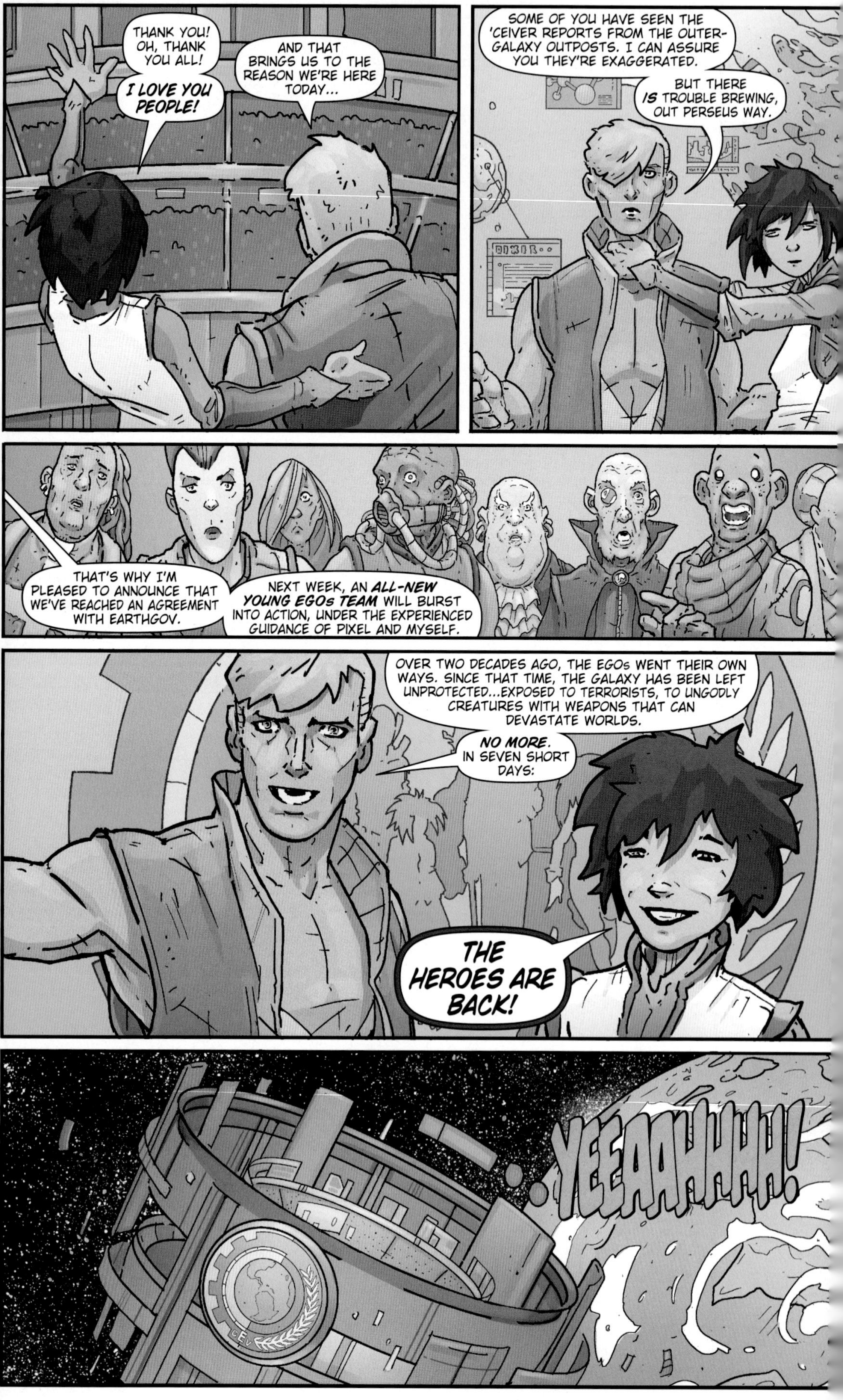
THANK YOU! OH, THANK YOU ALL!
I LOVE YOU PEOPLE!
AND THAT BRINGS US TO THE REASON WE'RE HERE TODAY...
SOME OF YOU HAVE SEEN THE 'CEIVER REPORTS FROM THE OUTER-GALAXY OUTPOSTS. I CAN ASSURE YOU THEY'RE EXAGGERATED.
BUT THERE IS TROUBLE BREWING, OUT PERSEUS WAY.
THAT'S WHY I'M PLEASED TO ANNOUNCE THAT WE'VE REACHED AN AGREEMENT WITH EARTHGOV.
NEXT WEEK, AN ALL-NEW YOUNG EGOs TEAM WILL BURST INTO ACTION, UNDER THE EXPERIENCED GUIDANCE OF PIXEL AND MYSELF.
OVER TWO DECADES AGO, THE EGOs WENT THEIR OWN WAYS. SINCE THAT TIME, THE GALAXY HAS BEEN LEFT UNPROTECTED...EXPOSED TO TERRORISTS, TO UNGODLY CREATURES WITH WEAPONS THAT CAN DEVASTATE WORLDS.
NO MORE. IN SEVEN SHORT DAYS:
THE HEROES ARE BACK!
YEEAAHHHH!

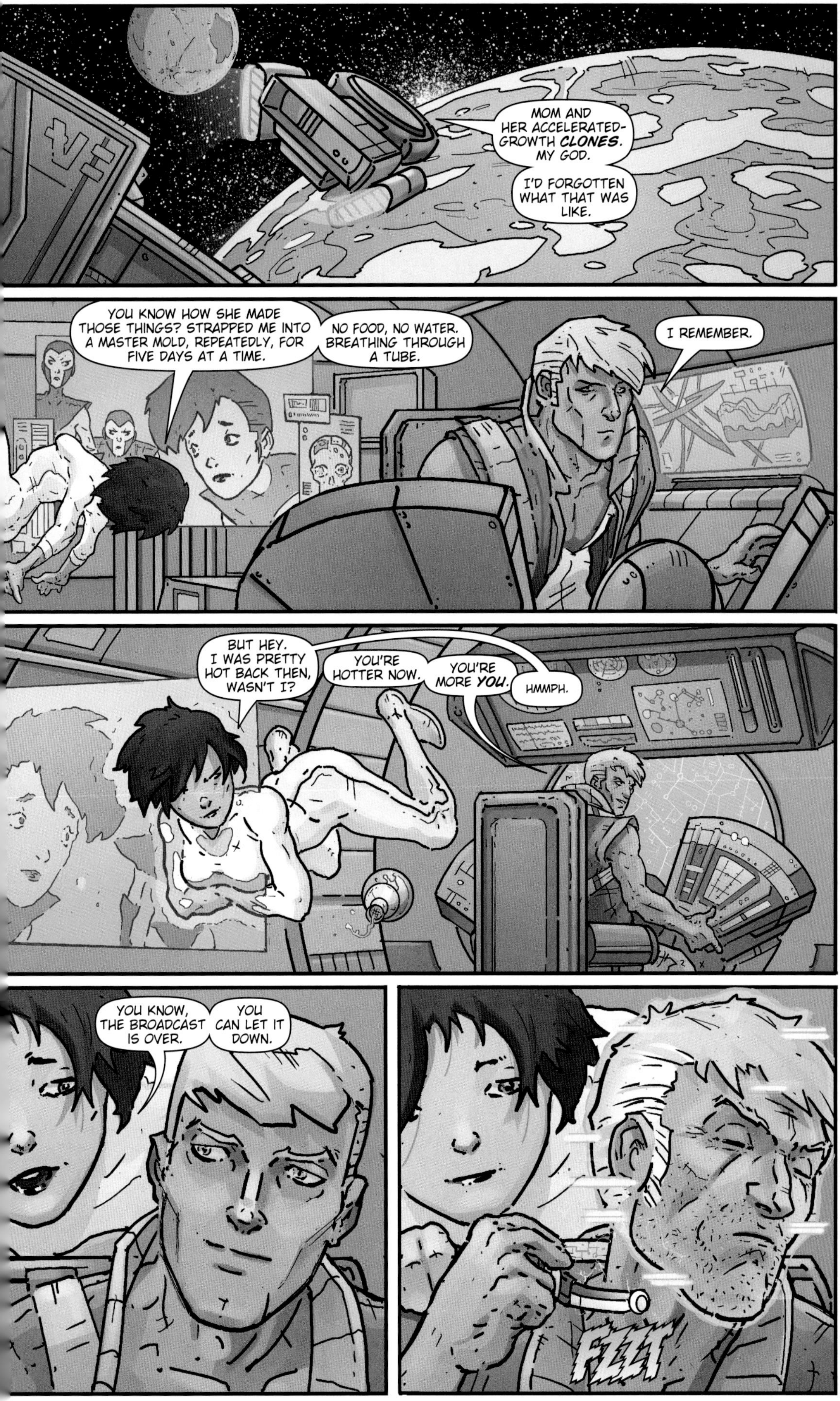
MOM AND HER ACCELERATED-GROWTH **CLONES**. MY GOD.
I'D FORGOTTEN WHAT THAT WAS LIKE.
YOU KNOW HOW SHE MADE THOSE THINGS? STRAPPED ME INTO A MASTER MOLD, REPEATEDLY, FOR FIVE DAYS AT A TIME.
NO FOOD, NO WATER. BREATHING THROUGH A TUBE.
I REMEMBER.
BUT HEY. I WAS PRETTY HOT BACK THEN, WASN'T I?
YOU'RE HOTTER NOW.
YOU'RE MORE ***YOU***.
HMMPH.
YOU KNOW, THE BROADCAST IS OVER.
YOU CAN LET IT DOWN.
FZZT

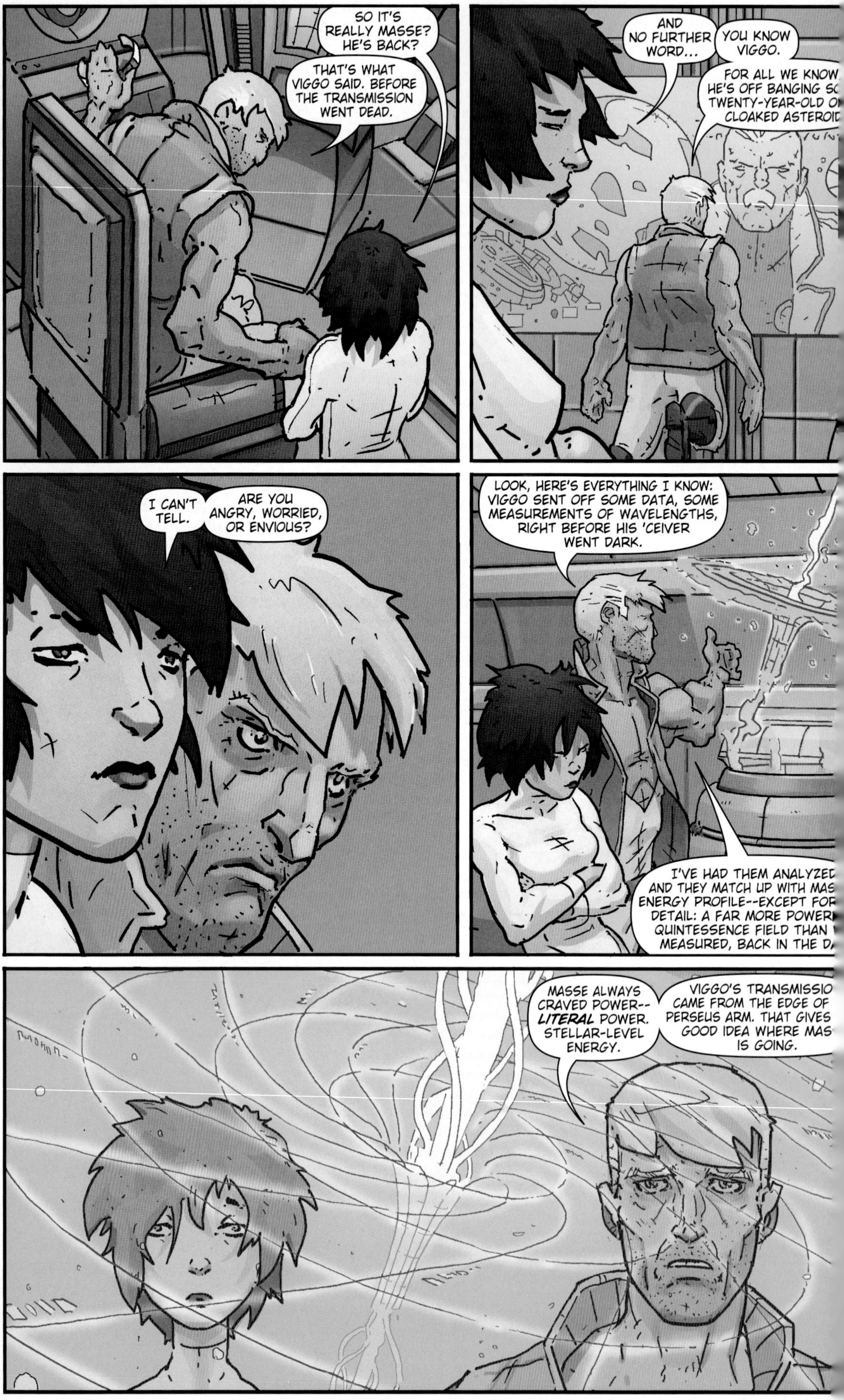
SO IT'S REALLY MASSE? HE'S BACK?
THAT'S WHAT VIGGO SAID. BEFORE THE TRANSMISSION WENT DEAD.
AND NO FURTHER WORD...
YOU KNOW VIGGO.
FOR ALL WE KNOW HE'S OFF BANGING SO TWENTY-YEAR-OLD O CLOAKED ASTEROID
I CAN'T TELL.
ARE YOU ANGRY, WORRIED, OR ENVIOUS?
LOOK, HERE'S EVERYTHING I KNOW: VIGGO SENT OFF SOME DATA, SOME MEASUREMENTS OF WAVELENGTHS, RIGHT BEFORE HIS 'CEIVER WENT DARK.
I'VE HAD THEM ANALYZED AND THEY MATCH UP WITH MAS ENERGY PROFILE--EXCEPT FOR DETAIL: A FAR MORE POWER QUINTESSENCE FIELD THAN MEASURED, BACK IN THE DA
MASSE ALWAYS CRAVED POWER-- *LITERAL* POWER. STELLAR-LEVEL ENERGY.
VIGGO'S TRANSMISSIO CAME FROM THE EDGE OF PERSEUS ARM. THAT GIVES GOOD IDEA WHERE MAS IS GOING.

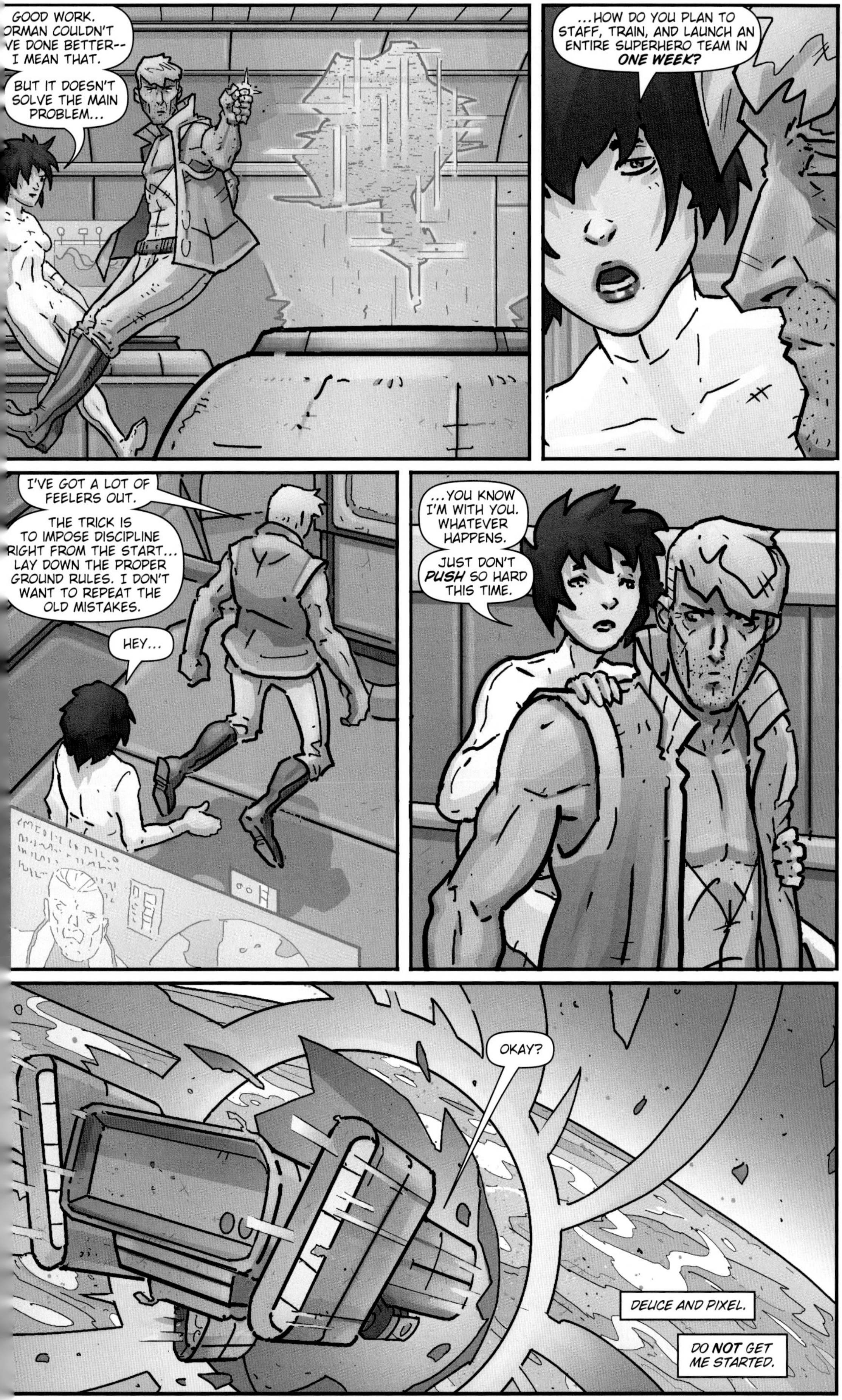
GOOD WORK. ORMAN COULDN'T VE DONE BETTER-- I MEAN THAT.
BUT IT DOESN'T SOLVE THE MAIN PROBLEM...
...HOW DO YOU PLAN TO STAFF, TRAIN, AND LAUNCH AN ENTIRE SUPERHERO TEAM IN ONE WEEK?
I'VE GOT A LOT OF FEELERS OUT.
THE TRICK IS TO IMPOSE DISCIPLINE RIGHT FROM THE START... LAY DOWN THE PROPER GROUND RULES. I DON'T WANT TO REPEAT THE OLD MISTAKES.
HEY...
...YOU KNOW I'M WITH YOU. WHATEVER HAPPENS.
JUST DON'T PUSH SO HARD THIS TIME.
OKAY?
DEUCE AND PIXEL.
DO NOT GET ME STARTED.

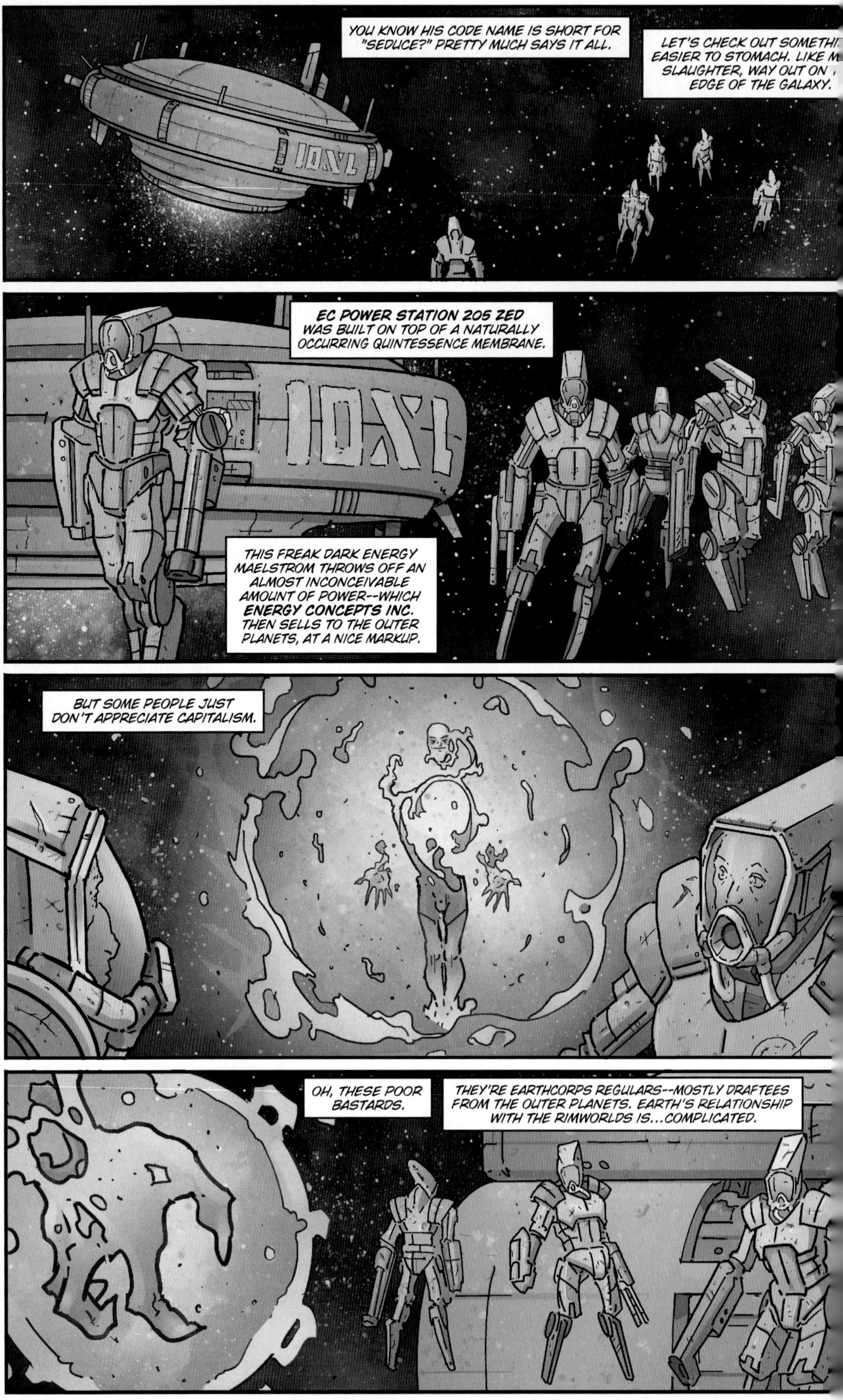
YOU KNOW HIS CODE NAME IS SHORT FOR "SEDUCE?" PRETTY MUCH SAYS IT ALL.
LET'S CHECK OUT SOMETHI EASIER TO STOMACH. LIKE M SLAUGHTER, WAY OUT ON EDGE OF THE GALAXY.
10XL
EC POWER STATION 205 ZED WAS BUILT ON TOP OF A NATURALLY OCCURRING QUINTESSENCE MEMBRANE.
10XL
THIS FREAK DARK ENERGY MAELSTROM THROWS OFF AN ALMOST INCONCEIVABLE AMOUNT OF POWER--WHICH ENERGY CONCEPTS INC. THEN SELLS TO THE OUTER PLANETS, AT A NICE MARKUP.
BUT SOME PEOPLE JUST DON'T APPRECIATE CAPITALISM.
OH, THESE POOR BASTARDS.
THEY'RE EARTHCORPS REGULARS--MOSTLY DRAFTEES FROM THE OUTER PLANETS. EARTH'S RELATIONSHIP WITH THE RIMWORLDS IS...COMPLICATED.

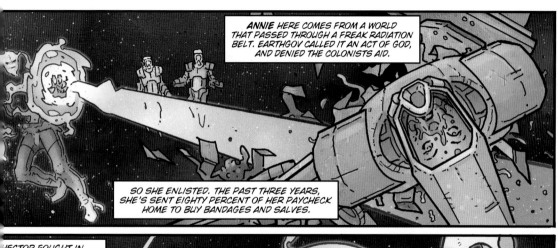

ANNIE HERE COMES FROM A WORLD THAT PASSED THROUGH A FREAK RADIATION BELT. EARTHGOV CALLED IT AN ACT OF GOD, AND DENIED THE COLONISTS AID.

SO SHE ENLISTED. THE PAST THREE YEARS, SHE'S SENT EIGHTY PERCENT OF HER PAYCHECK HOME TO BUY BANDAGES AND SALVES.

HECTOR FOUGHT IN CRUNCH WAR. THAT'S RIGHT, THE BIG ONE.

HE OUTLIVED ALL OF 'EM, AND THEN HIS PENSION RAN OUT. WHAT ELSE WAS THERE TO DO BUT REENLIST?

SUCKS TO BE JUST ABOUT EVERYONE, THESE DAYS.

OH! OH, I JUST REALIZED SOMETHING!

YOU PROBABLY THINK THIS GUY IS MASSE, DON'T YOU?

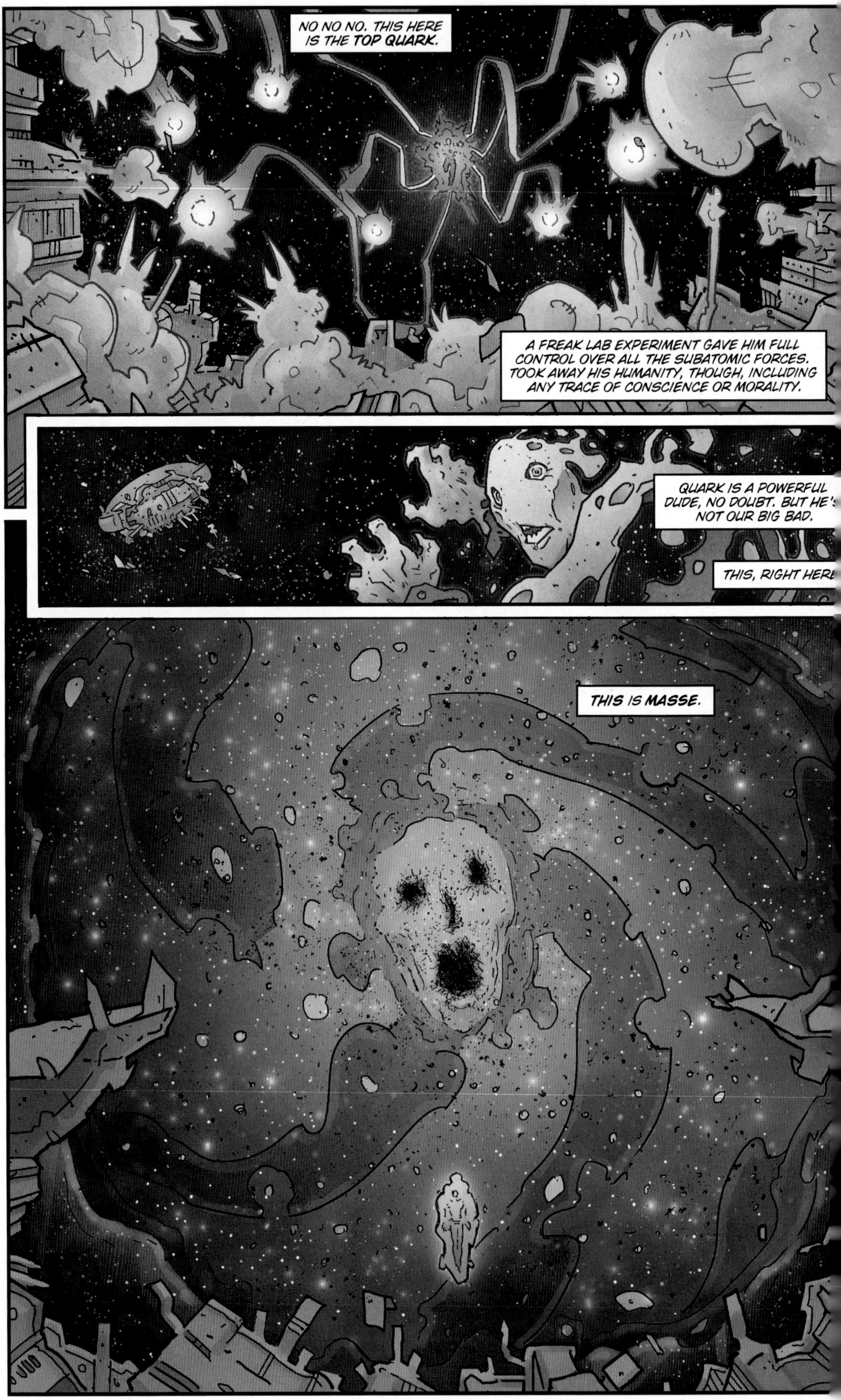

NO NO NO. THIS HERE IS THE TOP QUARK.
A FREAK LAB EXPERIMENT GAVE HIM FULL CONTROL OVER ALL THE SUBATOMIC FORCES. TOOK AWAY HIS HUMANITY, THOUGH, INCLUDING ANY TRACE OF CONSCIENCE OR MORALITY.
QUARK IS A POWERFUL DUDE, NO DOUBT. BUT HE'S NOT OUR BIG BAD.
THIS, RIGHT HERE
THIS IS MASSE.

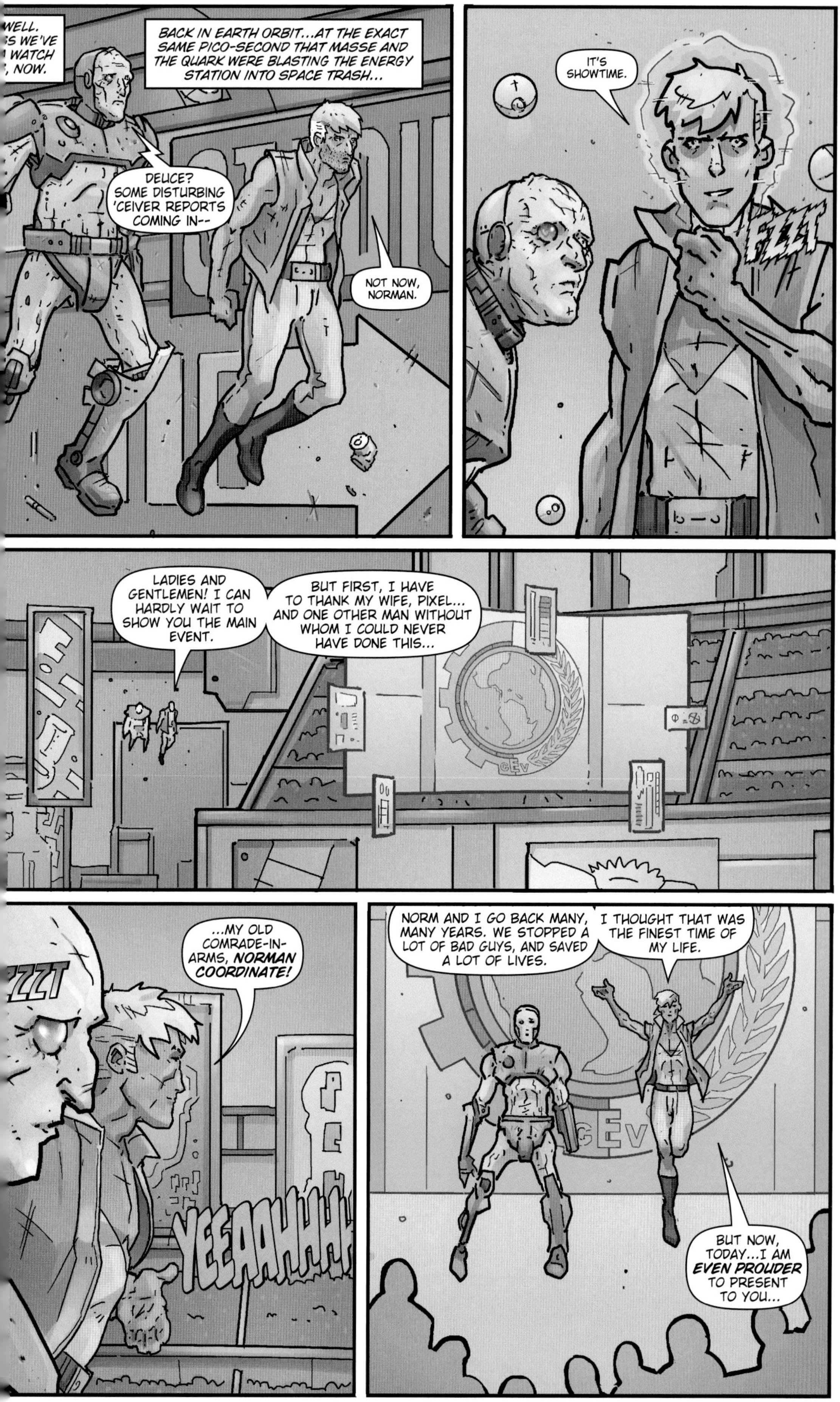

WELL.
S WE'VE
WATCH
, NOW.
BACK IN EARTH ORBIT...AT THE EXACT SAME PICO-SECOND THAT MASSE AND THE QUARK WERE BLASTING THE ENERGY STATION INTO SPACE TRASH...
DEUCE? SOME DISTURBING 'CEIVER REPORTS COMING IN--
NOT NOW, NORMAN.
IT'S SHOWTIME.
FZZT
LADIES AND GENTLEMEN! I CAN HARDLY WAIT TO SHOW YOU THE MAIN EVENT.
BUT FIRST, I HAVE TO THANK MY WIFE, PIXEL... AND ONE OTHER MAN WITHOUT WHOM I COULD NEVER HAVE DONE THIS...
GEV
ZZZT
...MY OLD COMRADE-IN-ARMS, NORMAN COORDINATE!
YEEAAHHH
NORM AND I GO BACK MANY, MANY YEARS. WE STOPPED A LOT OF BAD GUYS, AND SAVED A LOT OF LIVES.
I THOUGHT THAT WAS THE FINEST TIME OF MY LIFE.
GEV
BUT NOW, TODAY...I AM EVEN PROUDER TO PRESENT TO YOU...

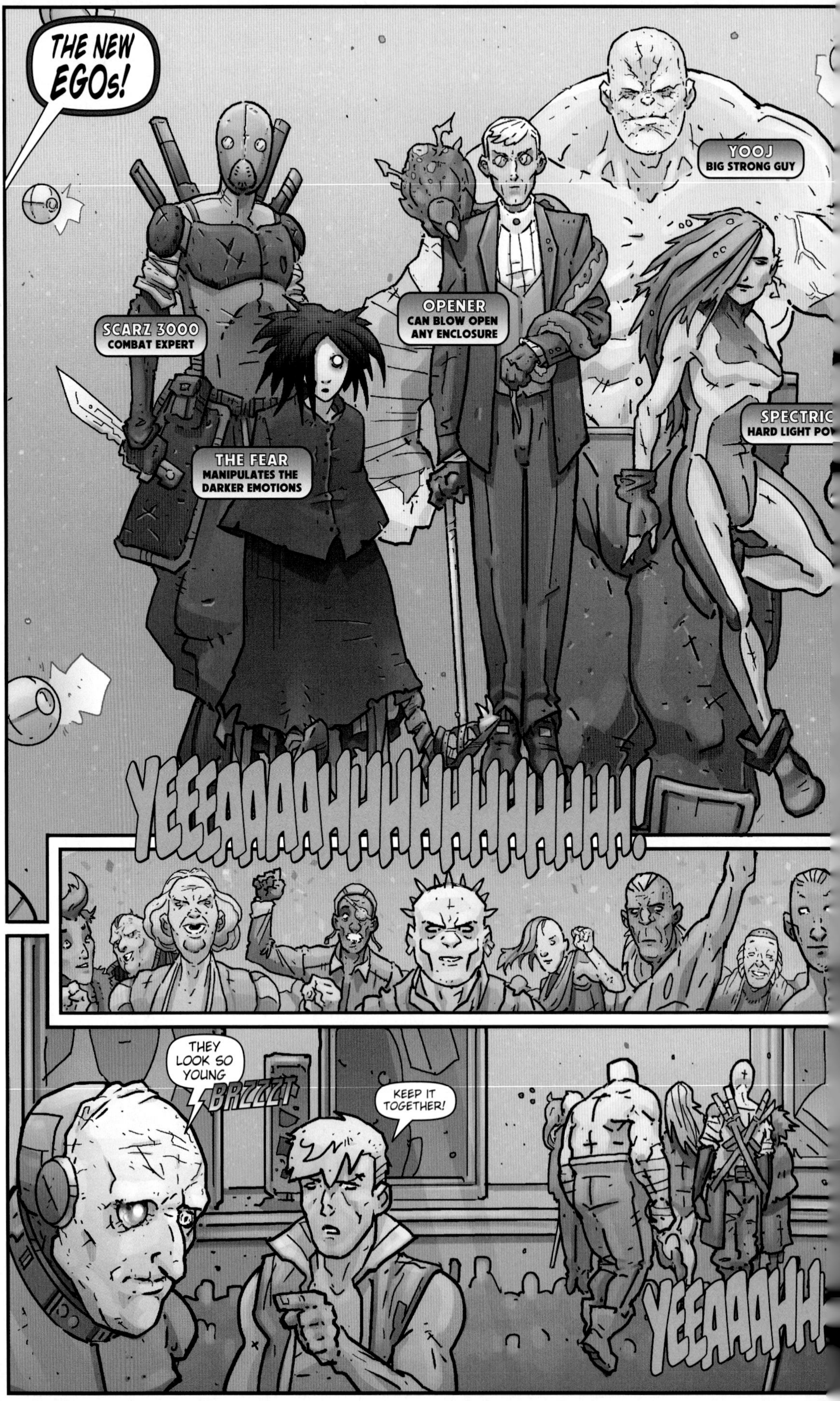

THE NEW EGOs!
YOOJ
BIG STRONG GUY
OPENER
CAN BLOW OPEN ANY ENCLOSURE
SCARZ 3000
COMBAT EXPERT
SPECTRIC
HARD LIGHT POW
THE FEAR
MANIPULATES THE DARKER EMOTIONS
YEEEAAAAHHHHHHHHHHHH!
THEY LOOK SO YOUNG
BRZZZT
KEEP IT TOGETHER!
YEEAAAHH

EUROPA CITY, GREATER JUPITER CONFEDERATION

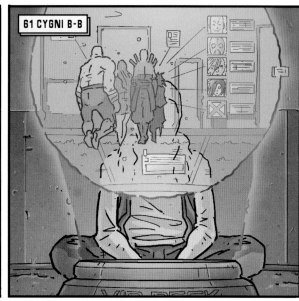

61 CYGNI B-B

...NON COLLEGE, HOURGLASS NEBULA

(THIS IS ME)

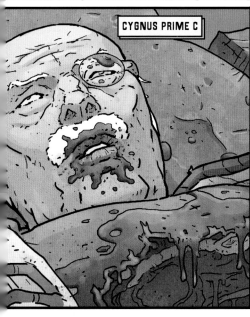

CYGNUS PRIME C

YES. THAT. *THAT'S* WHAT I WANT.

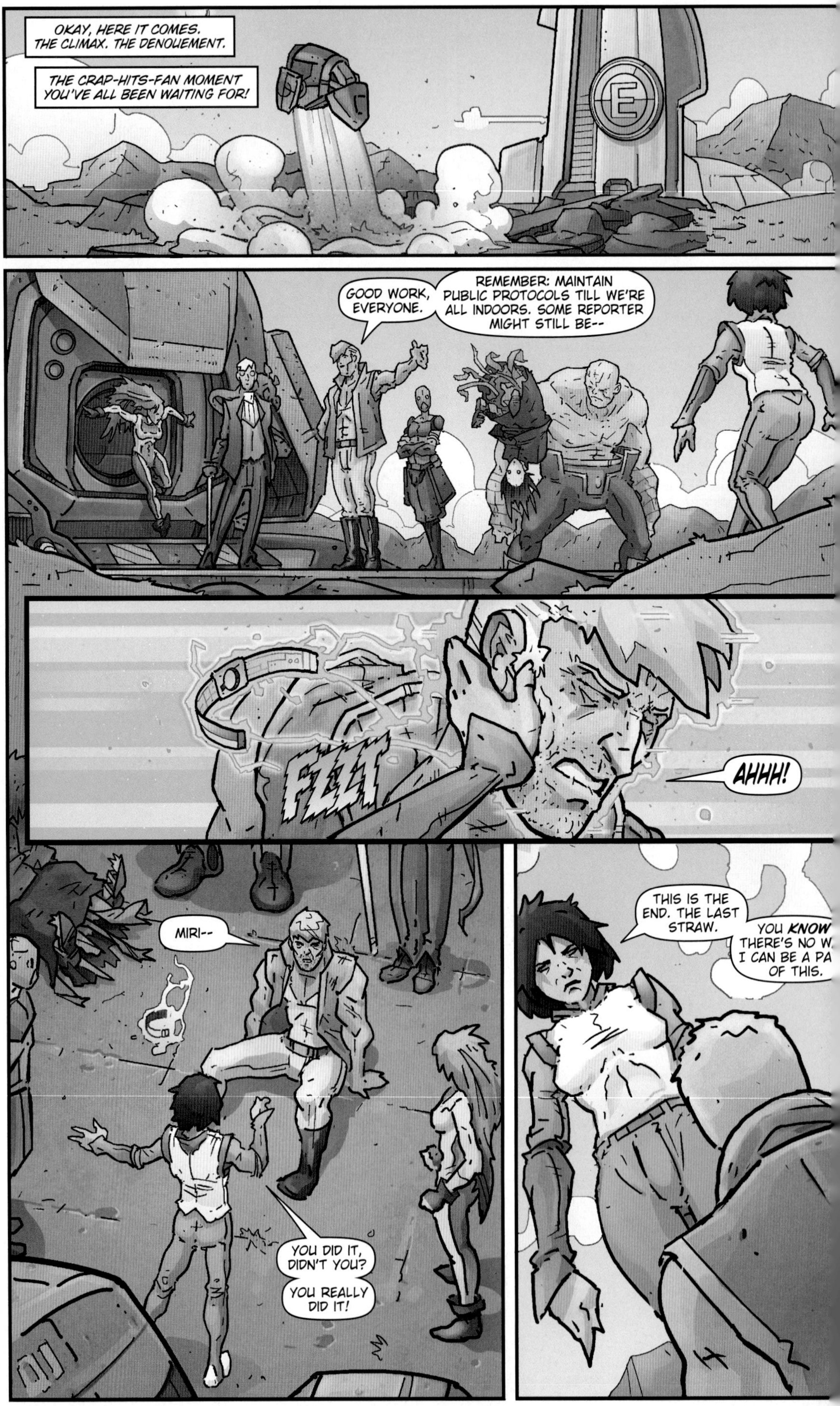
OKAY, HERE IT COMES. THE CLIMAX. THE DENOUEMENT.
THE CRAP-HITS-FAN MOMENT YOU'VE ALL BEEN WAITING FOR!
GOOD WORK, EVERYONE.
REMEMBER: MAINTAIN PUBLIC PROTOCOLS TILL WE'RE ALL INDOORS. SOME REPORTER MIGHT STILL BE--
FZZT
AHHH!
MIRI--
YOU DID IT, DIDN'T YOU?
YOU REALLY DID IT!
THIS IS THE END. THE LAST STRAW.
YOU KNOW THERE'S NO W
I CAN BE A PA
OF THIS.

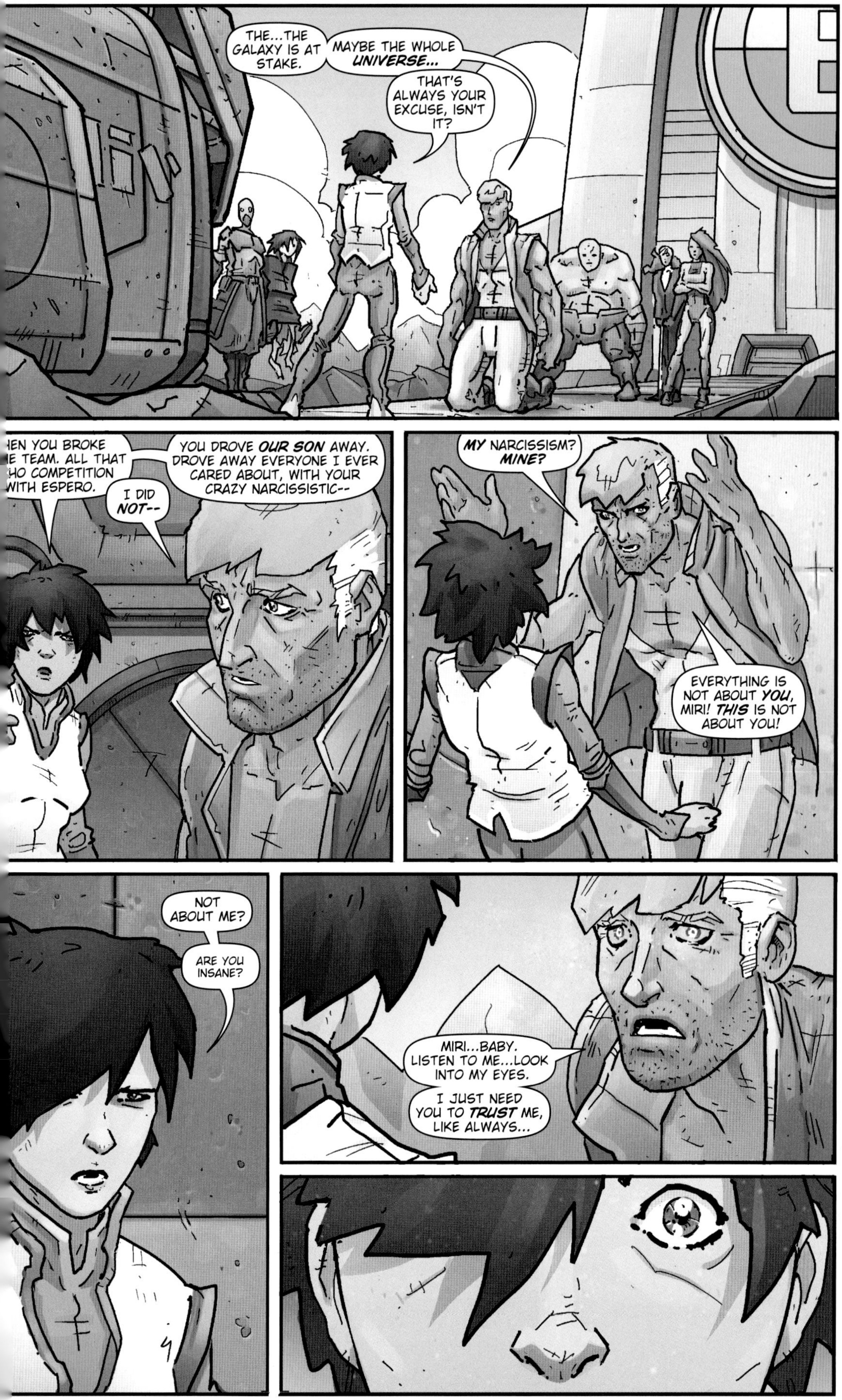

THE...THE GALAXY IS AT STAKE.
MAYBE THE WHOLE UNIVERSE...
THAT'S ALWAYS YOUR EXCUSE, ISN'T IT?
HEN YOU BROKE E TEAM. ALL THAT HO COMPETITION WITH ESPERO.
YOU DROVE OUR SON AWAY. DROVE AWAY EVERYONE I EVER CARED ABOUT, WITH YOUR CRAZY NARCISSISTIC--
I DID NOT--
MY NARCISSISM? MINE?
EVERYTHING IS NOT ABOUT YOU, MIRI! THIS IS NOT ABOUT YOU!
NOT ABOUT ME?
ARE YOU INSANE?
MIRI...BABY. LISTEN TO ME...LOOK INTO MY EYES.
I JUST NEED YOU TO TRUST ME, LIKE ALWAYS...

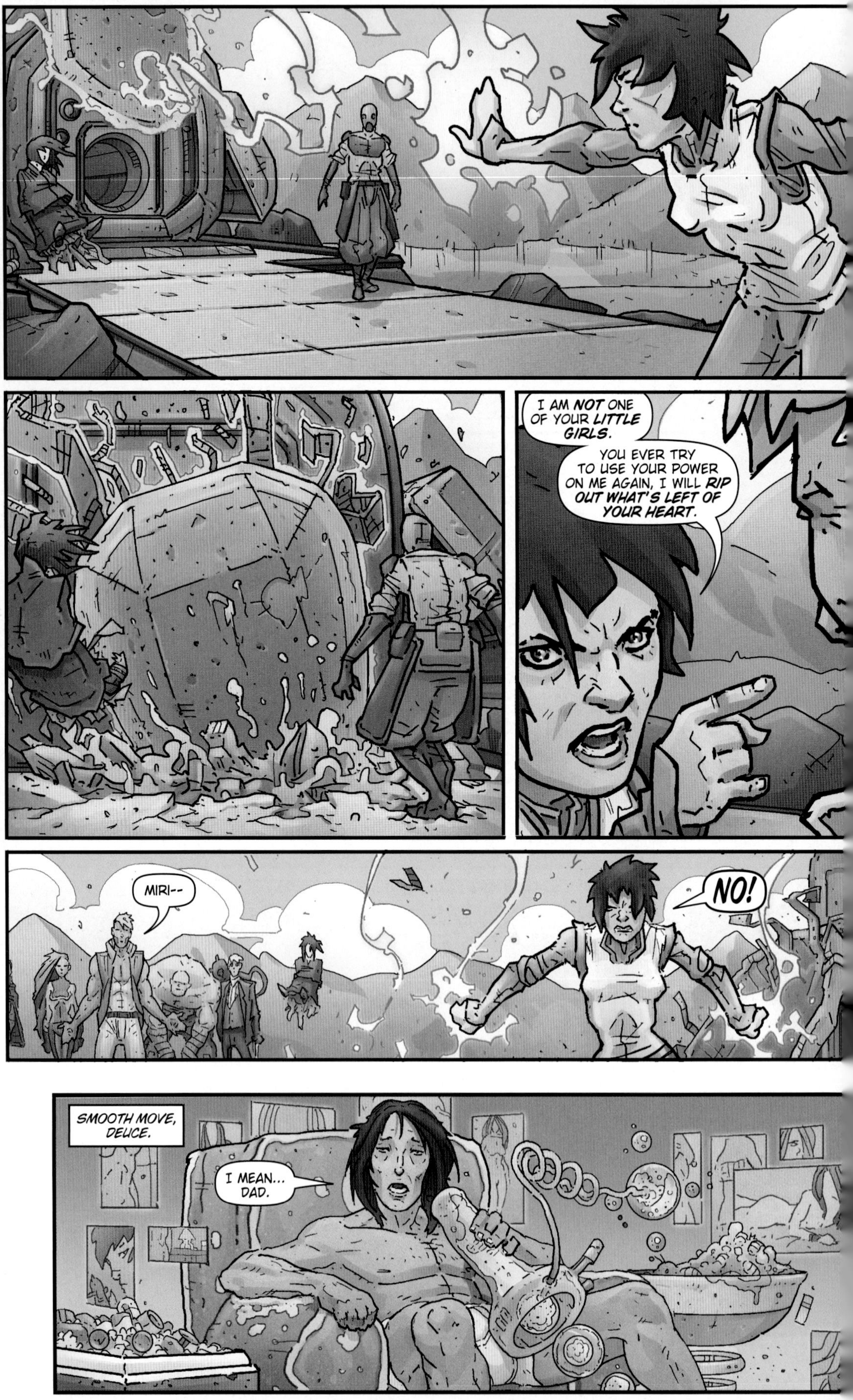
I AM **NOT** ONE OF YOUR ***LITTLE GIRLS***.
YOU EVER TRY TO USE YOUR POWER ON ME AGAIN, I WILL ***RIP OUT WHAT'S LEFT OF YOUR HEART***.
MIRI--
NO!
SMOOTH MOVE, DEUCE.
I MEAN... DAD.

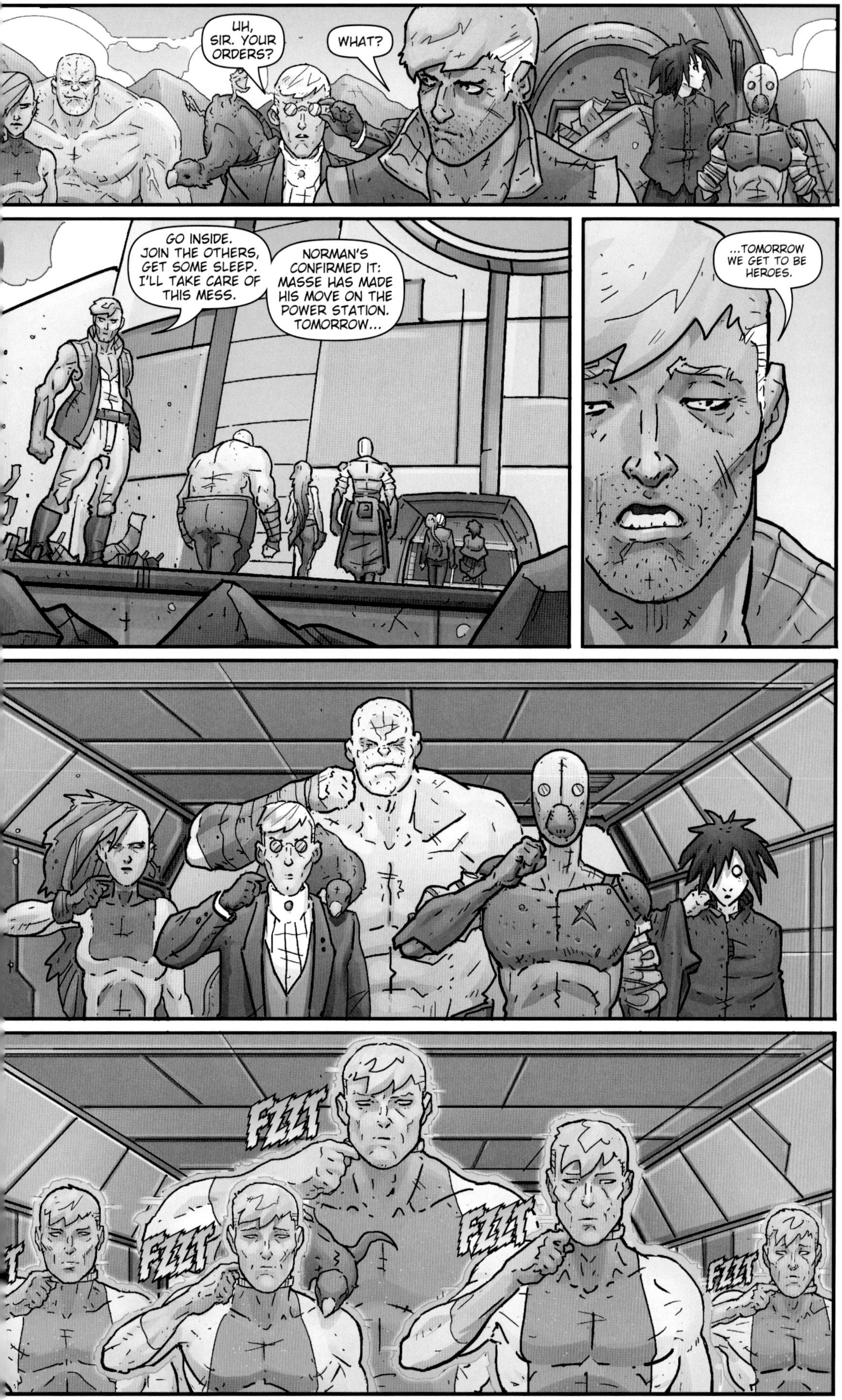
UH, SIR. YOUR ORDERS?
WHAT?
GO INSIDE. JOIN THE OTHERS, GET SOME SLEEP. I'LL TAKE CARE OF THIS MESS.
NORMAN'S CONFIRMED IT: MASSE HAS MADE HIS MOVE ON THE POWER STATION. TOMORROW...
...TOMORROW WE GET TO BE HEROES.
FZZT
FZZT
FZZT
FZZT

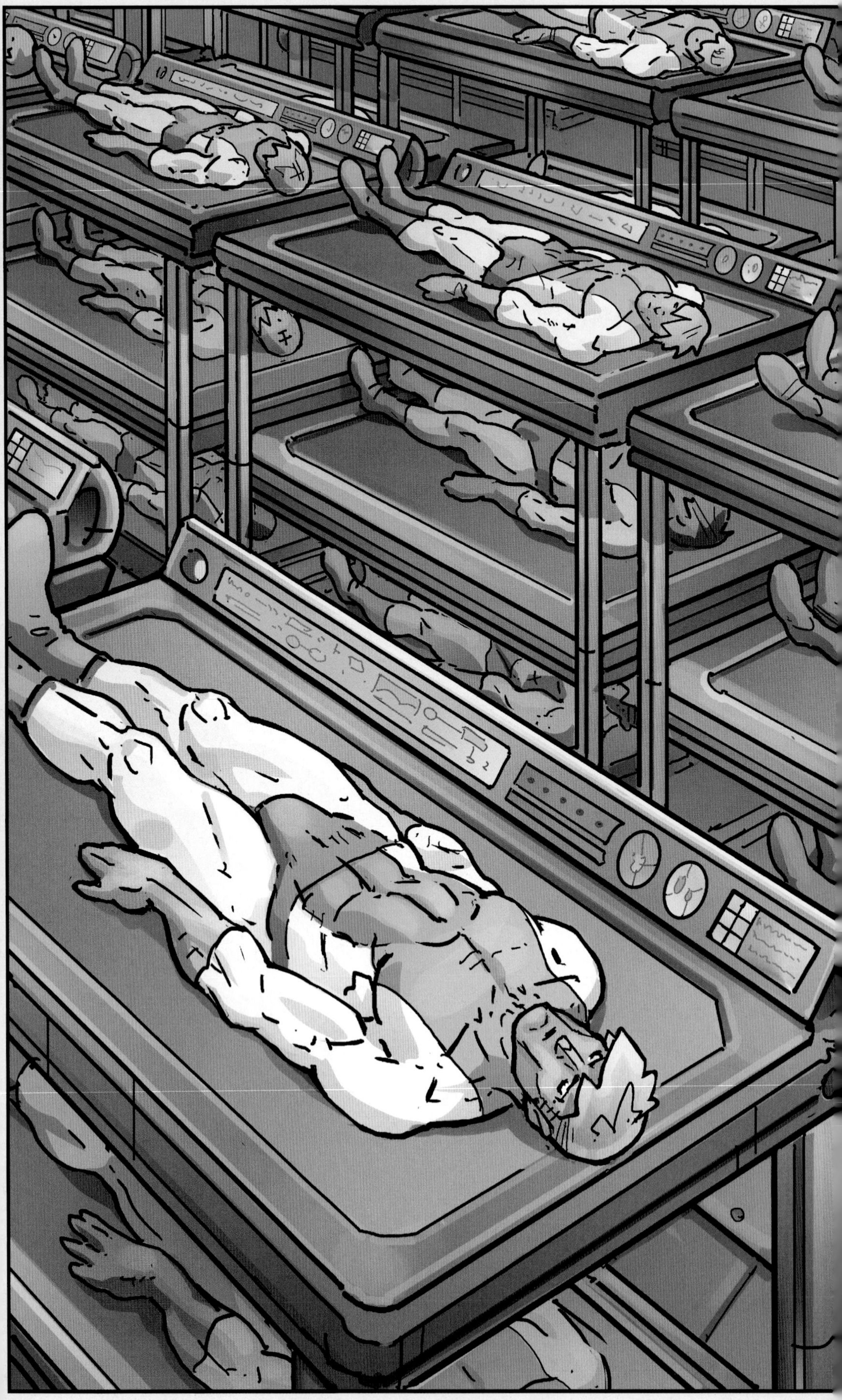

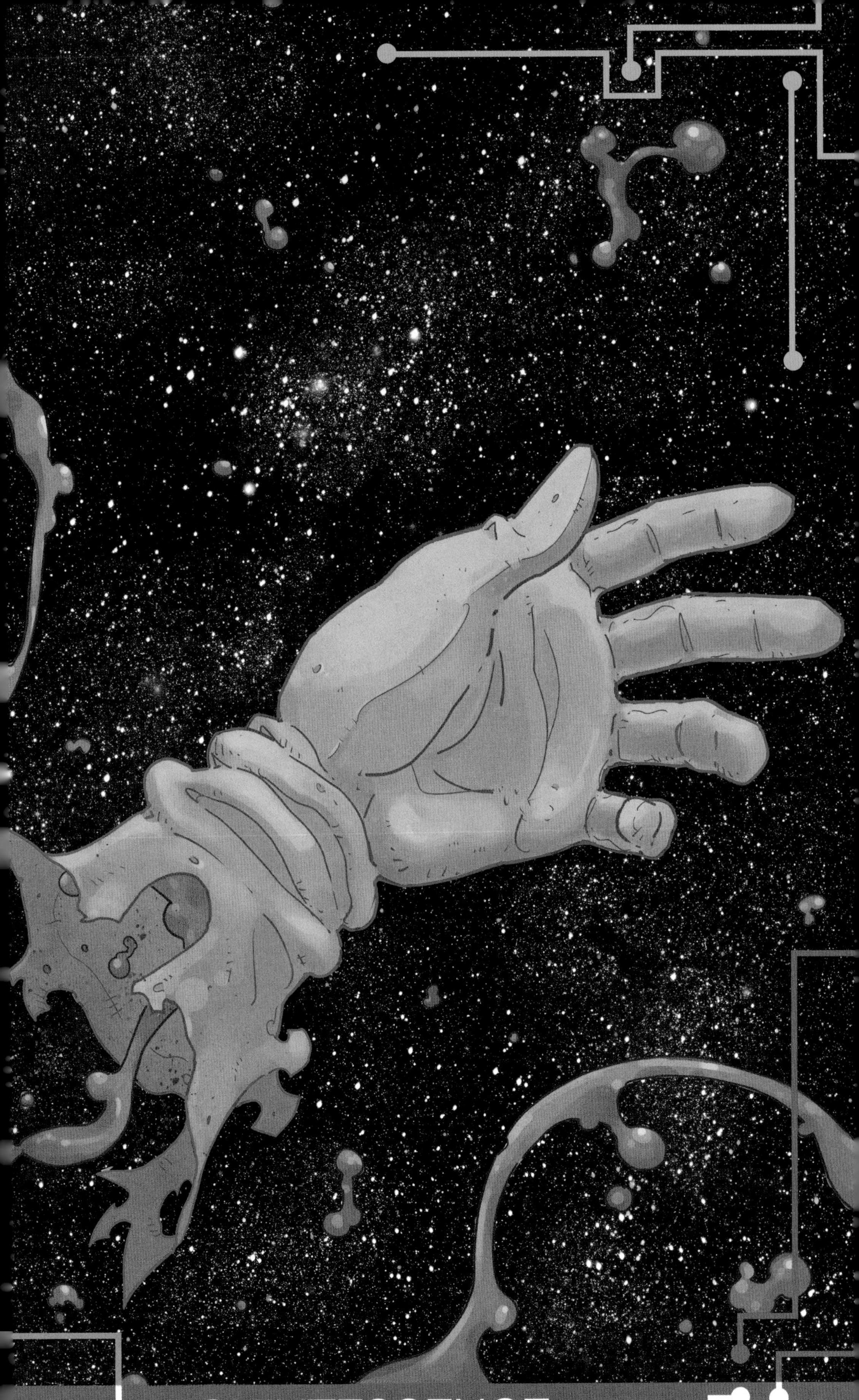

2 QUINTESSENCE

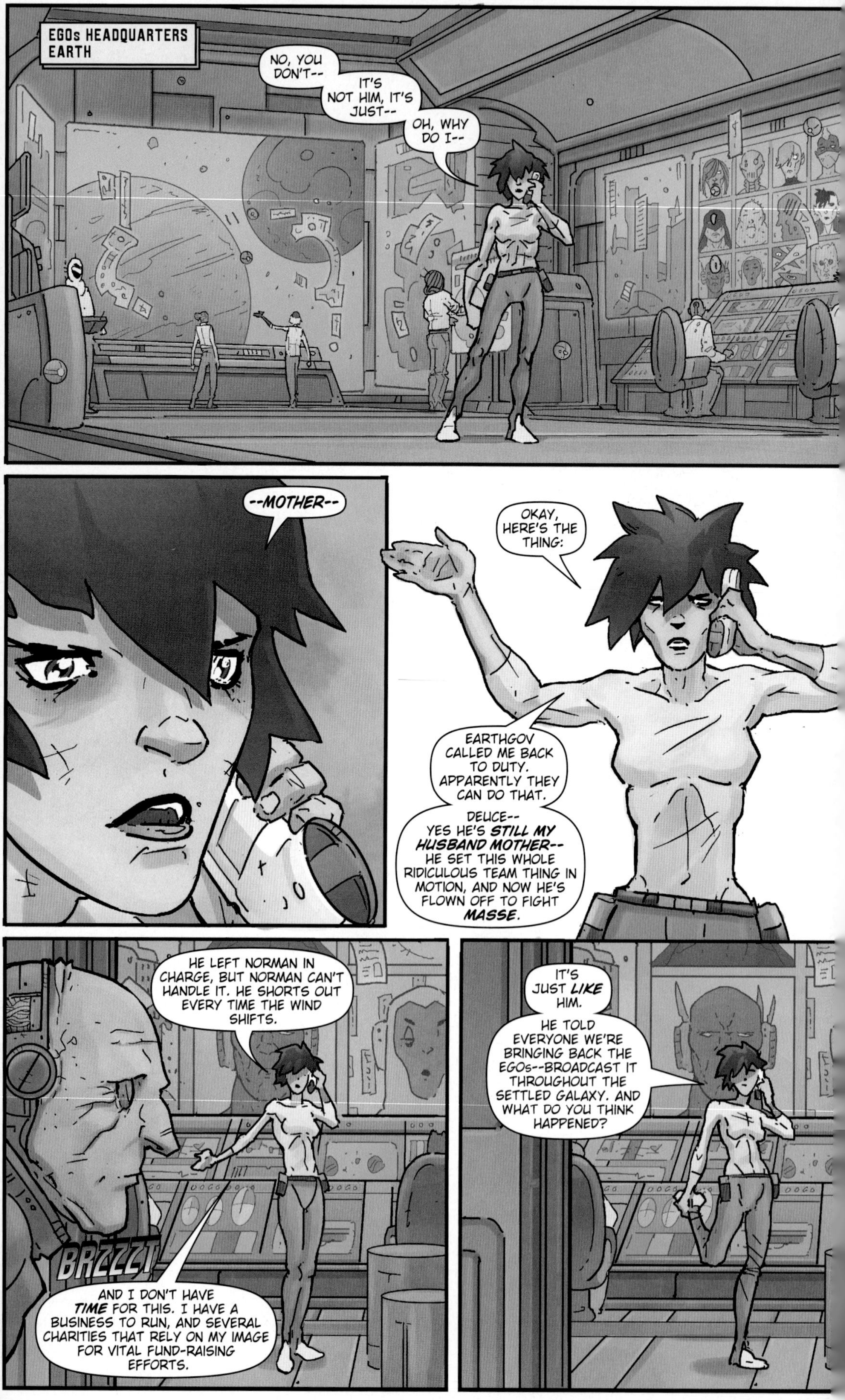

EGOs HEADQUARTERS EARTH
NO, YOU DON'T--
IT'S NOT HIM, IT'S JUST--
OH, WHY DO I--
--MOTHER--
OKAY, HERE'S THE THING:
EARTHGOV CALLED ME BACK TO DUTY. APPARENTLY THEY CAN DO THAT.
DEUCE-- YES HE'S STILL MY HUSBAND MOTHER-- HE SET THIS WHOLE RIDICULOUS TEAM THING IN MOTION, AND NOW HE'S FLOWN OFF TO FIGHT MASSE.
HE LEFT NORMAN IN CHARGE, BUT NORMAN CAN'T HANDLE IT. HE SHORTS OUT EVERY TIME THE WIND SHIFTS.
BRZZZT
AND I DON'T HAVE TIME FOR THIS. I HAVE A BUSINESS TO RUN, AND SEVERAL CHARITIES THAT RELY ON MY IMAGE FOR VITAL FUND-RAISING EFFORTS.
IT'S JUST LIKE HIM.
HE TOLD EVERYONE WE'RE BRINGING BACK THE EGOs--BROADCAST IT THROUGHOUT THE SETTLED GALAXY. AND WHAT DO YOU THINK HAPPENED?

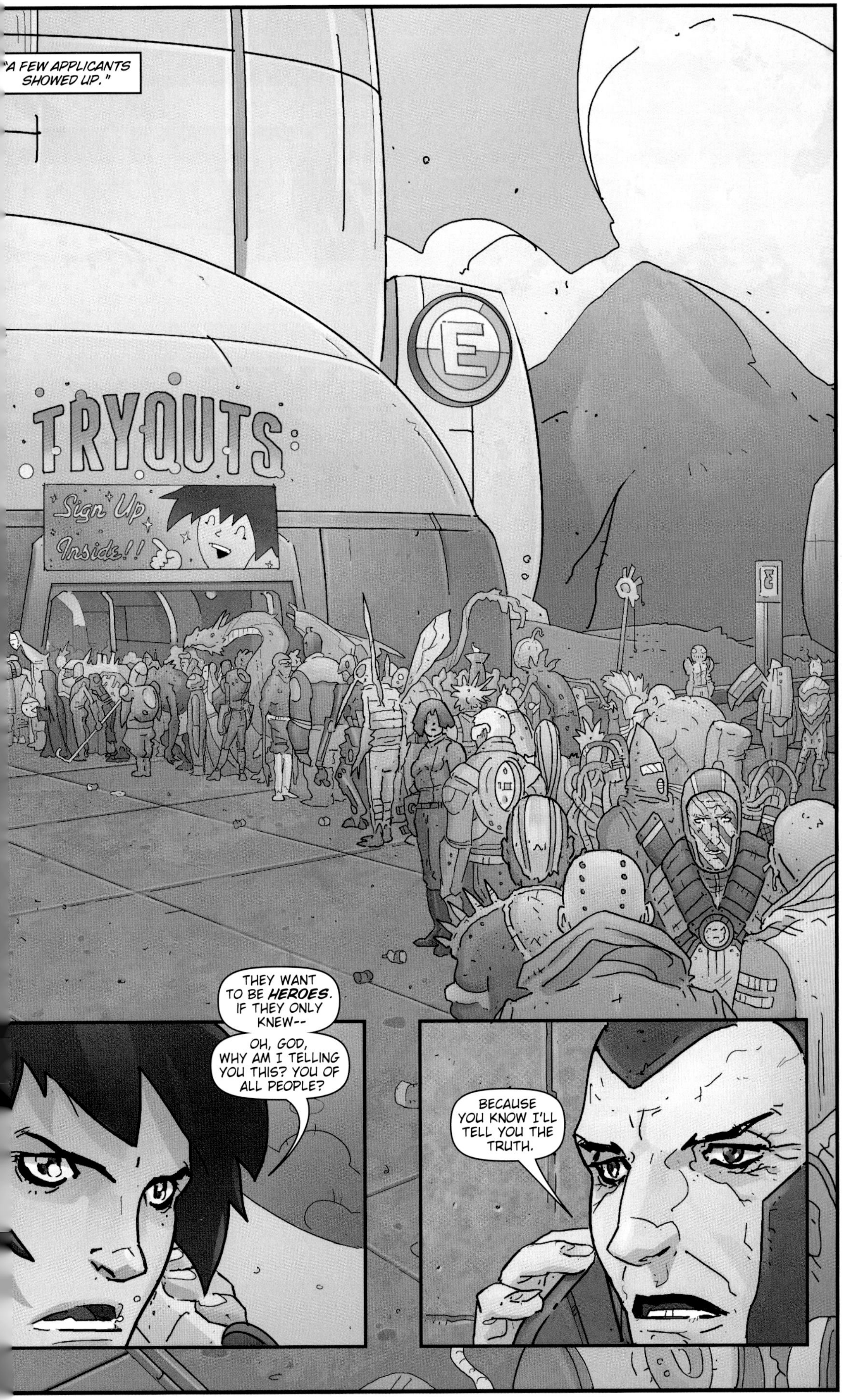
"A FEW APPLICANTS SHOWED UP."
TRYOUTS
Sign Up Inside!!
THEY WANT TO BE **HEROES**. IF THEY ONLY KNEW--
OH, GOD, WHY AM I TELLING YOU THIS? YOU OF ALL PEOPLE?
BECAUSE YOU KNOW I'LL TELL YOU THE TRUTH.

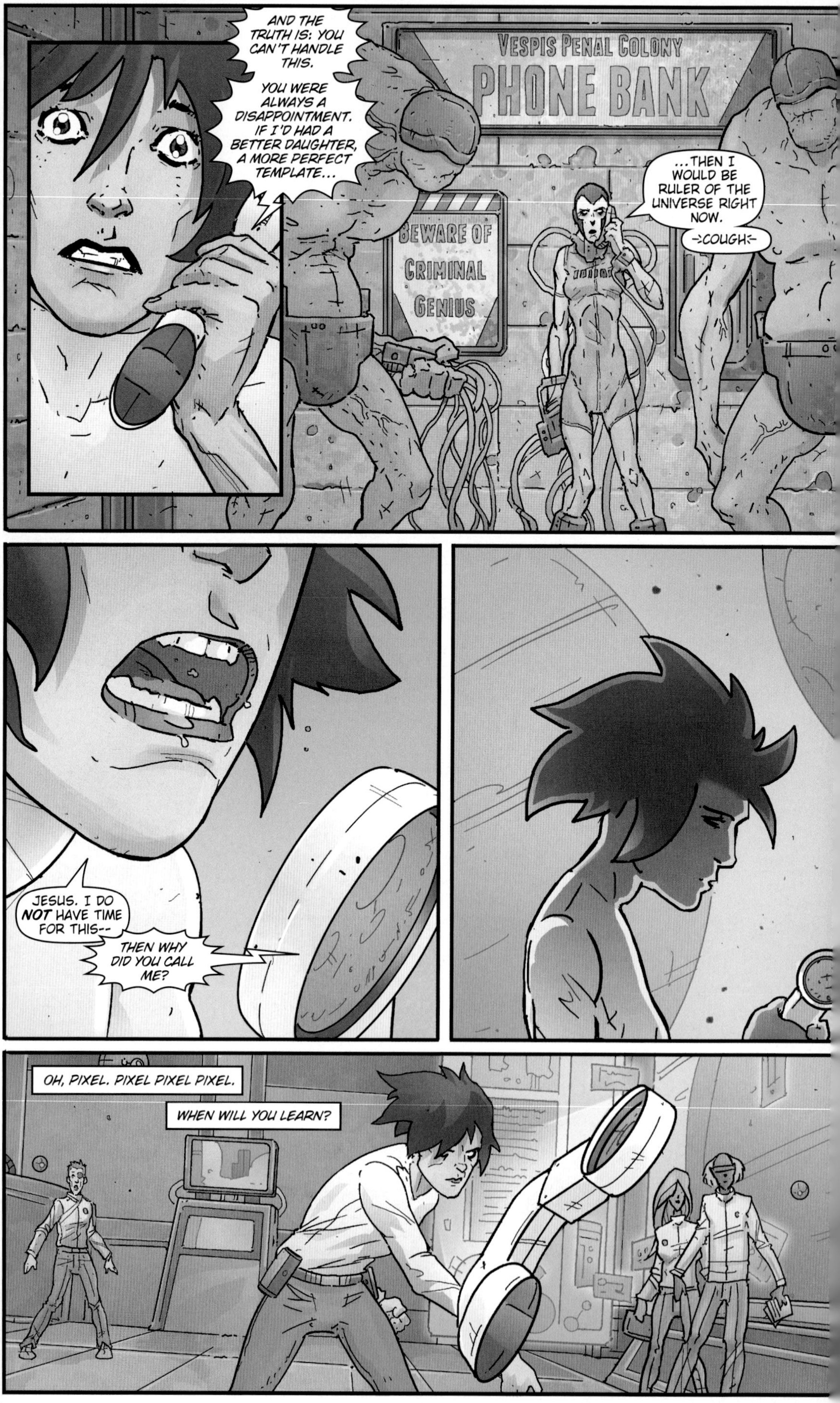
AND THE TRUTH IS: YOU CAN'T HANDLE THIS.
YOU WERE ALWAYS A DISAPPOINTMENT. IF I'D HAD A BETTER DAUGHTER, A MORE PERFECT TEMPLATE...
VESPIS PENAL COLONY
PHONE BANK
BEWARE OF CRIMINAL GENIUS
...THEN I WOULD BE RULER OF THE UNIVERSE RIGHT NOW.
COUGH
JESUS. I DO NOT HAVE TIME FOR THIS--
THEN WHY DID YOU CALL ME?
OH, PIXEL. PIXEL PIXEL PIXEL.
WHEN WILL YOU LEARN?

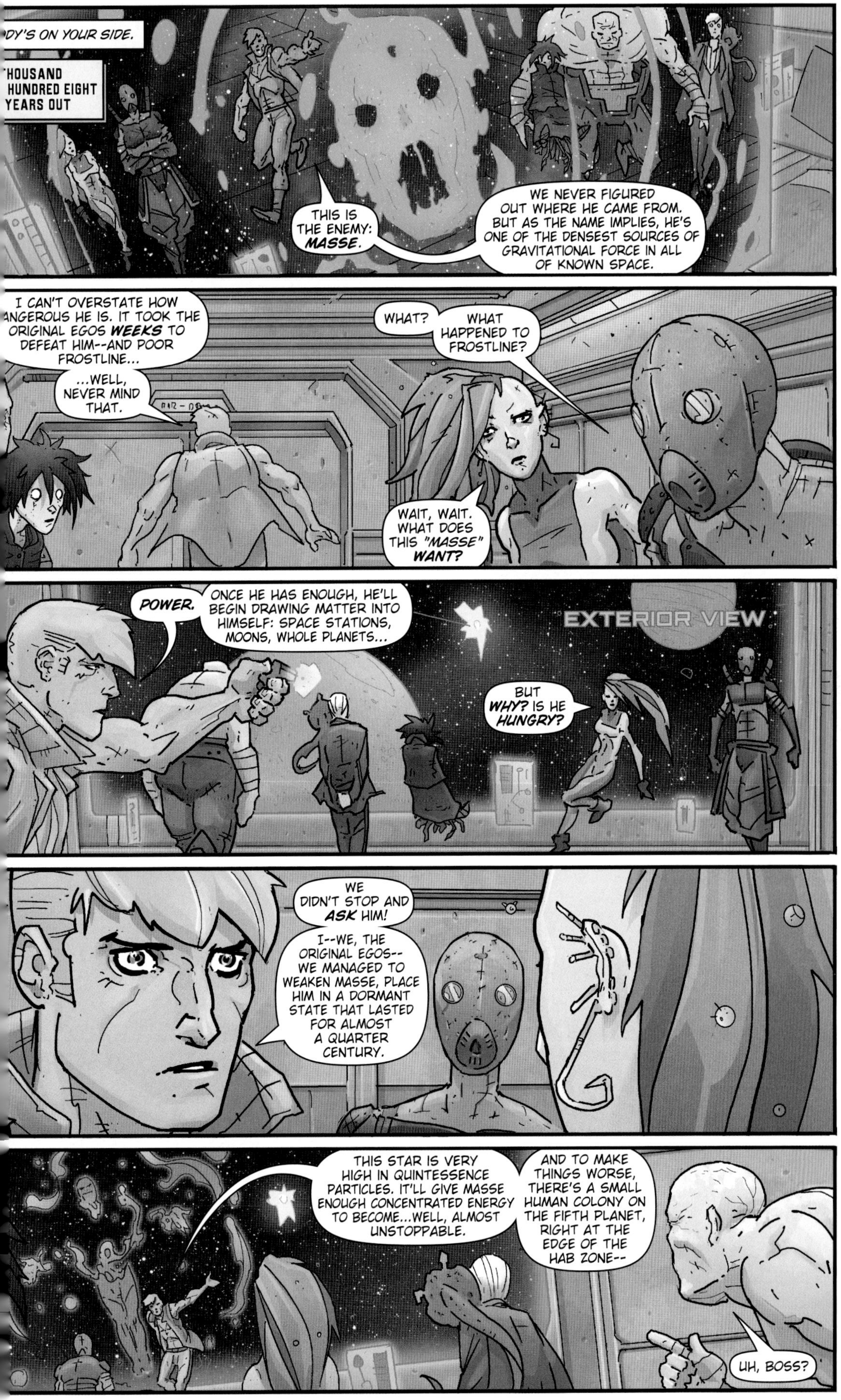

DY'S ON YOUR SIDE.
THOUSAND HUNDRED EIGHT YEARS OUT
THIS IS THE ENEMY: MASSE.
WE NEVER FIGURED OUT WHERE HE CAME FROM. BUT AS THE NAME IMPLIES, HE'S ONE OF THE DENSEST SOURCES OF GRAVITATIONAL FORCE IN ALL OF KNOWN SPACE.
I CAN'T OVERSTATE HOW ANGEROUS HE IS. IT TOOK THE ORIGINAL EGOS WEEKS TO DEFEAT HIM--AND POOR FROSTLINE...
...WELL, NEVER MIND THAT.
WHAT?
WHAT HAPPENED TO FROSTLINE?
WAIT, WAIT. WHAT DOES THIS "MASSE" WANT?
POWER.
ONCE HE HAS ENOUGH, HE'LL BEGIN DRAWING MATTER INTO HIMSELF: SPACE STATIONS, MOONS, WHOLE PLANETS...
EXTERIOR VIEW
BUT WHY? IS HE HUNGRY?
WE DIDN'T STOP AND ASK HIM!
I--WE, THE ORIGINAL EGOS-- WE MANAGED TO WEAKEN MASSE, PLACE HIM IN A DORMANT STATE THAT LASTED FOR ALMOST A QUARTER CENTURY.
THIS STAR IS VERY HIGH IN QUINTESSENCE PARTICLES. IT'LL GIVE MASSE ENOUGH CONCENTRATED ENERGY TO BECOME...WELL, ALMOST UNSTOPPABLE.
AND TO MAKE THINGS WORSE, THERE'S A SMALL HUMAN COLONY ON THE FIFTH PLANET, RIGHT AT THE EDGE OF THE HAB ZONE--
UH, BOSS?

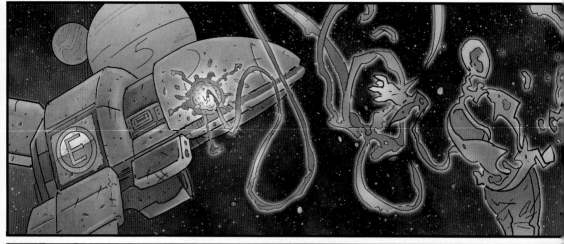

GO! AND REMEMBER TO KEEP YOUR IMAGERS UP. THIS IS BEING RECORDED FOR BROADCAST!

SCARZ, SPECTRICA. YOU TW TAKE POINT!

WHOEVER THIS GU IS, HE HAS ENERG POWERS--

--WHICH MAKES YOU THE FIRST WAVE!

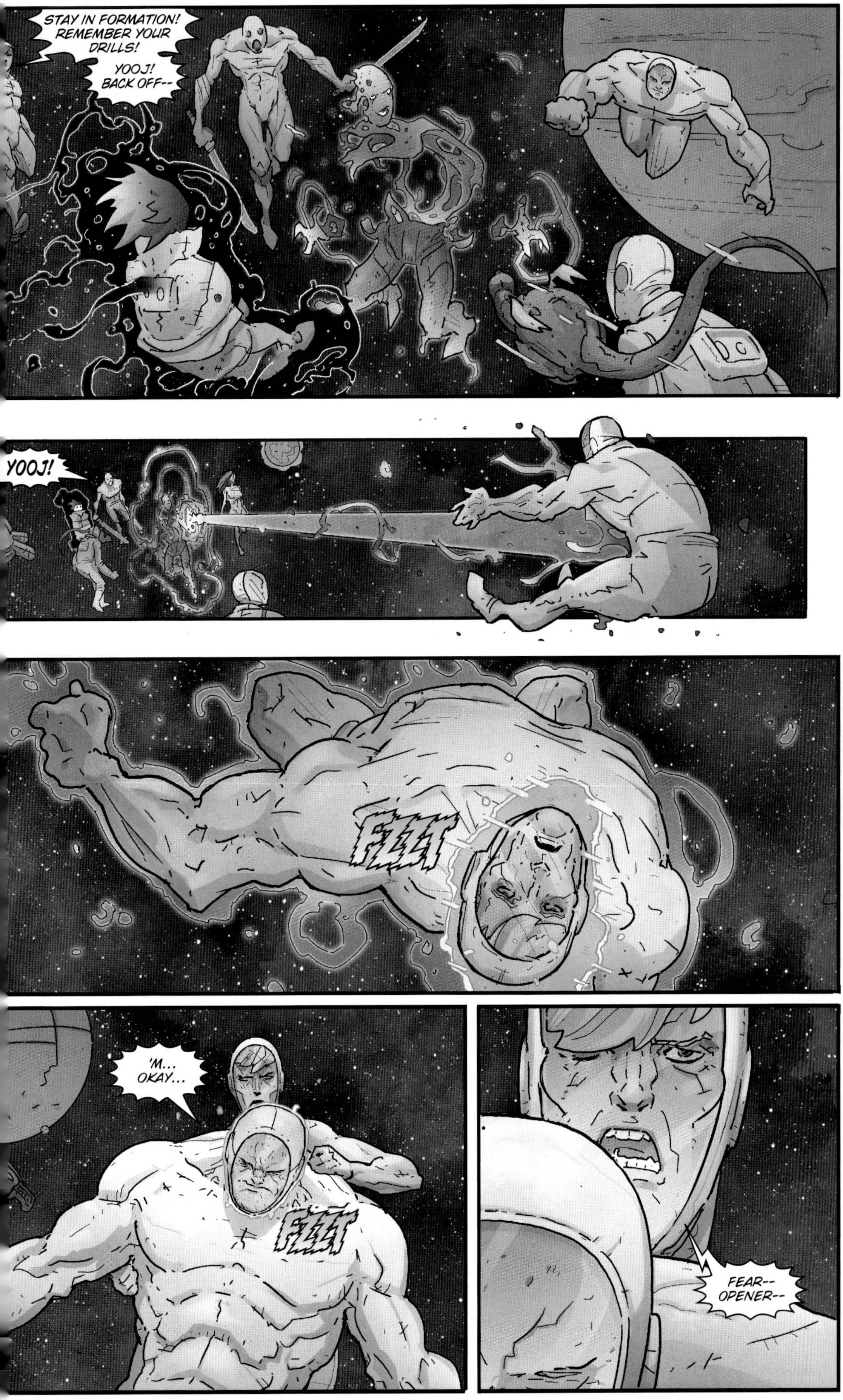
STAY IN FORMATION! REMEMBER YOUR DRILLS!
YOOJ! BACK OFF--
YOOJ!
FZZT
'M... OKAY...
FZZT
FEAR-- OPENER--

"--TAKE HIM!"

OPENER'S POWER IS TO BLOW ANYTHING APART FROM THE INSIDE.

PRETTY NASTY...

...BUT I THINK THE FEAR IS WORSE.

IMAGINE YOU'RE A CREATURE OF RAW MATTER... ELEMENTARY PARTICLES. THEN IMAGINE THOSE PARTICLES SUDDENLY START PULLING APART, SCATTERING IN A BILLION DIFFERENT DIRECTIONS.

YOU'D HA
WONDE

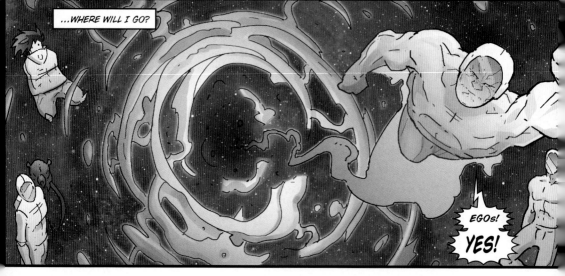

...WHERE WILL I GO?

EGOs!
YES!

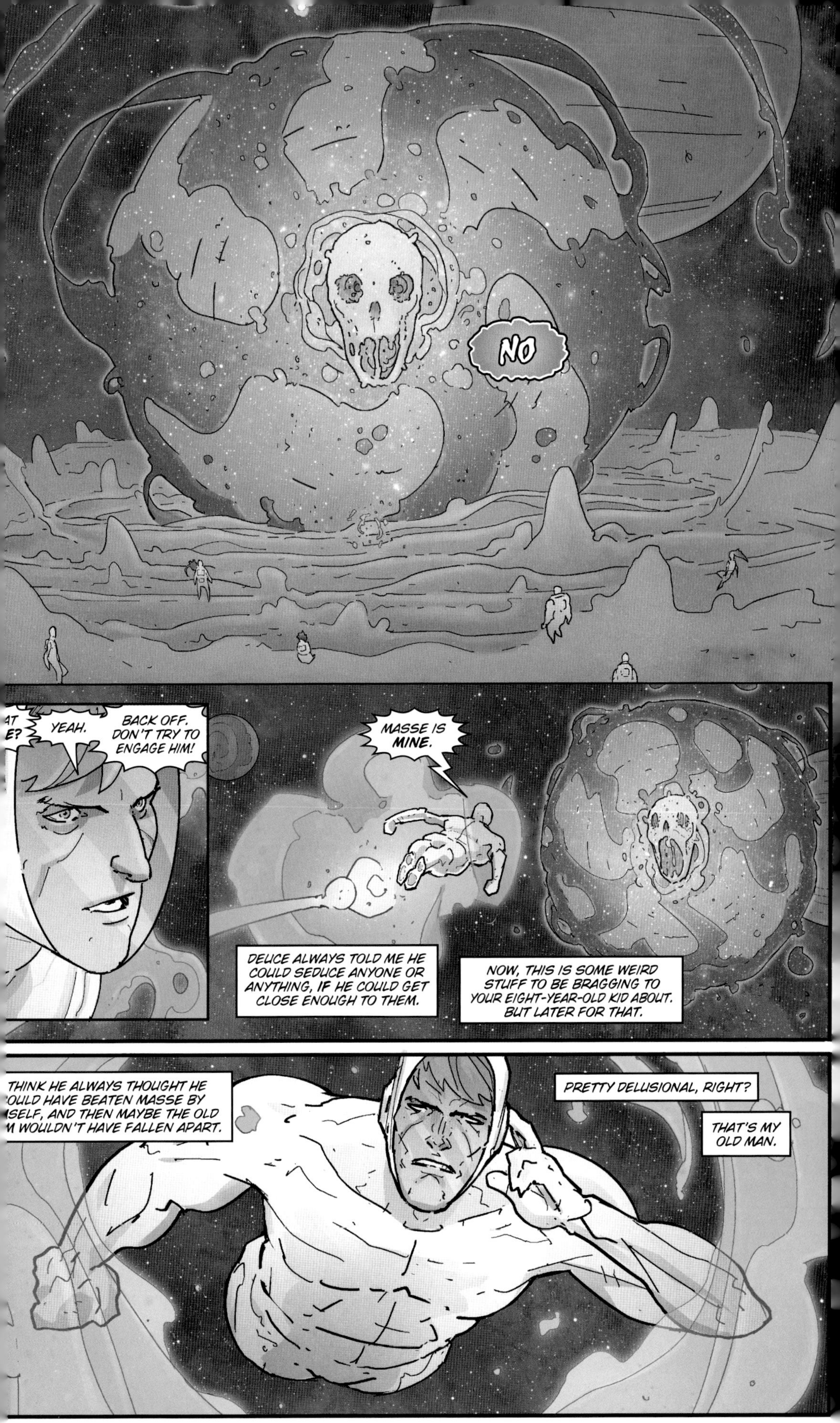

NO
...AT ...E?
YEAH.
BACK OFF. DON'T TRY TO ENGAGE HIM!
MASSE IS MINE.
DEUCE ALWAYS TOLD ME HE COULD SEDUCE ANYONE OR ANYTHING, IF HE COULD GET CLOSE ENOUGH TO THEM.
NOW, THIS IS SOME WEIRD STUFF TO BE BRAGGING TO YOUR EIGHT-YEAR-OLD KID ABOUT. BUT LATER FOR THAT.
...THINK HE ALWAYS THOUGHT HE ...OULD HAVE BEATEN MASSE BY ...SELF, AND THEN MAYBE THE OLD ...M WOULDN'T HAVE FALLEN APART.
PRETTY DELUSIONAL, RIGHT?
THAT'S MY OLD MAN.

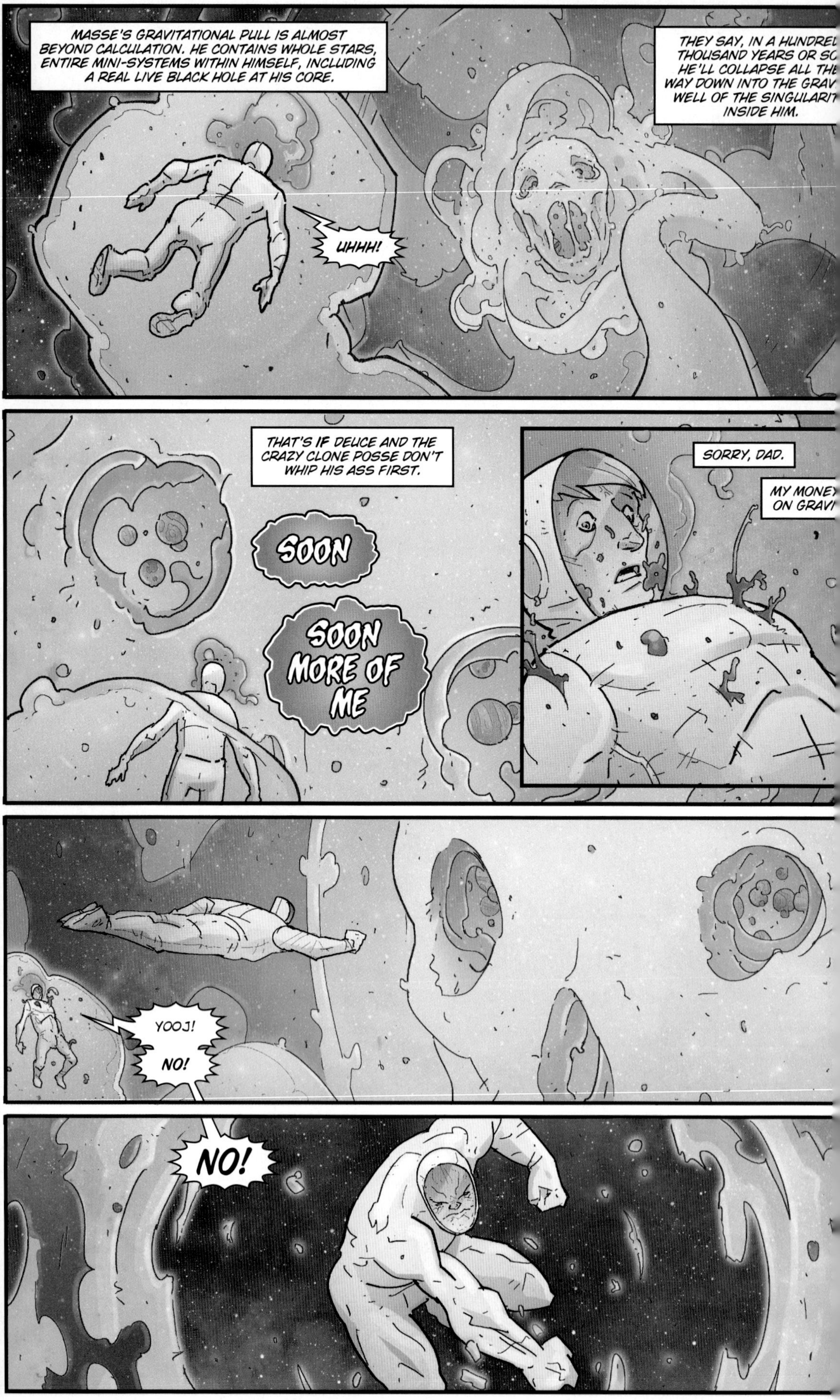
MASSE'S GRAVITATIONAL PULL IS ALMOST BEYOND CALCULATION. HE CONTAINS WHOLE STARS, ENTIRE MINI-SYSTEMS WITHIN HIMSELF, INCLUDING A REAL LIVE BLACK HOLE AT HIS CORE.
THEY SAY, IN A HUNDRE THOUSAND YEARS OR S HE'LL COLLAPSE ALL TH WAY DOWN INTO THE GRAV WELL OF THE SINGULARI INSIDE HIM.
UHHH!
THAT'S IF DEUCE AND THE CRAZY CLONE POSSE DON'T WHIP HIS ASS FIRST.
SOON
SOON MORE OF ME
SORRY, DAD.
MY MONE ON GRAV
YOOJ!
NO!
NO!

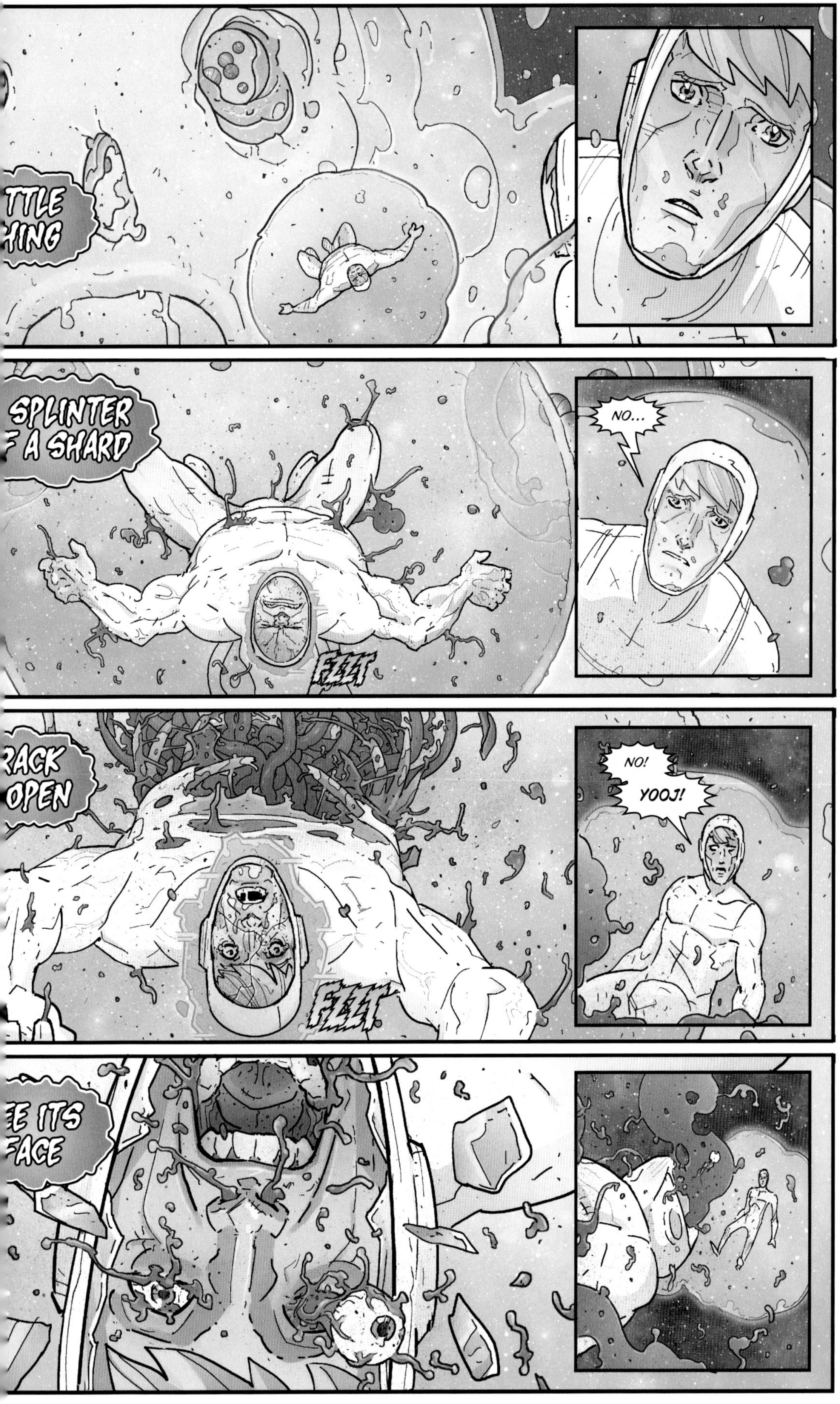

TTLE
HING
SPLINTER
F A SHARD
NO...
FZZT
RACK
OPEN
NO!
YOOJ!
FZZT
E ITS
FACE

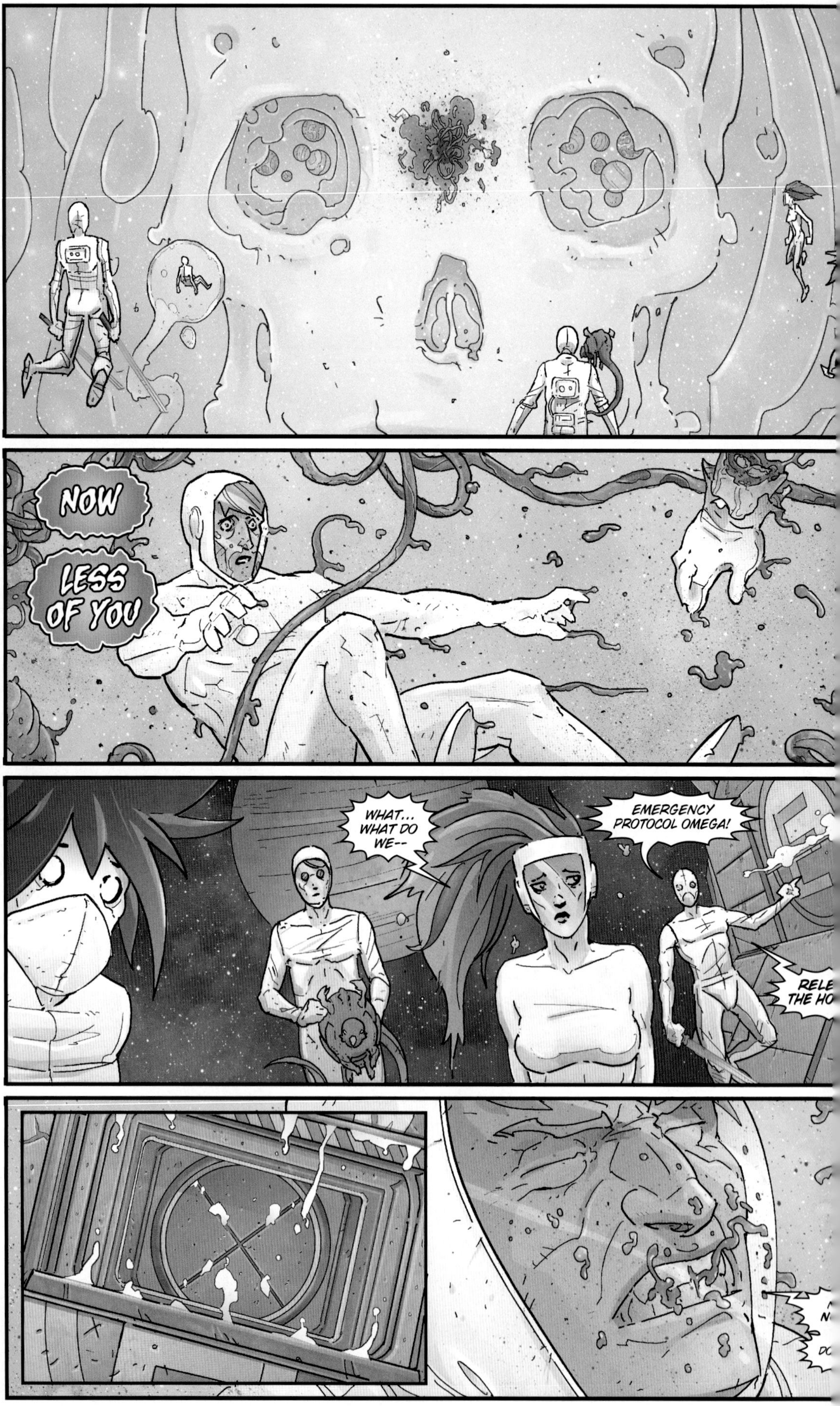
NOW
LESS OF YOU
WHAT... WHAT DO WE--
EMERGENCY PROTOCOL OMEGA!

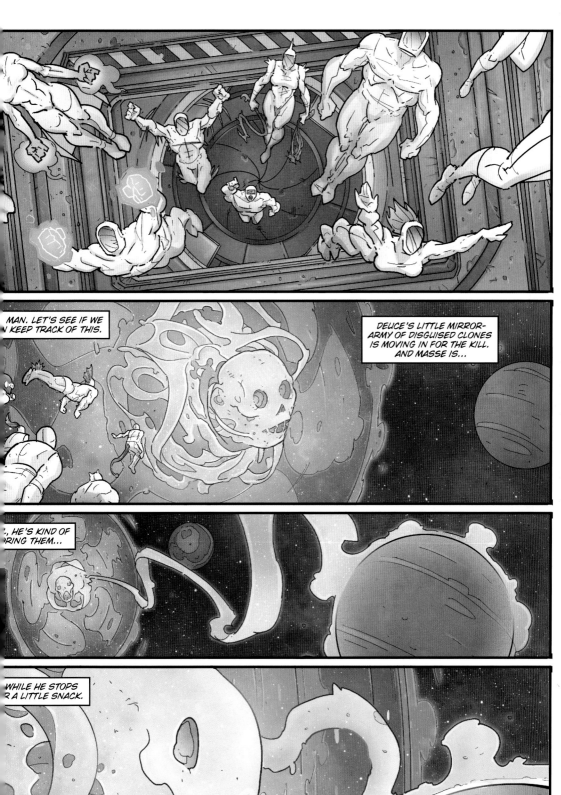

MAN. LET'S SEE IF WE [CA]N KEEP TRACK OF THIS.

DEUCE'S LITTLE MIRROR-ARMY OF DISGUISED CLONES IS MOVING IN FOR THE KILL. AND MASSE IS...

[BU]T, HE'S KIND OF [IGNO]RING THEM...

WHILE HE STOPS [FO]R A LITTLE SNACK.

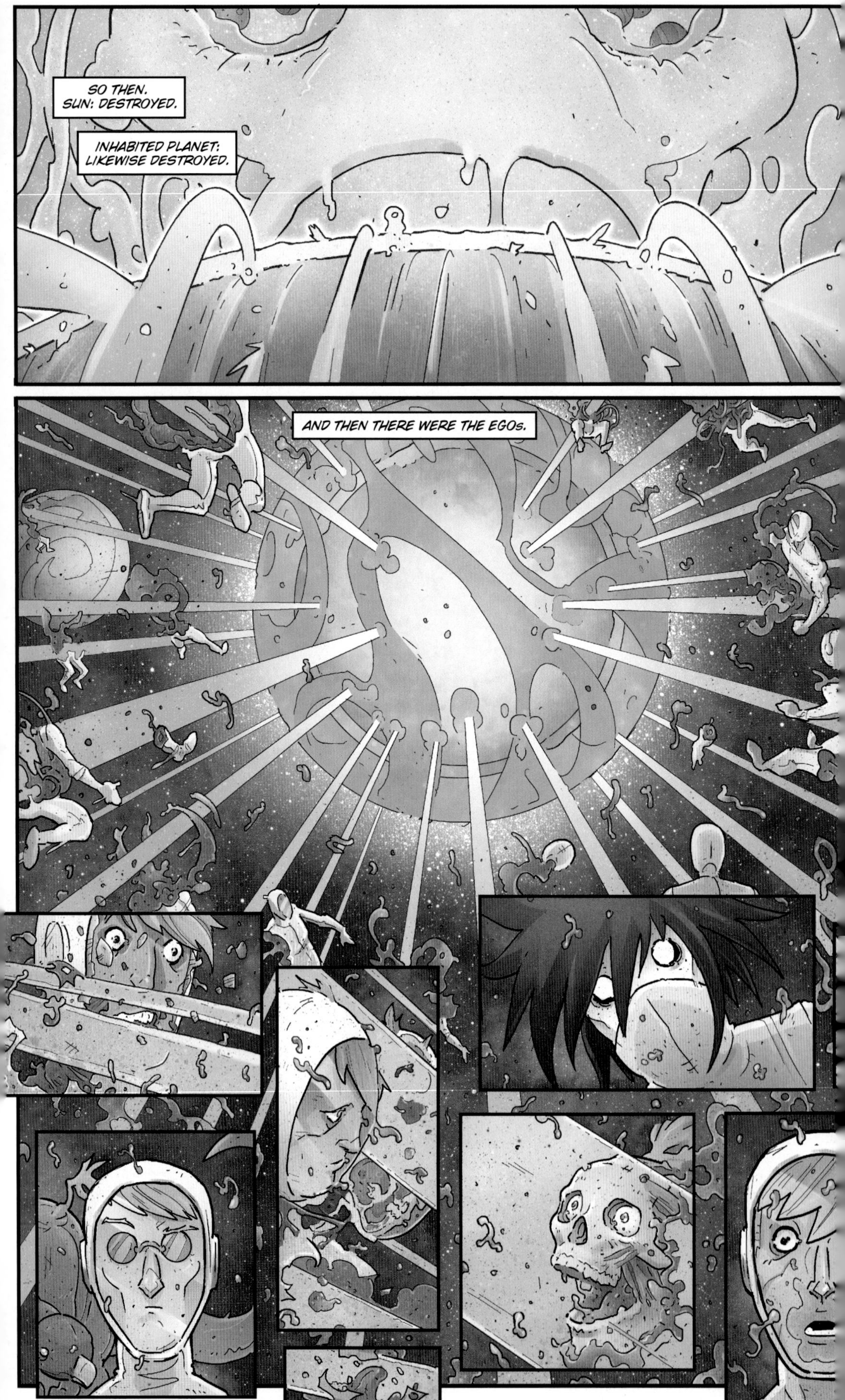
SO THEN.
SUN: DESTROYED.
INHABITED PLANET:
LIKEWISE DESTROYED.
AND THEN THERE WERE THE EGOs.

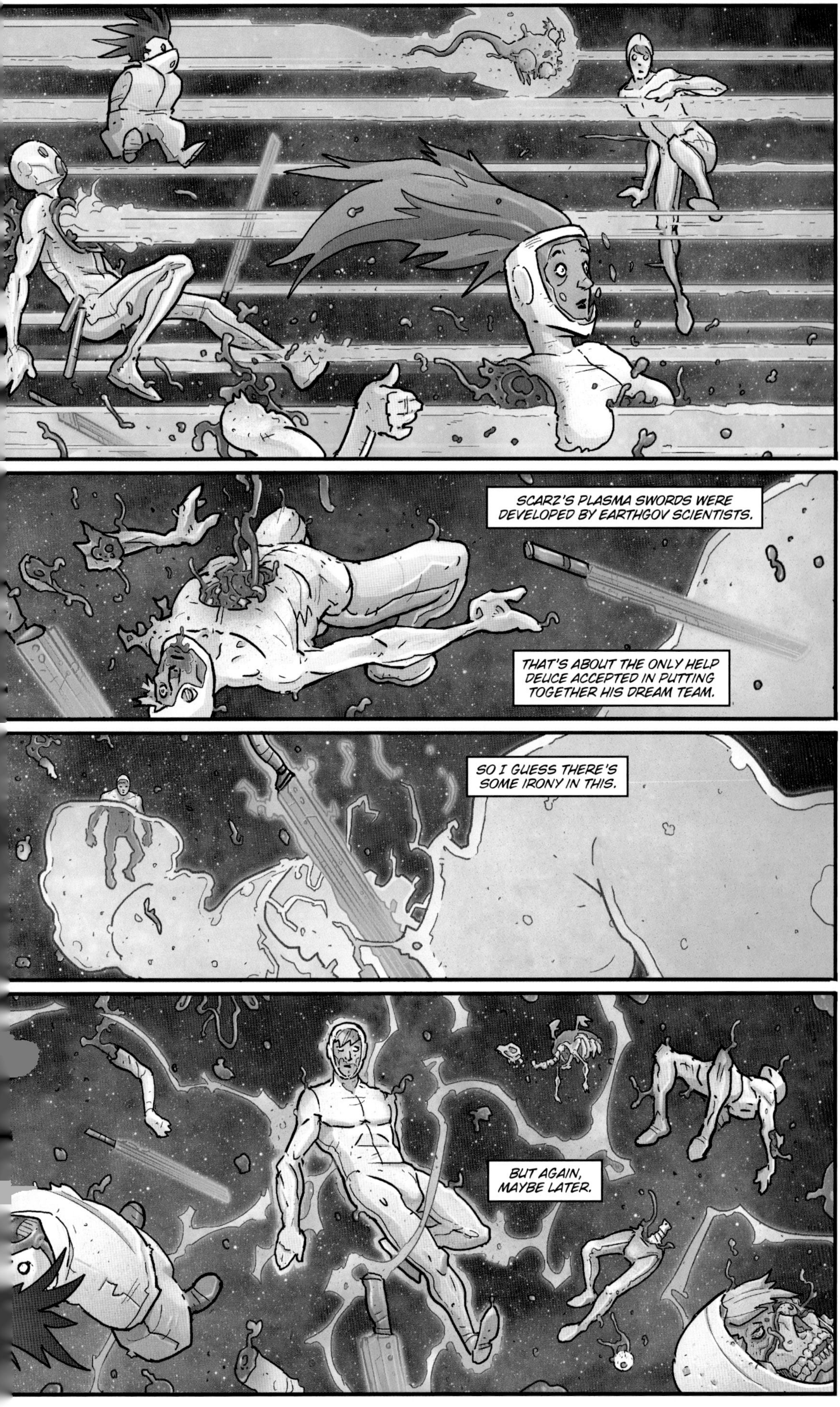
SCARZ'S PLASMA SWORDS WERE DEVELOPED BY EARTHGOV SCIENTISTS.
THAT'S ABOUT THE ONLY HELP DEUCE ACCEPTED IN PUTTING TOGETHER HIS DREAM TEAM.
SO I GUESS THERE'S SOME IRONY IN THIS.
BUT AGAIN, MAYBE LATER.

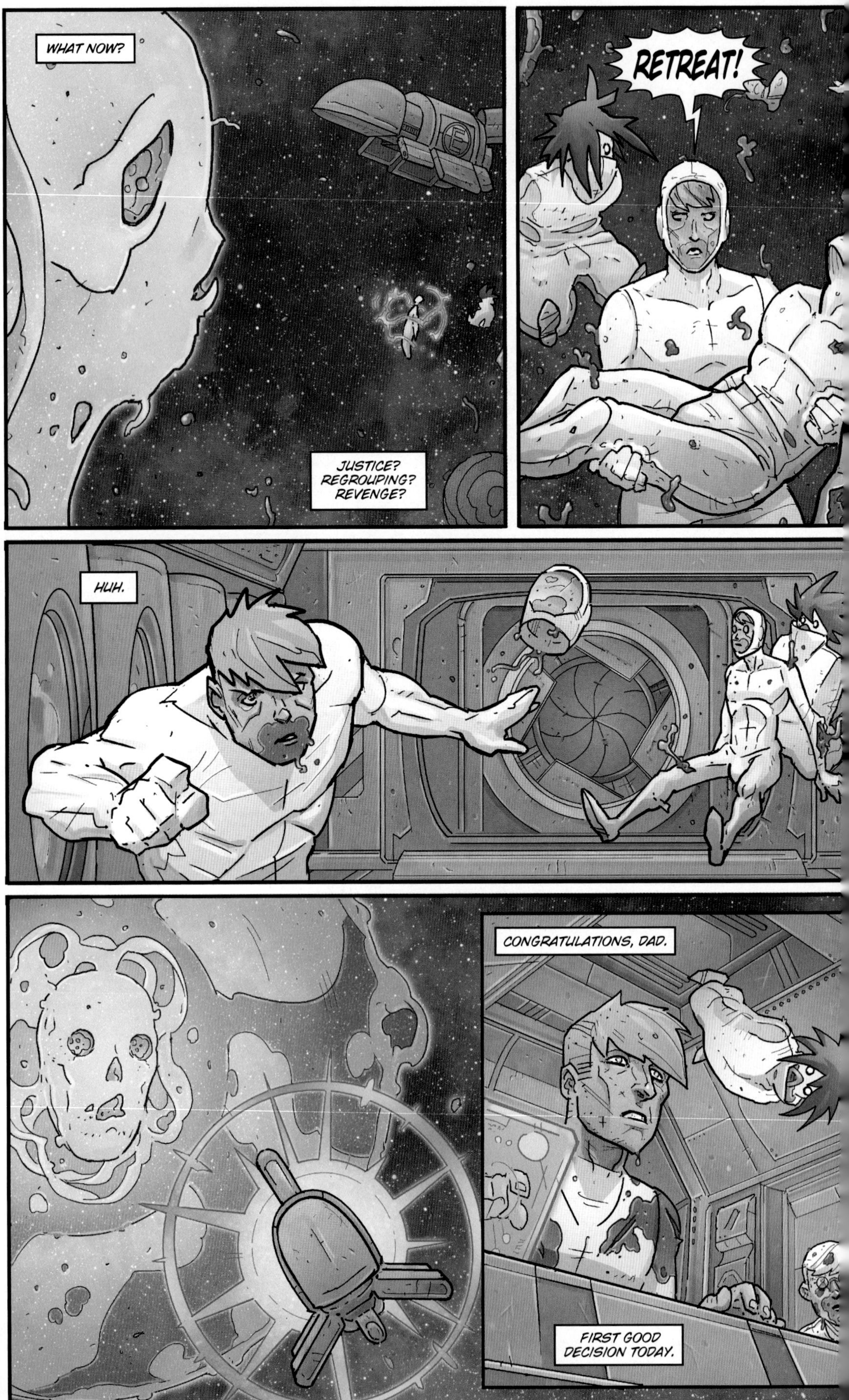
WHAT NOW?
JUSTICE? REGROUPING? REVENGE?
RETREAT!
HUH.
CONGRATULATIONS, DAD.
FIRST GOOD DECISION TODAY.

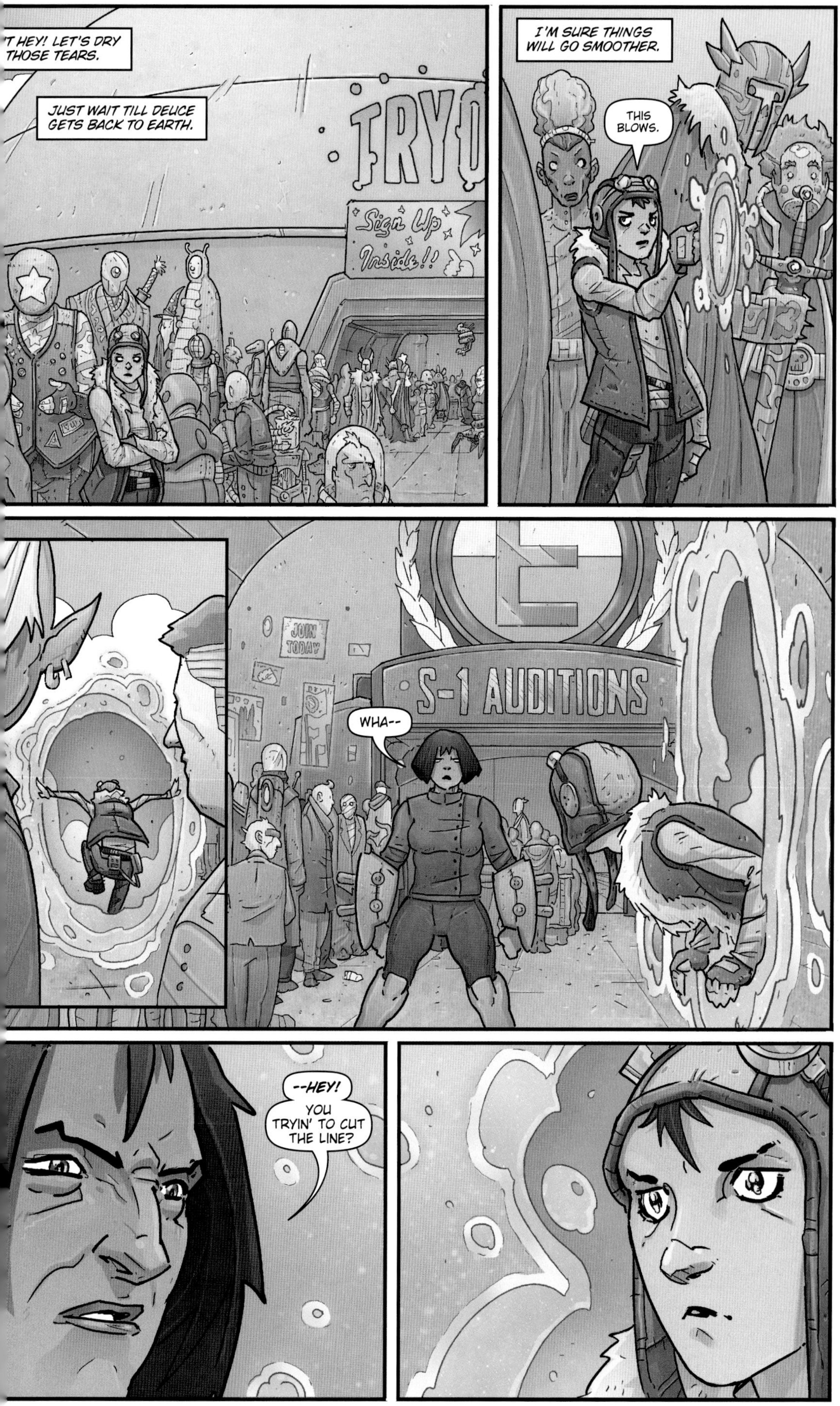
T HEY! LET'S DRY THOSE TEARS.
JUST WAIT TILL DEUCE GETS BACK TO EARTH.
TRYO
Sign Up Inside!!
I'M SURE THINGS WILL GO SMOOTHER.
THIS BLOWS.
JOIN TODAY
S-1 AUDITIONS
WHA--
--HEY! YOU TRYIN' TO CUT THE LINE?

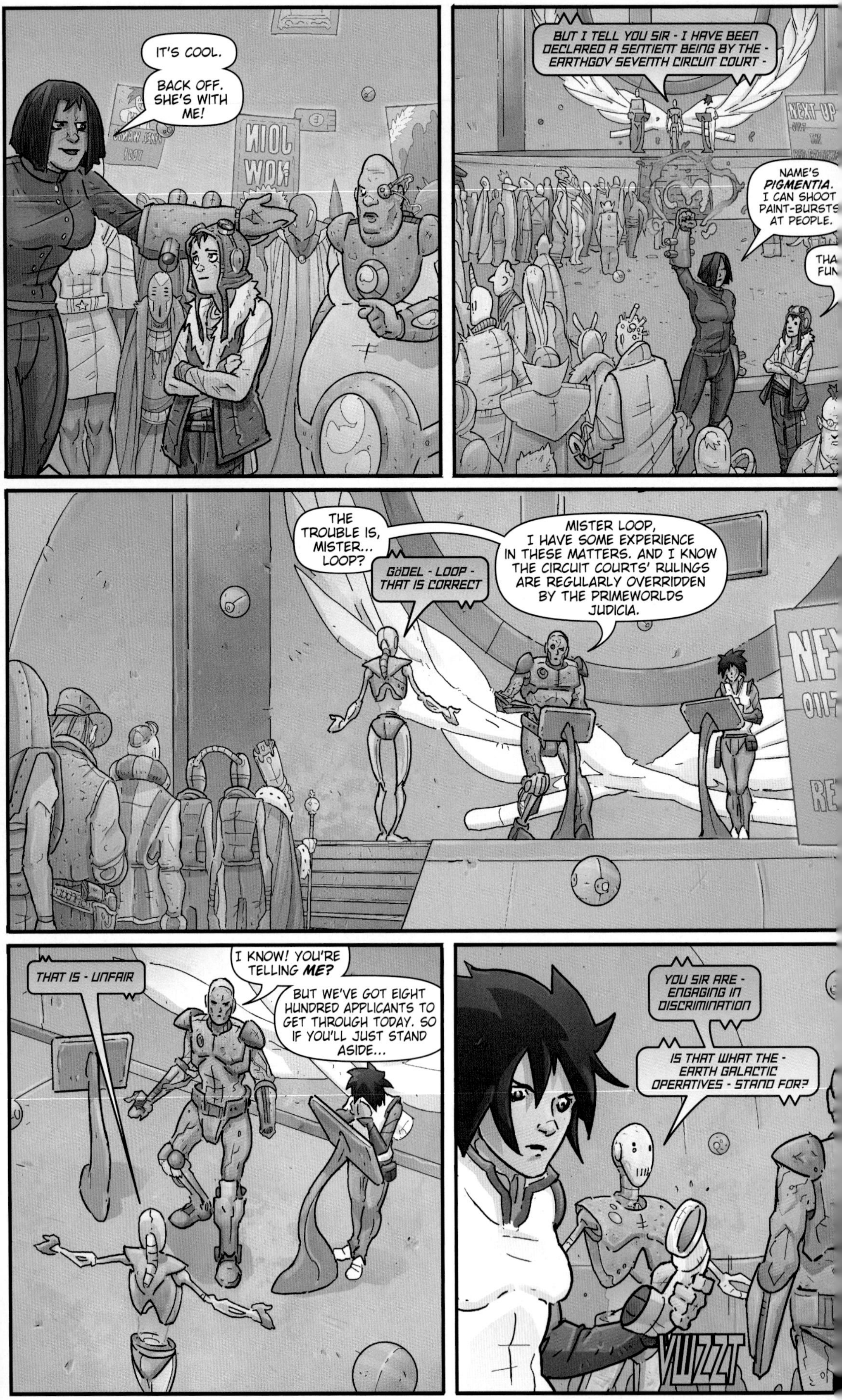

IT'S COOL.
BACK OFF. SHE'S WITH ME!
BUT I TELL YOU SIR - I HAVE BEEN DECLARED A SENTIENT BEING BY THE - EARTHGOV SEVENTH CIRCUIT COURT -
NAME'S **PIGMENTIA**. I CAN SHOOT PAINT-BURSTS AT PEOPLE.
THE TROUBLE IS, MISTER... LOOP?
GÖDEL - LOOP - THAT IS CORRECT
MISTER LOOP, I HAVE SOME EXPERIENCE IN THESE MATTERS. AND I KNOW THE CIRCUIT COURTS' RULINGS ARE REGULARLY OVERRIDDEN BY THE PRIMEWORLDS JUDICIA.
THAT IS - UNFAIR
I KNOW! YOU'RE TELLING **ME?**
BUT WE'VE GOT EIGHT HUNDRED APPLICANTS TO GET THROUGH TODAY. SO IF YOU'LL JUST STAND ASIDE...
YOU SIR ARE - ENGAGING IN DISCRIMINATION
IS THAT WHAT THE - EARTH GALACTIC OPERATIVES - STAND FOR?
VUZZT

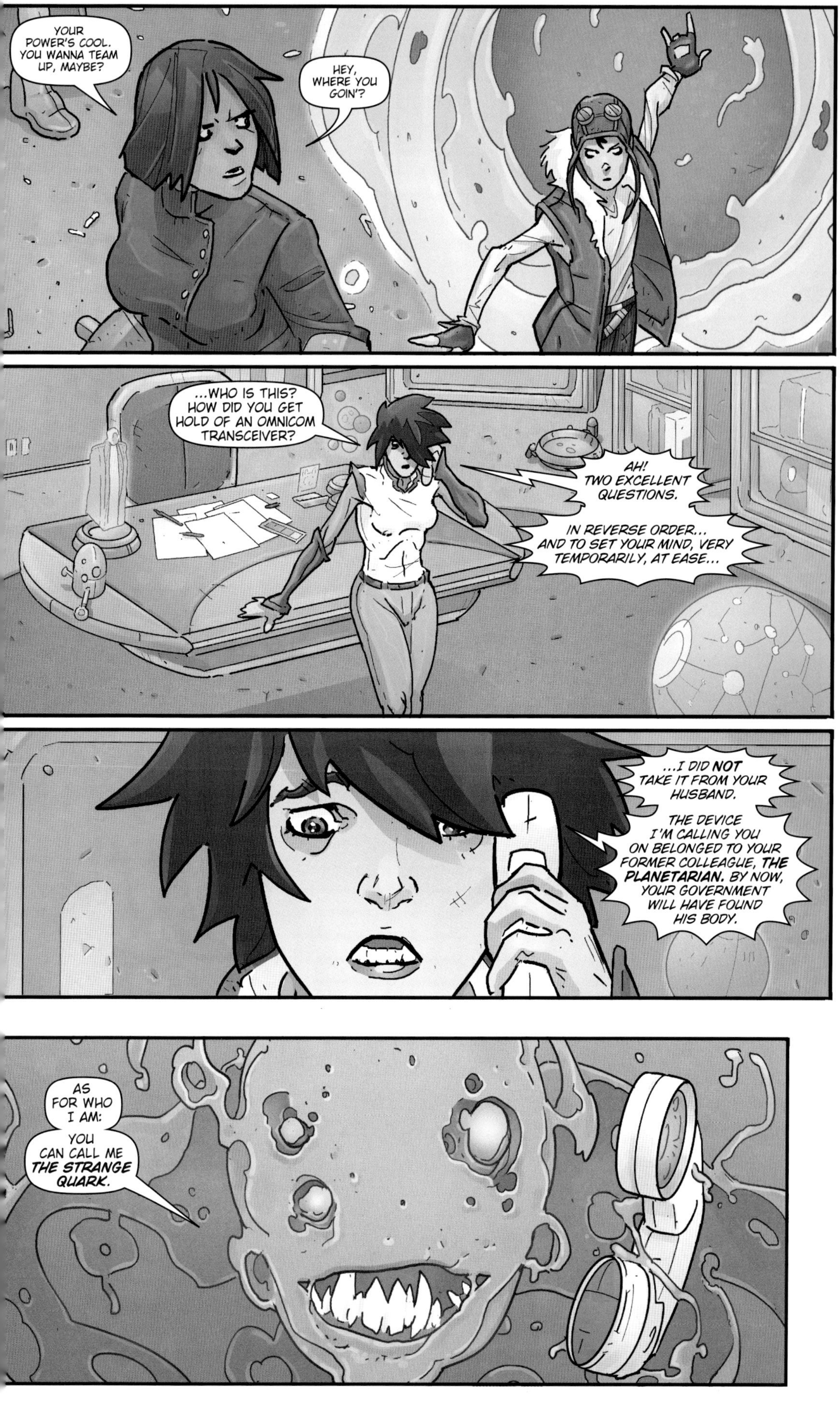
YOUR POWER'S COOL. YOU WANNA TEAM UP, MAYBE?
HEY, WHERE YOU GOIN'?
...WHO IS THIS? HOW DID YOU GET HOLD OF AN OMNICOM TRANSCEIVER?
AH! TWO EXCELLENT QUESTIONS.
IN REVERSE ORDER... AND TO SET YOUR MIND, VERY TEMPORARILY, AT EASE...
...I DID **NOT** TAKE IT FROM YOUR HUSBAND.
THE DEVICE I'M CALLING YOU ON BELONGED TO YOUR FORMER COLLEAGUE, **THE PLANETARIAN.** BY NOW, YOUR GOVERNMENT WILL HAVE FOUND HIS BODY.
AS FOR WHO I AM:
YOU CAN CALL ME ***THE STRANGE QUARK.***

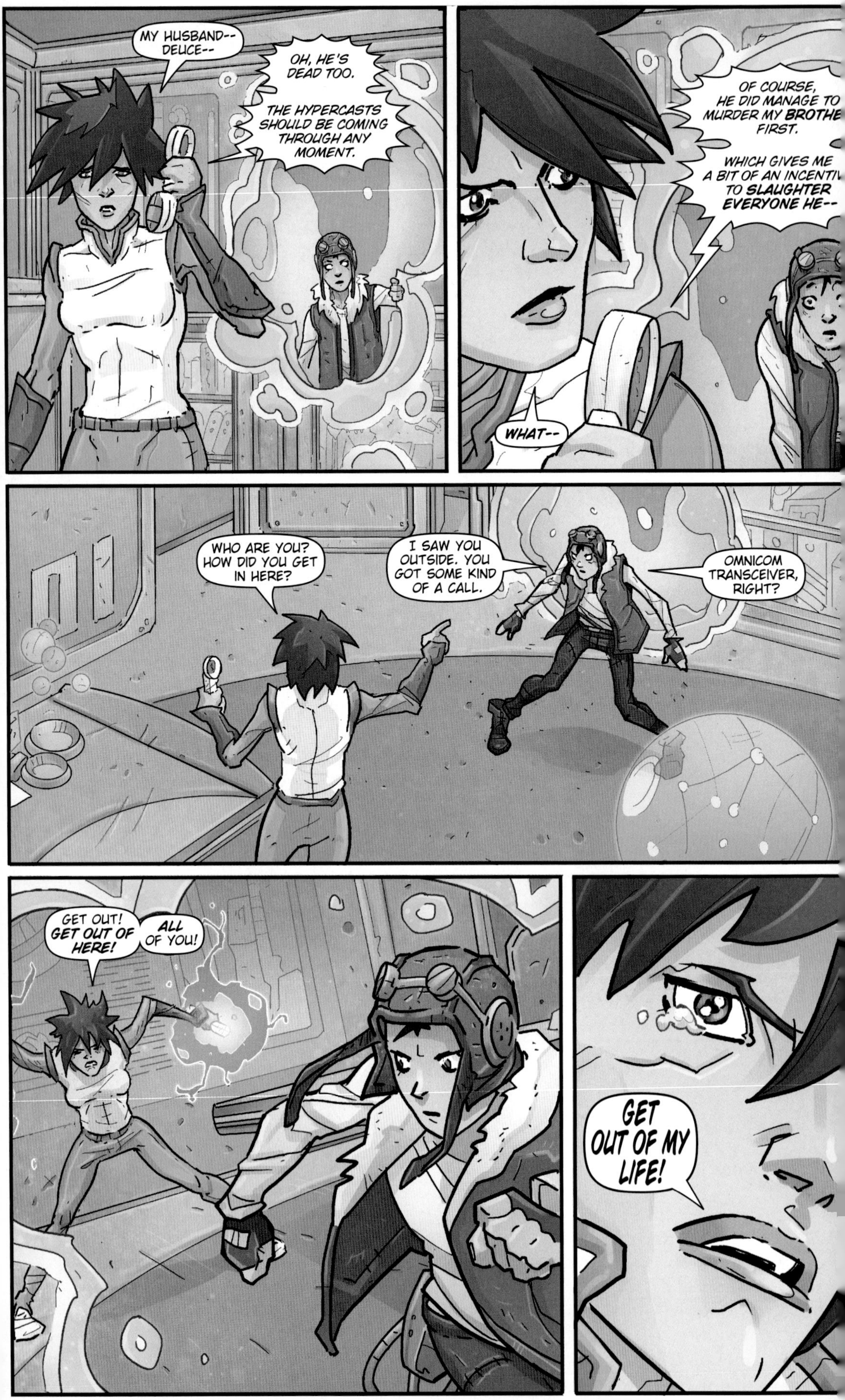
MY HUSBAND--
DEUCE--
OH, HE'S DEAD TOO.
THE HYPERCASTS SHOULD BE COMING THROUGH ANY MOMENT.
OF COURSE, HE DID MANAGE TO MURDER MY BROTHE FIRST.
WHICH GIVES ME A BIT OF AN INCENTIV TO SLAUGHTER EVERYONE HE--
WHAT--
WHO ARE YOU? HOW DID YOU GET IN HERE?
I SAW YOU OUTSIDE. YOU GOT SOME KIND OF A CALL.
OMNICOM TRANSCEIVER, RIGHT?
GET OUT! GET OUT OF HERE!
ALL OF YOU!
GET OUT OF MY LIFE!

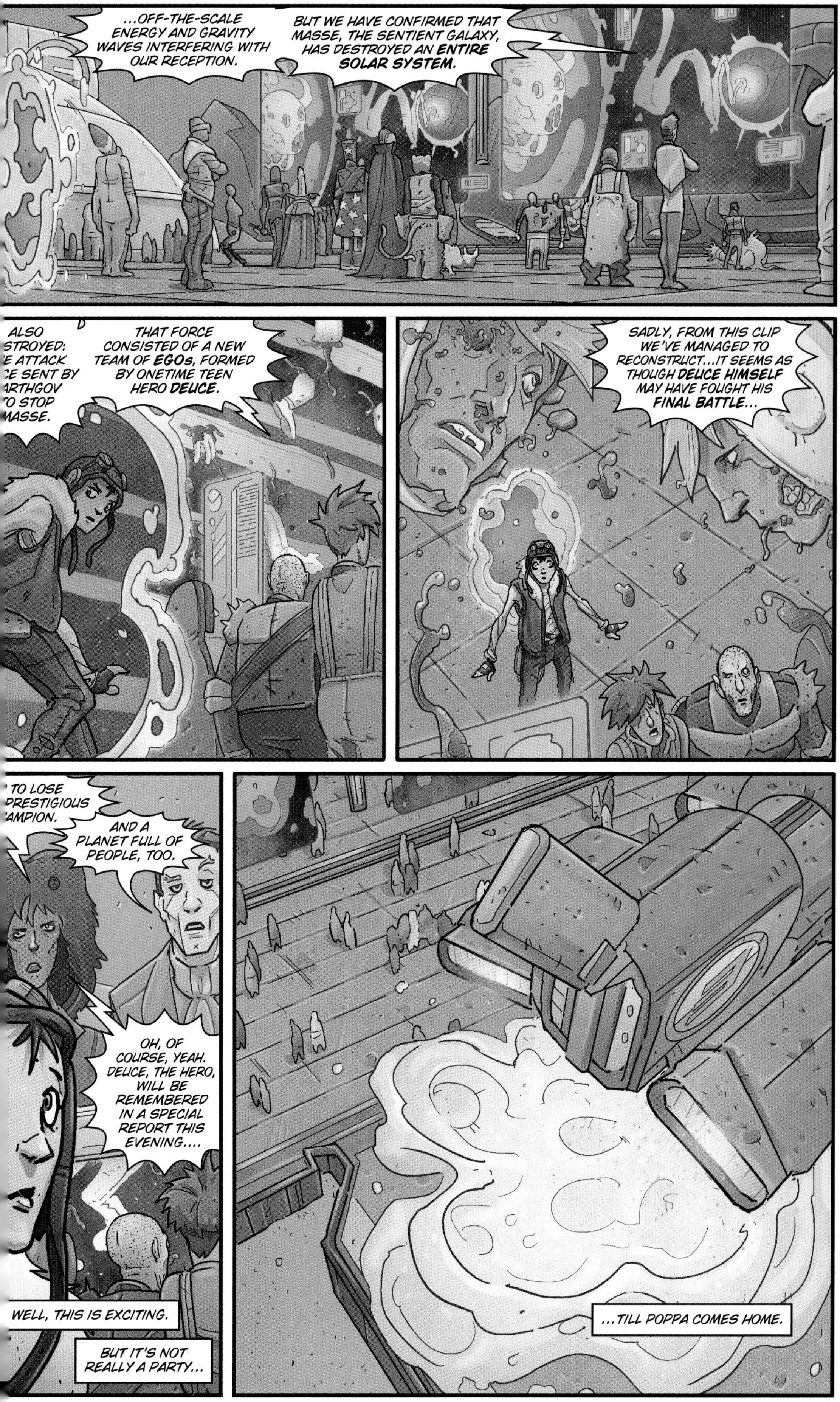
...OFF-THE-SCALE ENERGY AND GRAVITY WAVES INTERFERING WITH OUR RECEPTION.
BUT WE HAVE CONFIRMED THAT MASSE, THE SENTIENT GALAXY, HAS DESTROYED AN ENTIRE SOLAR SYSTEM.
ALSO STROYED: E ATTACK E SENT BY ARTHGOV O STOP MASSE.
THAT FORCE CONSISTED OF A NEW TEAM OF EGOs, FORMED BY ONETIME TEEN HERO DEUCE.
SADLY, FROM THIS CLIP WE'VE MANAGED TO RECONSTRUCT...IT SEEMS AS THOUGH DEUCE HIMSELF MAY HAVE FOUGHT HIS FINAL BATTLE...
TO LOSE PRESTIGIOUS AMPION.
AND A PLANET FULL OF PEOPLE, TOO.
OH, OF COURSE, YEAH. DEUCE, THE HERO, WILL BE REMEMBERED IN A SPECIAL REPORT THIS EVENING....
WELL, THIS IS EXCITING.
BUT IT'S NOT REALLY A PARTY...
...TILL POPPA COMES HOME.

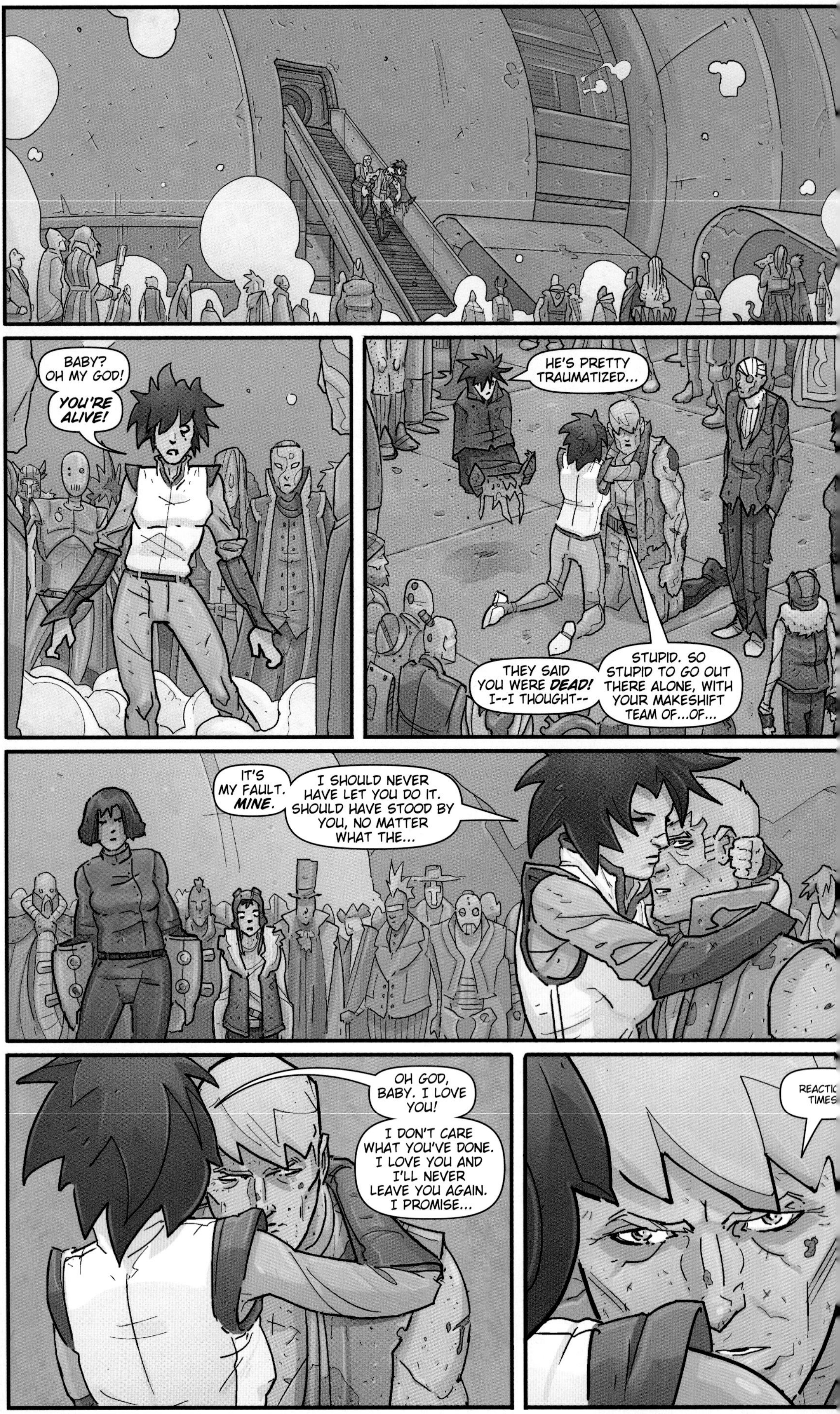
BABY? OH MY GOD! YOU'RE ALIVE!
HE'S PRETTY TRAUMATIZED...
THEY SAID YOU WERE DEAD! I--I THOUGHT--
STUPID. SO STUPID TO GO OUT THERE ALONE, WITH YOUR MAKESHIFT TEAM OF...OF...
IT'S MY FAULT. MINE.
I SHOULD NEVER HAVE LET YOU DO IT. SHOULD HAVE STOOD BY YOU, NO MATTER WHAT THE...
OH GOD, BABY. I LOVE YOU!
I DON'T CARE WHAT YOU'VE DONE. I LOVE YOU AND I'LL NEVER LEAVE YOU AGAIN. I PROMISE...

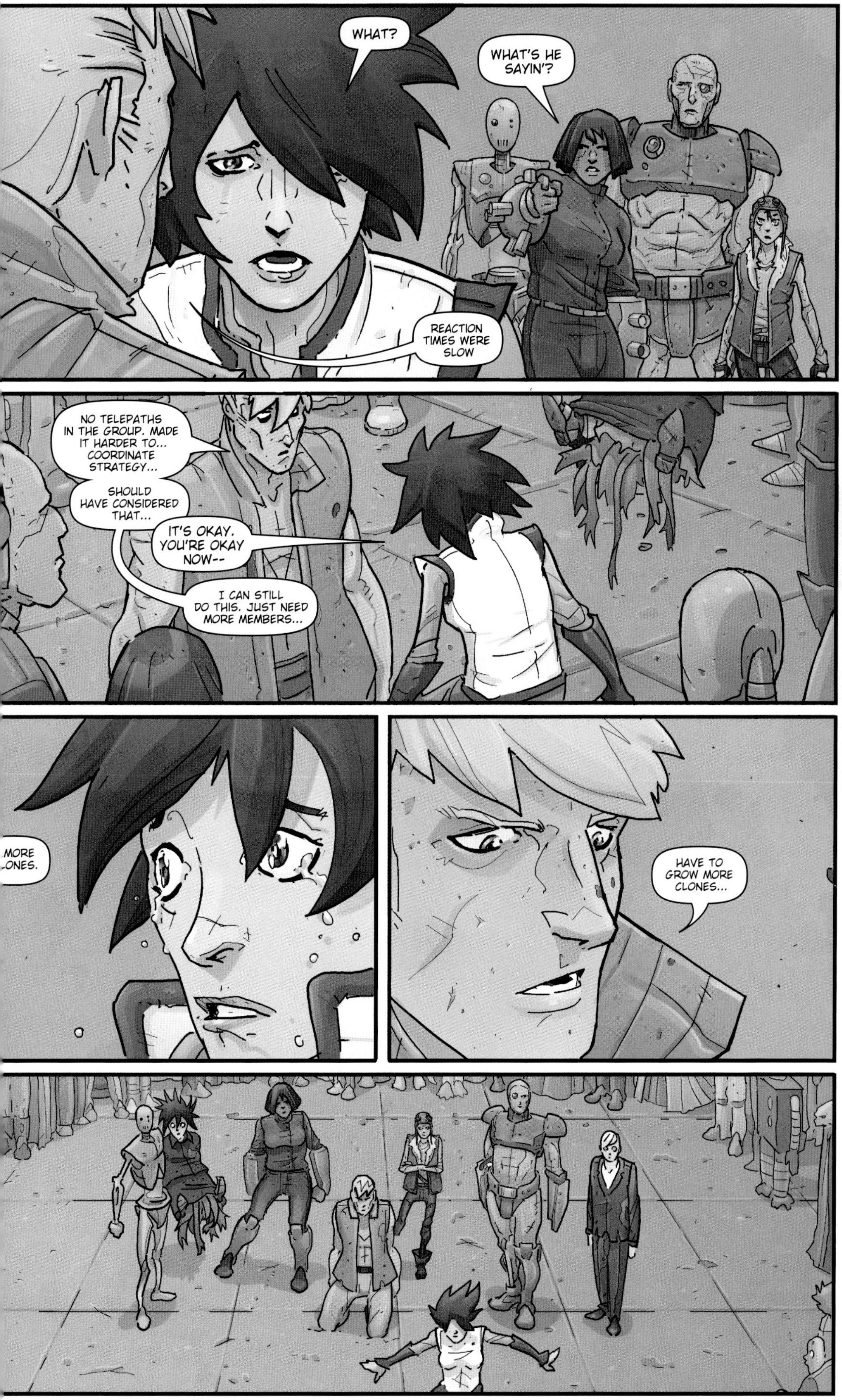
WHAT?
WHAT'S HE SAYIN'?
REACTION TIMES WERE SLOW
NO TELEPATHS IN THE GROUP. MADE IT HARDER TO... COORDINATE STRATEGY...
SHOULD HAVE CONSIDERED THAT...
IT'S OKAY. YOU'RE OKAY NOW--
I CAN STILL DO THIS. JUST NEED MORE MEMBERS...
MORE ONES.
HAVE TO GROW MORE CLONES...

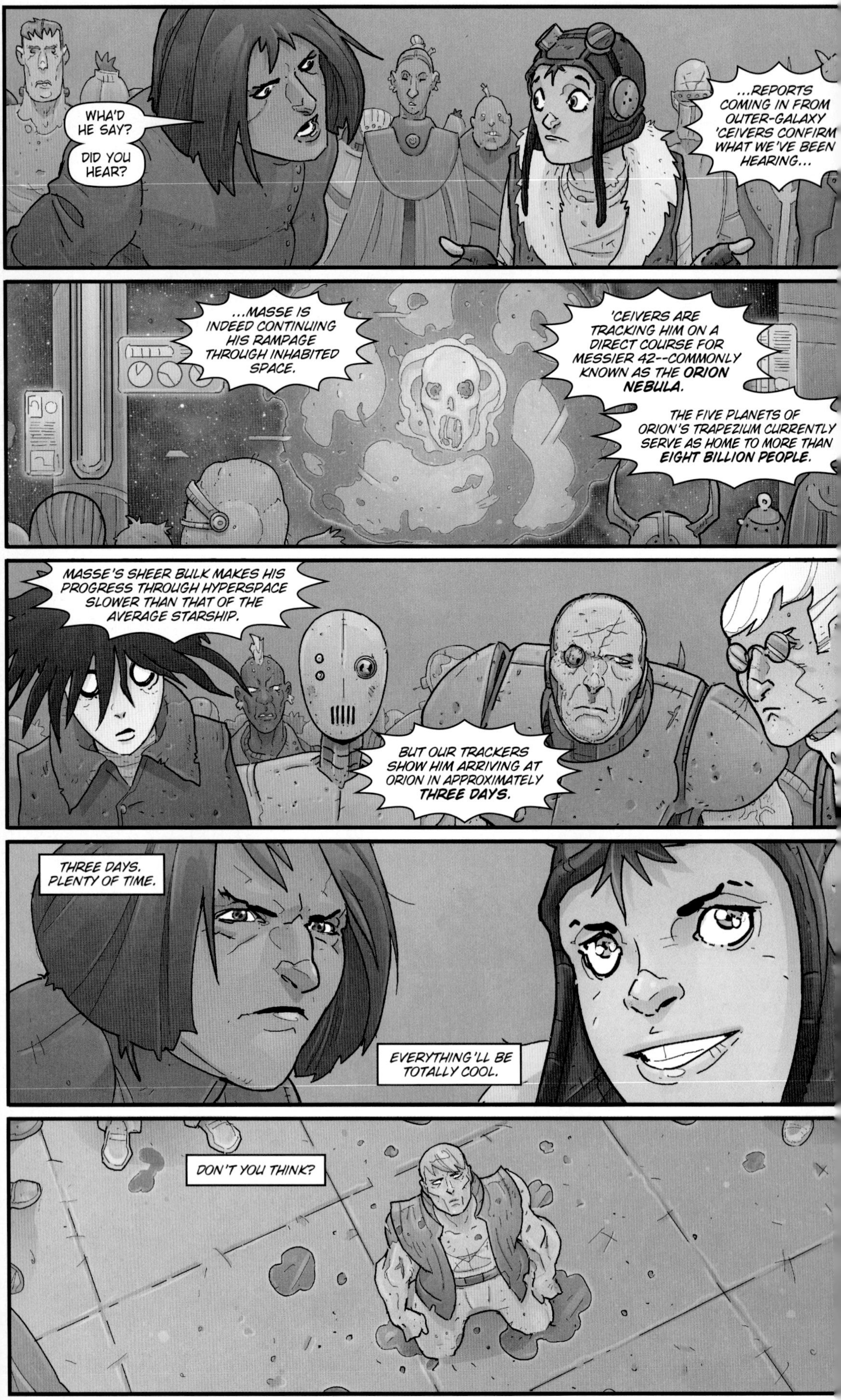
WHA'D HE SAY?
DID YOU HEAR?
...REPORTS COMING IN FROM OUTER-GALAXY 'CEIVERS CONFIRM WHAT WE'VE BEEN HEARING...
...MASSE IS INDEED CONTINUING HIS RAMPAGE THROUGH INHABITED SPACE.
'CEIVERS ARE TRACKING HIM ON A DIRECT COURSE FOR MESSIER 42--COMMONLY KNOWN AS THE ORION NEBULA.
THE FIVE PLANETS OF ORION'S TRAPEZIUM CURRENTLY SERVE AS HOME TO MORE THAN EIGHT BILLION PEOPLE.
MASSE'S SHEER BULK MAKES HIS PROGRESS THROUGH HYPERSPACE SLOWER THAN THAT OF THE AVERAGE STARSHIP.
BUT OUR TRACKERS SHOW HIM ARRIVING AT ORION IN APPROXIMATELY THREE DAYS.
THREE DAYS. PLENTY OF TIME.
EVERYTHING'LL BE TOTALLY COOL.
DON'T YOU THINK?

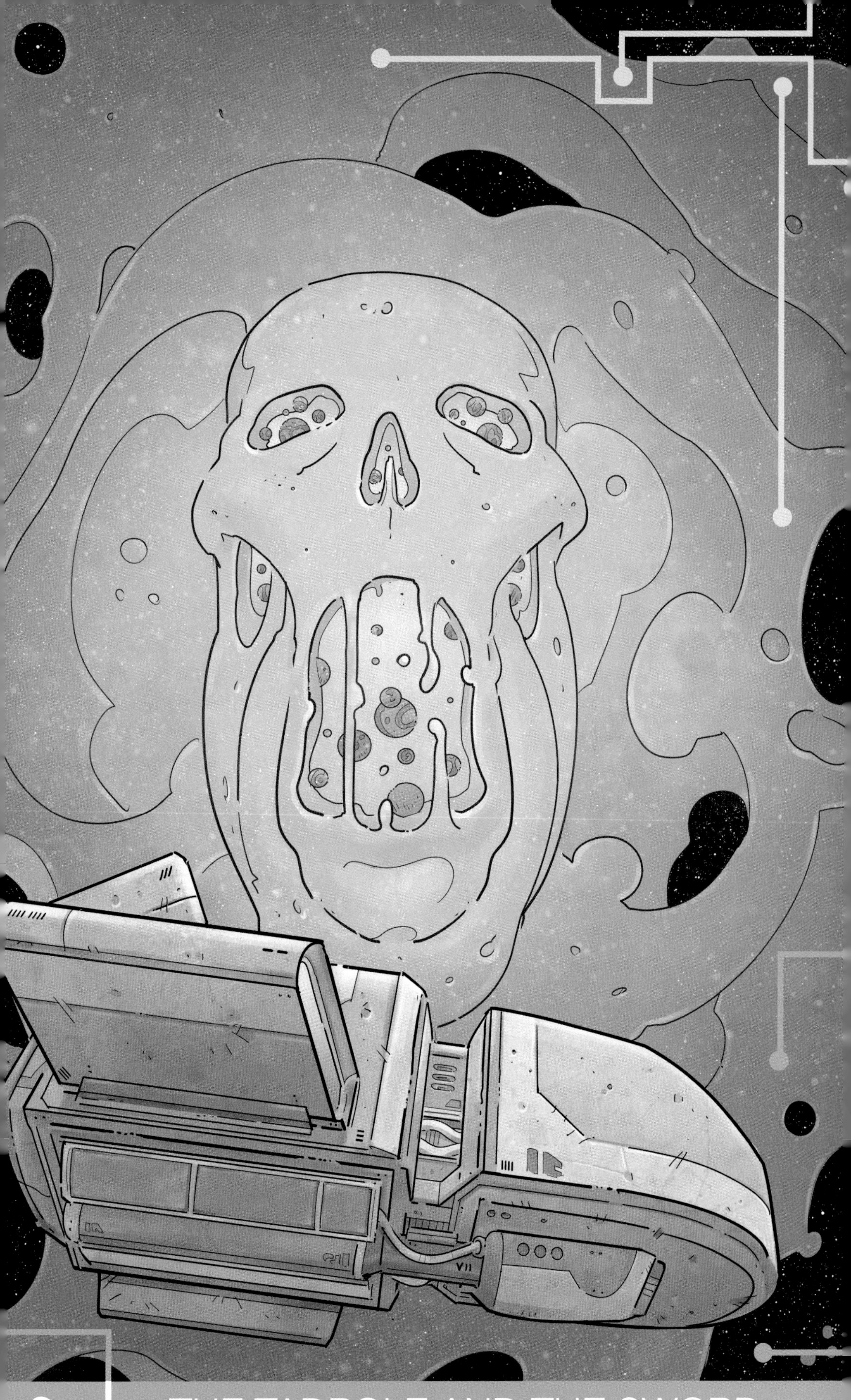

3 THE TADPOLE AND THE SWORD

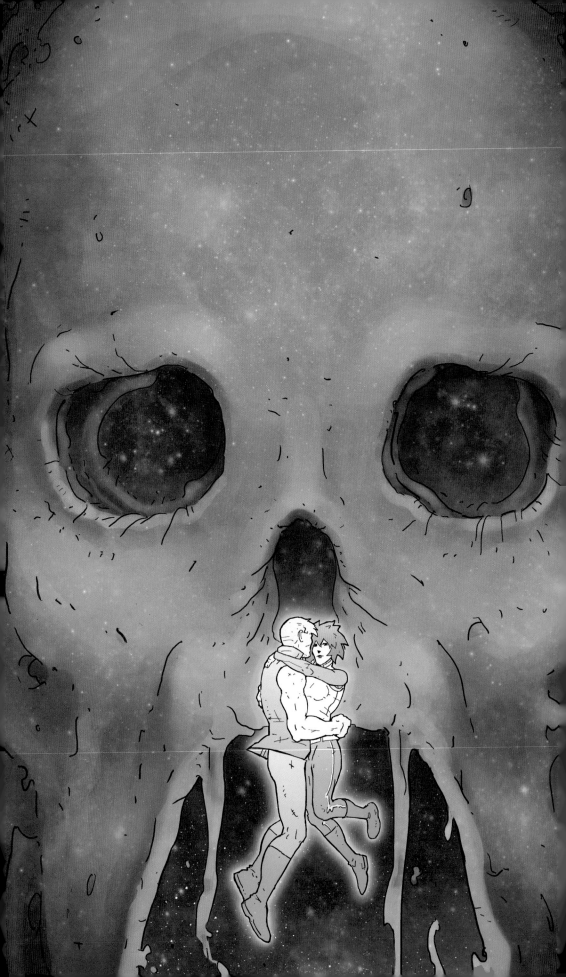

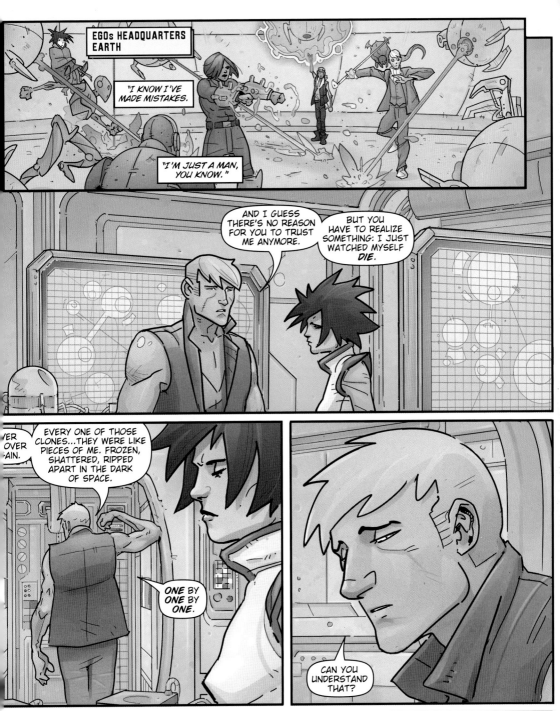

EGOs HEADQUARTERS
EARTH

"I KNOW I'VE MADE MISTAKES."

"I'M JUST A MAN, YOU KNOW."

AND I GUESS THERE'S NO REASON FOR YOU TO TRUST ME ANYMORE.

BUT YOU HAVE TO REALIZE SOMETHING: I JUST WATCHED MYSELF DIE.

...VER OVER ...AIN.

EVERY ONE OF THOSE CLONES...THEY WERE LIKE PIECES OF ME. FROZEN, SHATTERED, RIPPED APART IN THE DARK OF SPACE.

ONE BY ONE BY ONE.

CAN YOU UNDERSTAND THAT?

OH, I UNDERSTAND.

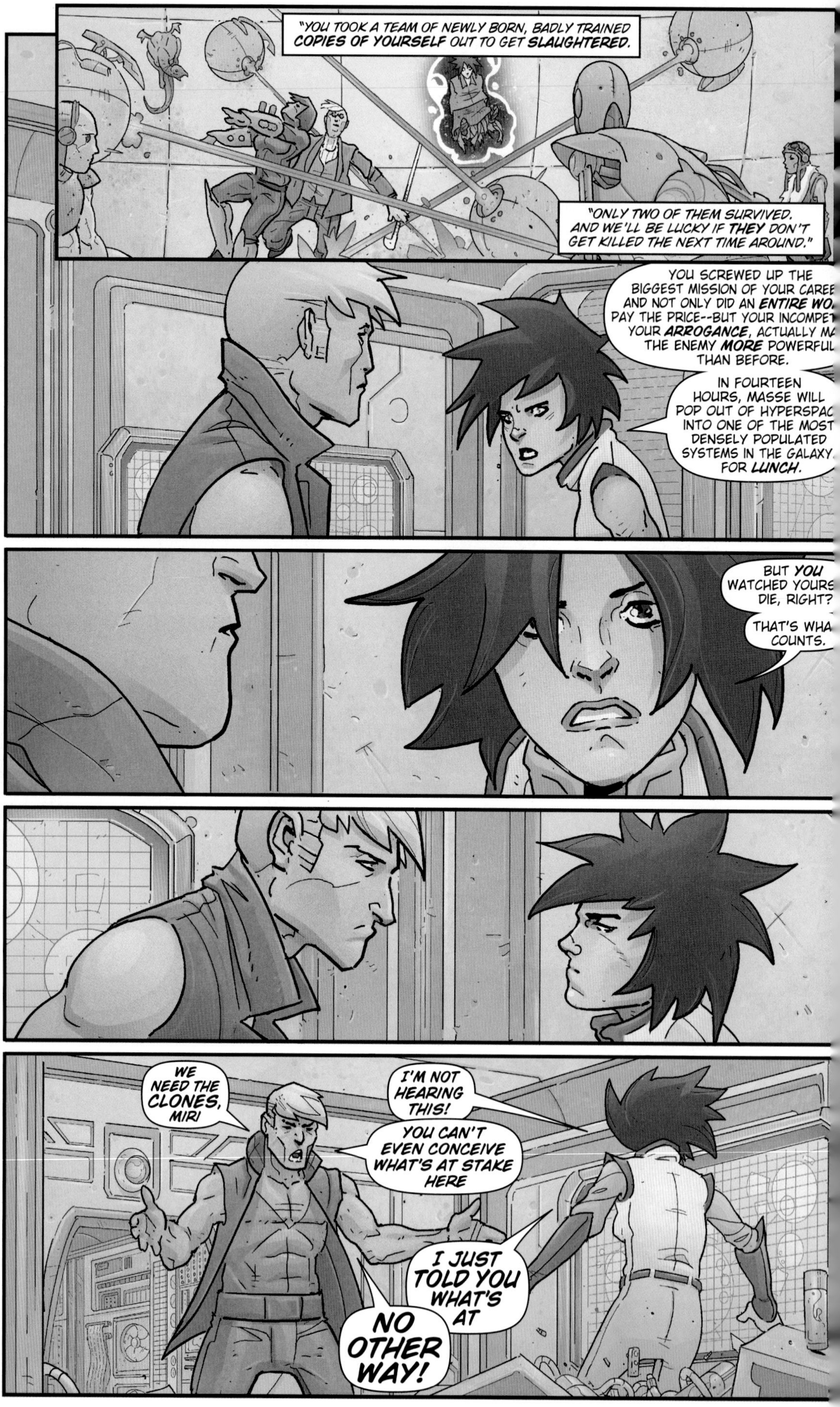
"YOU TOOK A TEAM OF NEWLY BORN, BADLY TRAINED COPIES OF YOURSELF OUT TO GET SLAUGHTERED.
"ONLY TWO OF THEM SURVIVED. AND WE'LL BE LUCKY IF THEY DON'T GET KILLED THE NEXT TIME AROUND."
YOU SCREWED UP THE BIGGEST MISSION OF YOUR CAREE AND NOT ONLY DID AN ENTIRE WO PAY THE PRICE--BUT YOUR INCOMPET YOUR ARROGANCE, ACTUALLY MA THE ENEMY MORE POWERFUL THAN BEFORE.
IN FOURTEEN HOURS, MASSE WILL POP OUT OF HYPERSPAC INTO ONE OF THE MOST DENSELY POPULATED SYSTEMS IN THE GALAXY. FOR LUNCH.
BUT YOU WATCHED YOURS DIE, RIGHT?
THAT'S WHA COUNTS.
WE NEED THE CLONES, MIRI
I'M NOT HEARING THIS!
YOU CAN'T EVEN CONCEIVE WHAT'S AT STAKE HERE
I JUST TOLD YOU WHAT'S AT
NO OTHER WAY!

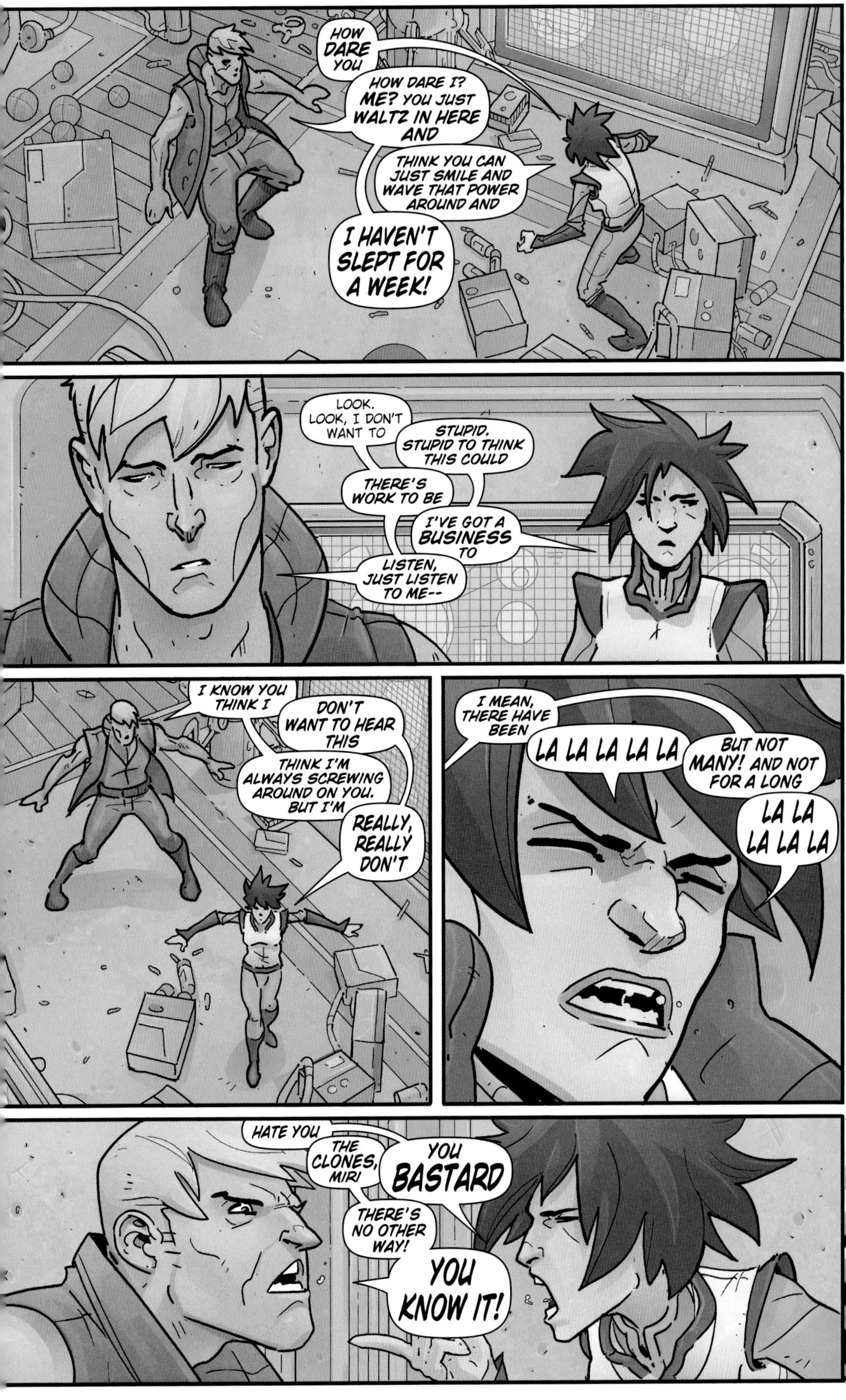
HOW DARE YOU
HOW DARE I? ME? YOU JUST WALTZ IN HERE AND
THINK YOU CAN JUST SMILE AND WAVE THAT POWER AROUND AND
I HAVEN'T SLEPT FOR A WEEK!
LOOK. LOOK, I DON'T WANT TO
STUPID. STUPID TO THINK THIS COULD
THERE'S WORK TO BE
I'VE GOT A BUSINESS TO
LISTEN, JUST LISTEN TO ME--
I KNOW YOU THINK I
DON'T WANT TO HEAR THIS
THINK I'M ALWAYS SCREWING AROUND ON YOU. BUT I'M
REALLY, REALLY DON'T
I MEAN, THERE HAVE BEEN
LA LA LA LA LA
BUT NOT MANY! AND NOT FOR A LONG
LA LA LA LA LA
HATE YOU
THE CLONES, MIRI
YOU BASTARD
THERE'S NO OTHER WAY!
YOU KNOW IT!

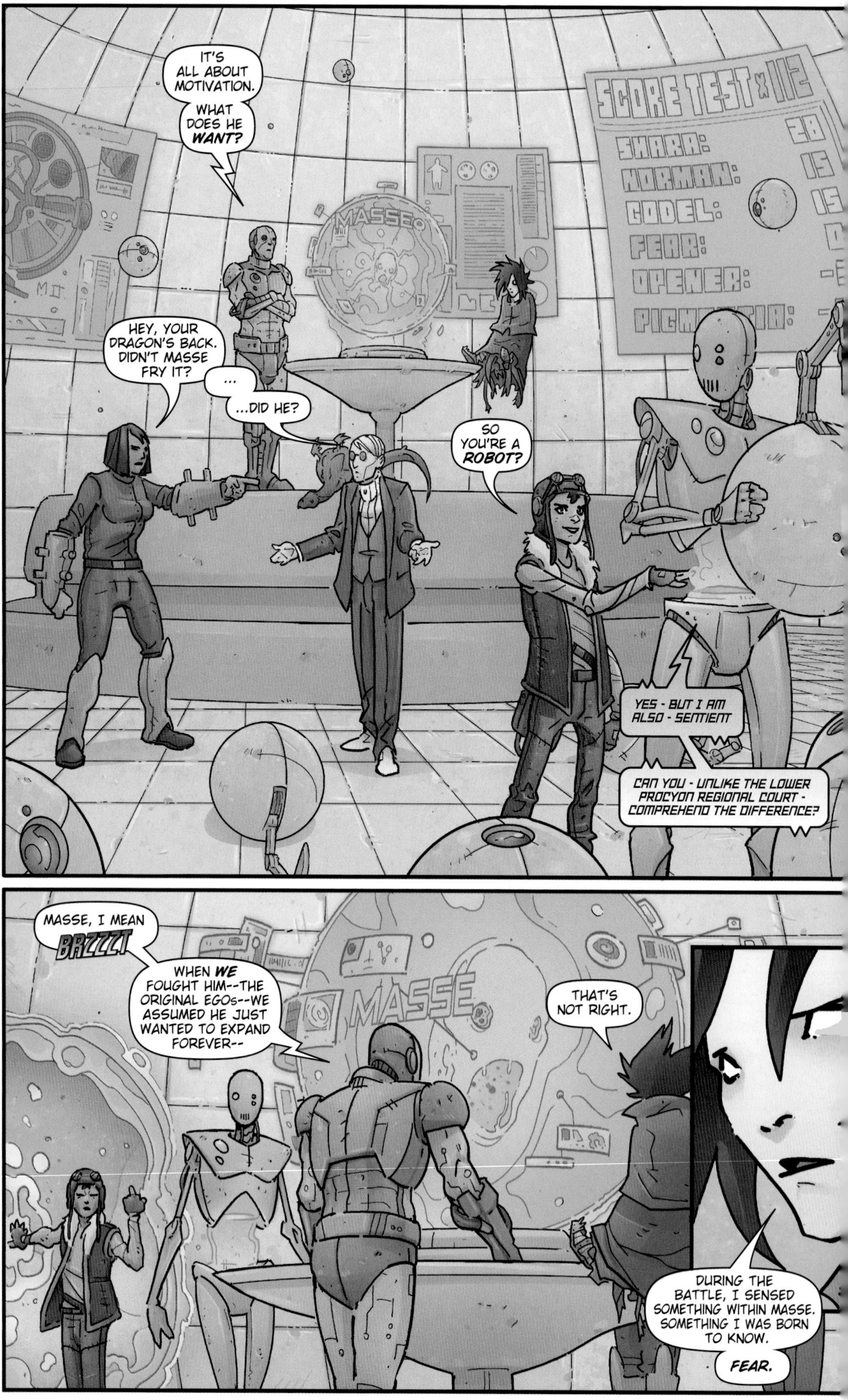

SCORE TEST x 112
SHARA: 28
NORMAN: 15
GODEL:
FEAR:
OPENER:
MASSE
IT'S ALL ABOUT MOTIVATION.
WHAT DOES HE ***WANT?***
HEY, YOUR DRAGON'S BACK. DIDN'T MASSE FRY IT?
...
...DID HE?
SO YOU'RE A ***ROBOT?***
YES - BUT I AM ALSO - SENTIENT
CAN YOU - UNLIKE THE LOWER PROCYON REGIONAL COURT - COMPREHEND THE DIFFERENCE?
MASSE, I MEAN
BRZZZT
WHEN ***WE*** FOUGHT HIM--THE ORIGINAL EGOs--WE ASSUMED HE JUST WANTED TO EXPAND FOREVER--
THAT'S NOT RIGHT.
DURING THE BATTLE, I SENSED SOMETHING WITHIN MASSE. SOMETHING I WAS BORN TO KNOW.
FEAR.

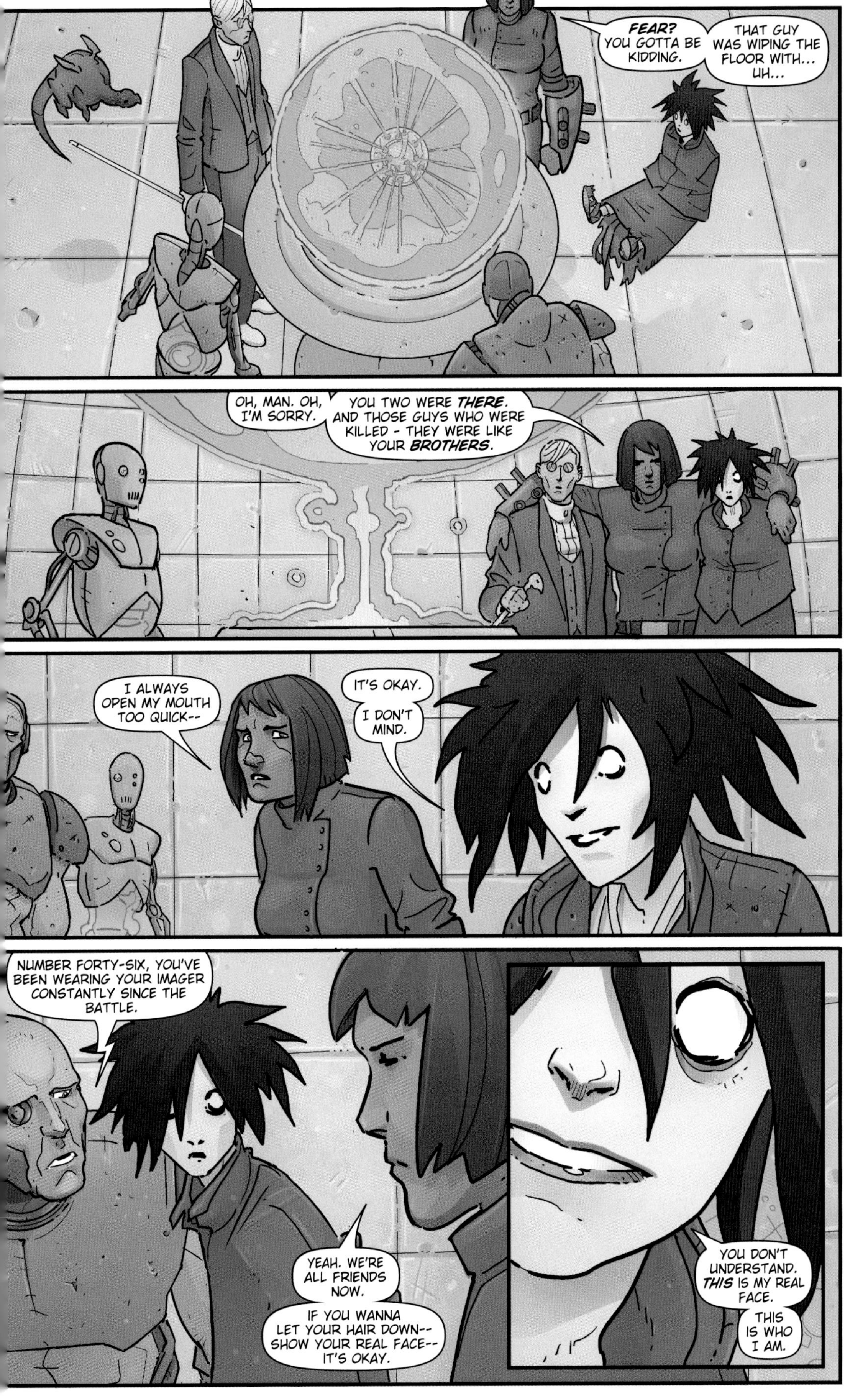
FEAR? YOU GOTTA BE KIDDING.
THAT GUY WAS WIPING THE FLOOR WITH... UH...
OH, MAN. OH, I'M SORRY.
YOU TWO WERE THERE. AND THOSE GUYS WHO WERE KILLED - THEY WERE LIKE YOUR BROTHERS.
I ALWAYS OPEN MY MOUTH TOO QUICK--
IT'S OKAY.
I DON'T MIND.
NUMBER FORTY-SIX, YOU'VE BEEN WEARING YOUR IMAGER CONSTANTLY SINCE THE BATTLE.
YEAH. WE'RE ALL FRIENDS NOW.
IF YOU WANNA LET YOUR HAIR DOWN-- SHOW YOUR REAL FACE-- IT'S OKAY.
YOU DON'T UNDERSTAND. THIS IS MY REAL FACE.
THIS IS WHO I AM.

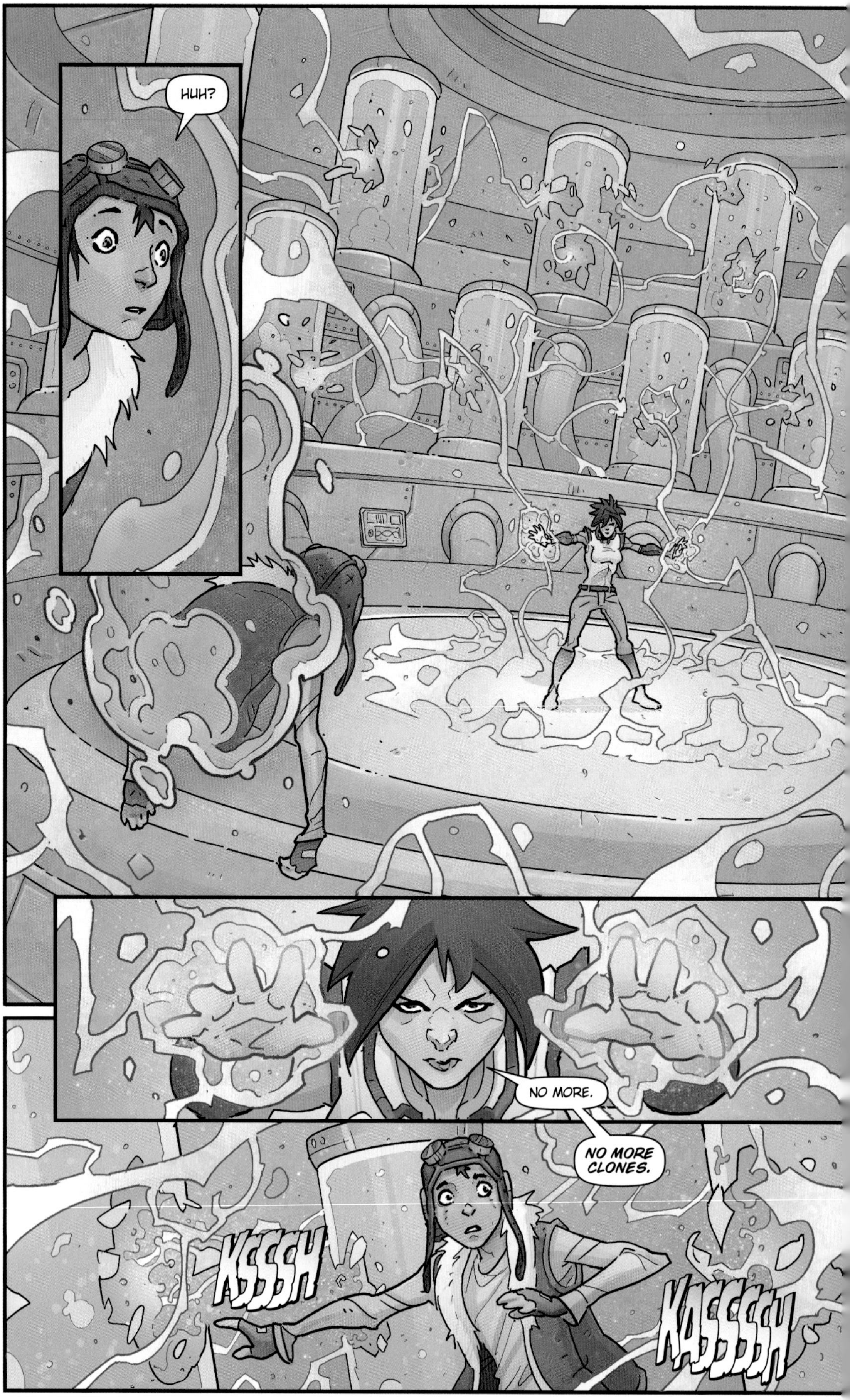
HUH?
NO MORE.
NO MORE CLONES.
KSSSH
KASSSSH

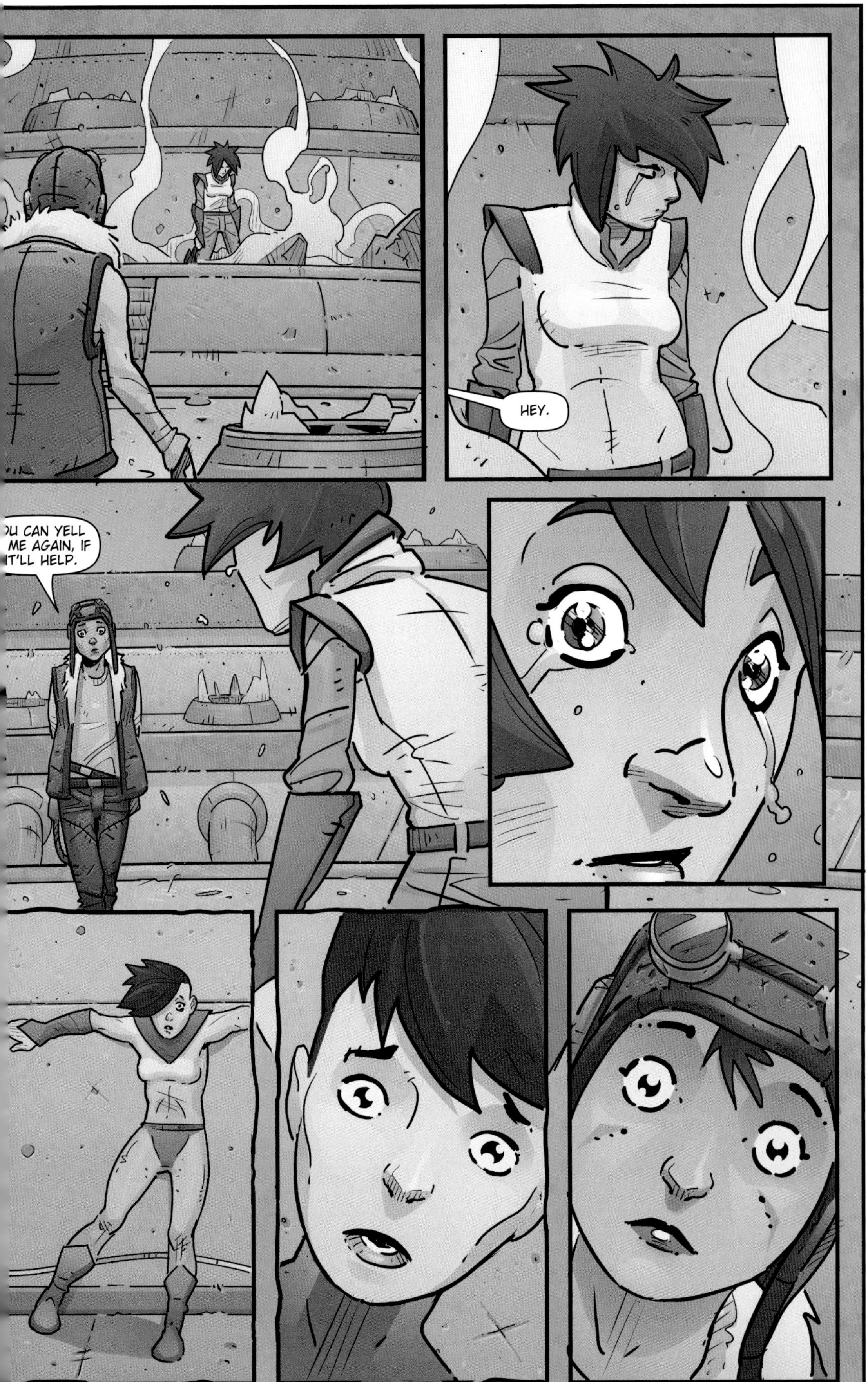
HEY.
OU CAN YELL
ME AGAIN, IF
IT'LL HELP.

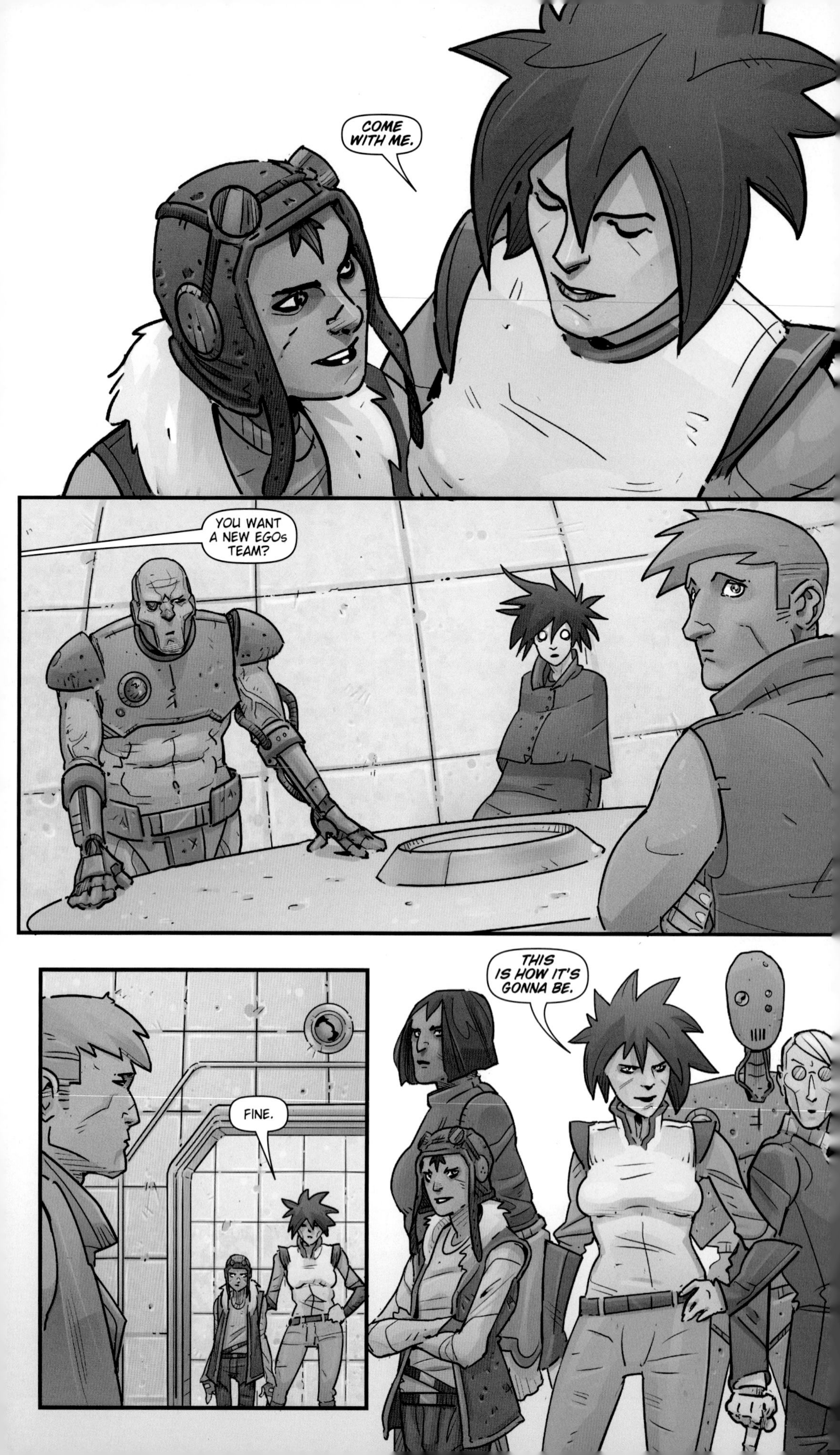
COME WITH ME.
YOU WANT A NEW EGOs TEAM?
FINE.
THIS IS HOW IT'S GONNA BE.

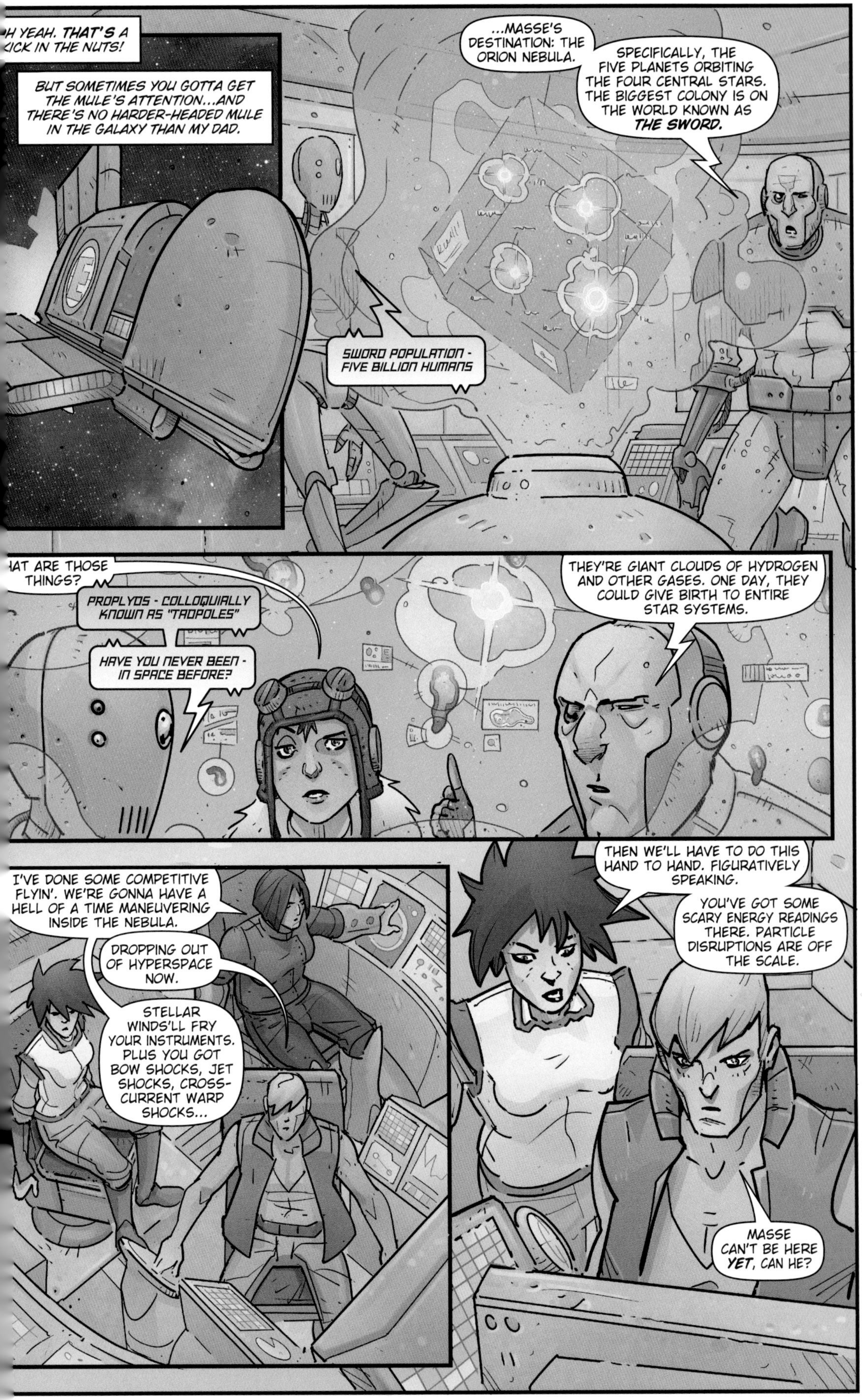
H YEAH. THAT'S A
KICK IN THE NUTS!
BUT SOMETIMES YOU GOTTA GET THE MULE'S ATTENTION...AND THERE'S NO HARDER-HEADED MULE IN THE GALAXY THAN MY DAD.
...MASSE'S DESTINATION: THE ORION NEBULA.
SPECIFICALLY, THE FIVE PLANETS ORBITING THE FOUR CENTRAL STARS. THE BIGGEST COLONY IS ON THE WORLD KNOWN AS THE SWORD.
SWORD POPULATION - FIVE BILLION HUMANS
HAT ARE THOSE THINGS?
PROPLYDS - COLLOQUIALLY KNOWN AS "TADPOLES"
HAVE YOU NEVER BEEN - IN SPACE BEFORE?
THEY'RE GIANT CLOUDS OF HYDROGEN AND OTHER GASES. ONE DAY, THEY COULD GIVE BIRTH TO ENTIRE STAR SYSTEMS.
I'VE DONE SOME COMPETITIVE FLYIN'. WE'RE GONNA HAVE A HELL OF A TIME MANEUVERING INSIDE THE NEBULA.
DROPPING OUT OF HYPERSPACE NOW.
STELLAR WINDS'LL FRY YOUR INSTRUMENTS. PLUS YOU GOT BOW SHOCKS, JET SHOCKS, CROSS-CURRENT WARP SHOCKS...
THEN WE'LL HAVE TO DO THIS HAND TO HAND. FIGURATIVELY SPEAKING.
YOU'VE GOT SOME SCARY ENERGY READINGS THERE. PARTICLE DISRUPTIONS ARE OFF THE SCALE.
MASSE CAN'T BE HERE YET, CAN HE?

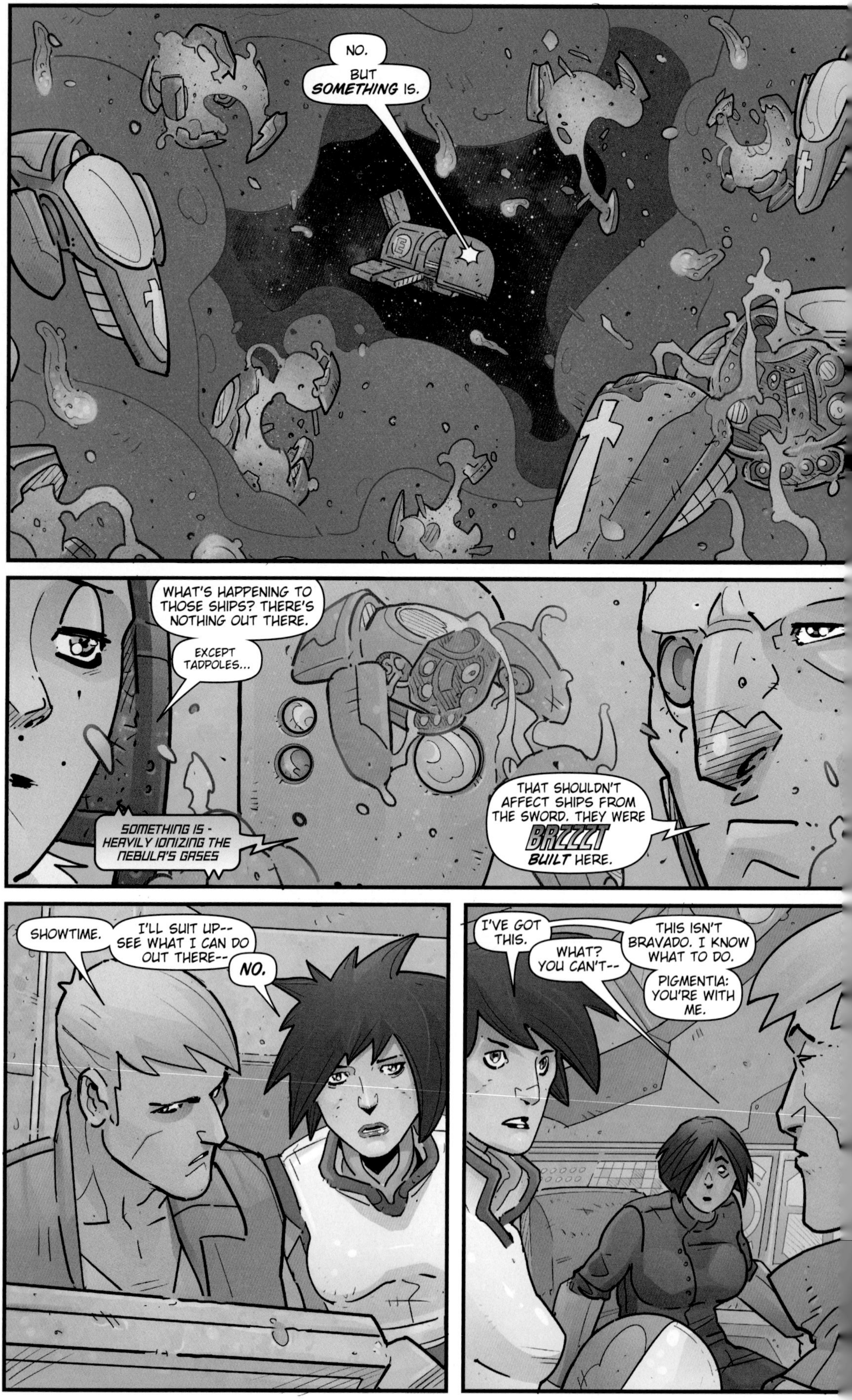
NO.
BUT SOMETHING IS.
WHAT'S HAPPENING TO THOSE SHIPS? THERE'S NOTHING OUT THERE.
EXCEPT TADPOLES...
SOMETHING IS - HEAVILY IONIZING THE NEBULA'S GASES
THAT SHOULDN'T AFFECT SHIPS FROM THE SWORD. THEY WERE BRZZZT BUILT HERE.
SHOWTIME.
I'LL SUIT UP-- SEE WHAT I CAN DO OUT THERE--
NO.
I'VE GOT THIS.
WHAT? YOU CAN'T--
THIS ISN'T BRAVADO. I KNOW WHAT TO DO.
PIGMENTIA: YOU'RE WITH ME.

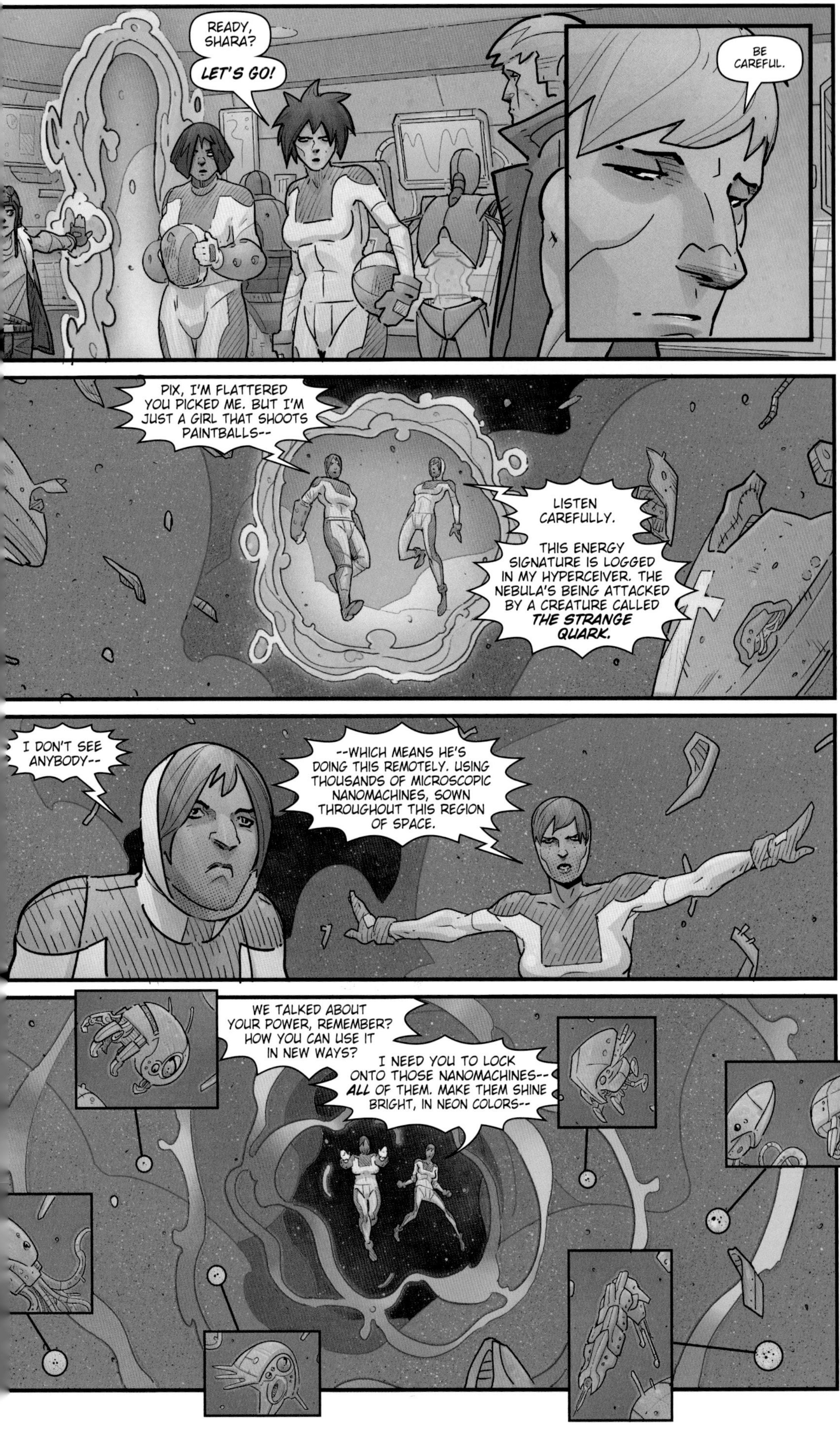
READY, SHARA?
LET'S GO!
BE CAREFUL.
PIX, I'M FLATTERED YOU PICKED ME. BUT I'M JUST A GIRL THAT SHOOTS PAINTBALLS--
LISTEN CAREFULLY.
THIS ENERGY SIGNATURE IS LOGGED IN MY HYPERCEIVER. THE NEBULA'S BEING ATTACKED BY A CREATURE CALLED THE STRANGE QUARK.
I DON'T SEE ANYBODY--
--WHICH MEANS HE'S DOING THIS REMOTELY. USING THOUSANDS OF MICROSCOPIC NANOMACHINES, SOWN THROUGHOUT THIS REGION OF SPACE.
WE TALKED ABOUT YOUR POWER, REMEMBER? HOW YOU CAN USE IT IN NEW WAYS?
I NEED YOU TO LOCK ONTO THOSE NANOMACHINES-- ALL OF THEM. MAKE THEM SHINE BRIGHT, IN NEON COLORS--

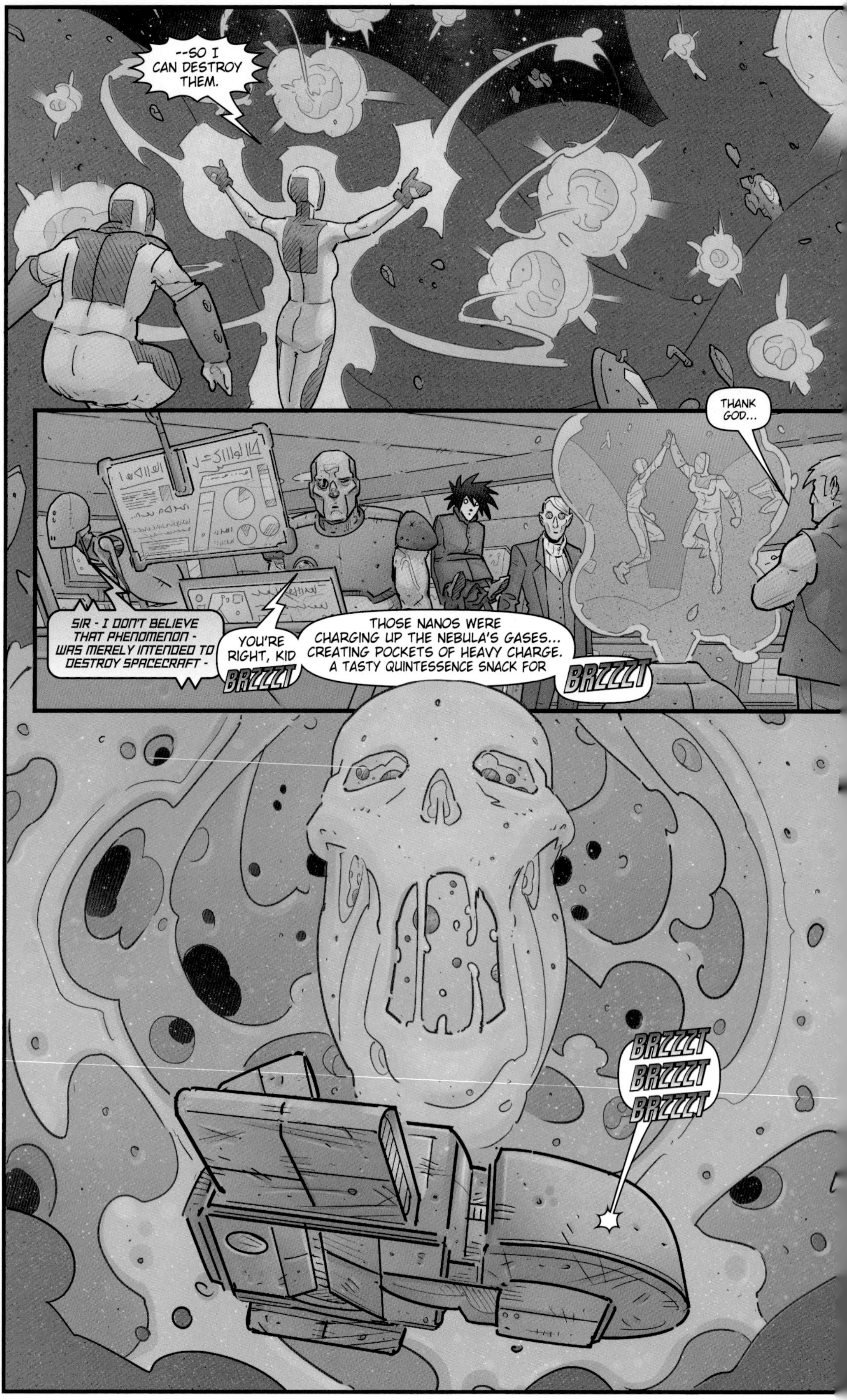
--SO I CAN DESTROY THEM.
THANK GOD...
SIR - I DON'T BELIEVE THAT PHENOMENON - WAS MERELY INTENDED TO DESTROY SPACECRAFT -
YOU'RE RIGHT, KID
BRZZZT
THOSE NANOS WERE CHARGING UP THE NEBULA'S GASES... CREATING POCKETS OF HEAVY CHARGE. A TASTY QUINTESSENCE SNACK FOR
BRZZZT
BRZZZT
BRZZZT
BRZZZT

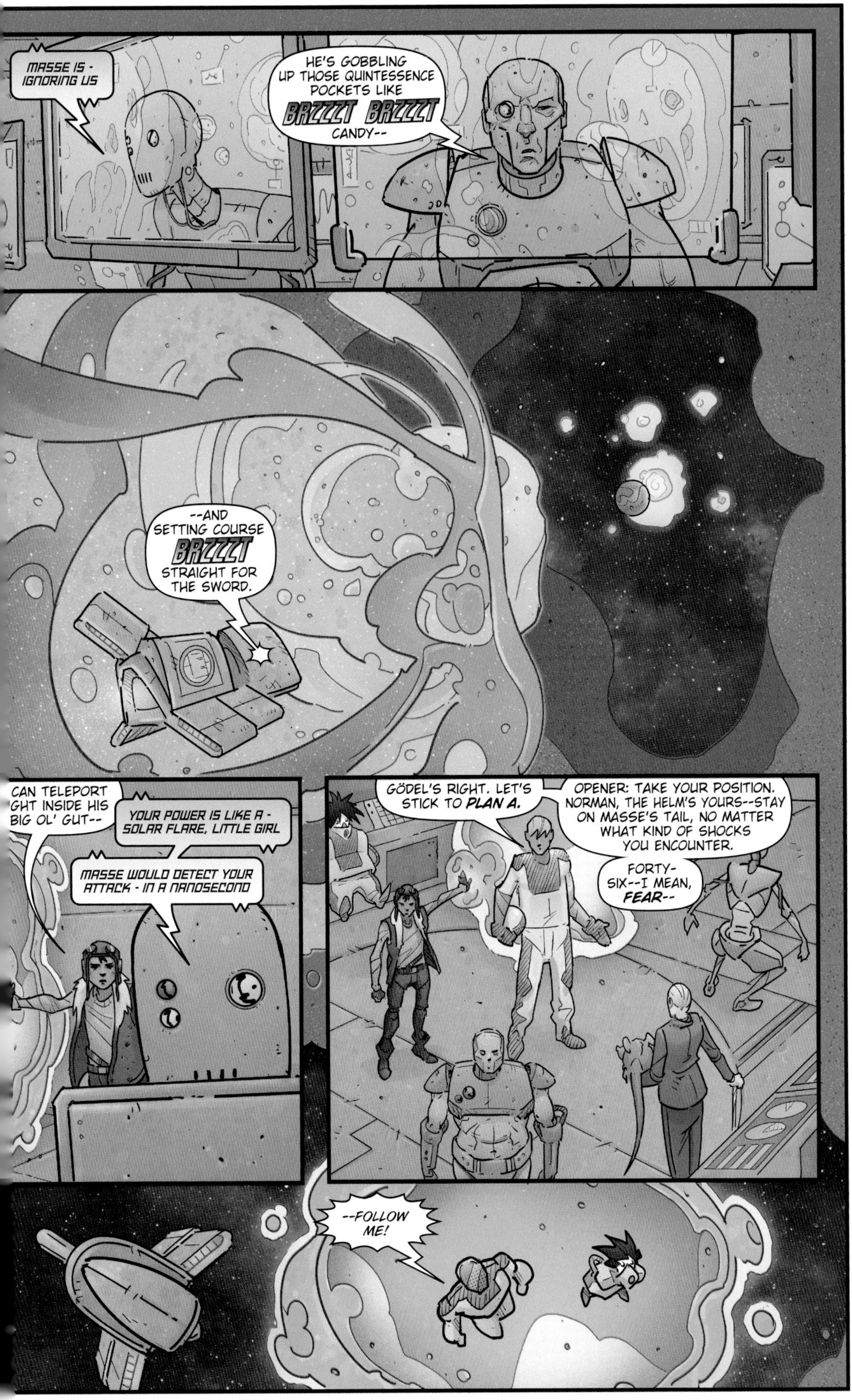
MASSE IS - IGNORING US
HE'S GOBBLING UP THOSE QUINTESSENCE POCKETS LIKE BRZZZT BRZZZT CANDY--
--AND SETTING COURSE BRZZZT STRAIGHT FOR THE SWORD.
CAN TELEPORT GHT INSIDE HIS BIG OL' GUT--
YOUR POWER IS LIKE A - SOLAR FLARE, LITTLE GIRL
MASSE WOULD DETECT YOUR ATTACK - IN A NANOSECOND
GÖDEL'S RIGHT. LET'S STICK TO PLAN A.
OPENER: TAKE YOUR POSITION. NORMAN, THE HELM'S YOURS--STAY ON MASSE'S TAIL, NO MATTER WHAT KIND OF SHOCKS YOU ENCOUNTER.
FORTY-SIX--I MEAN, FEAR--
--FOLLOW ME!

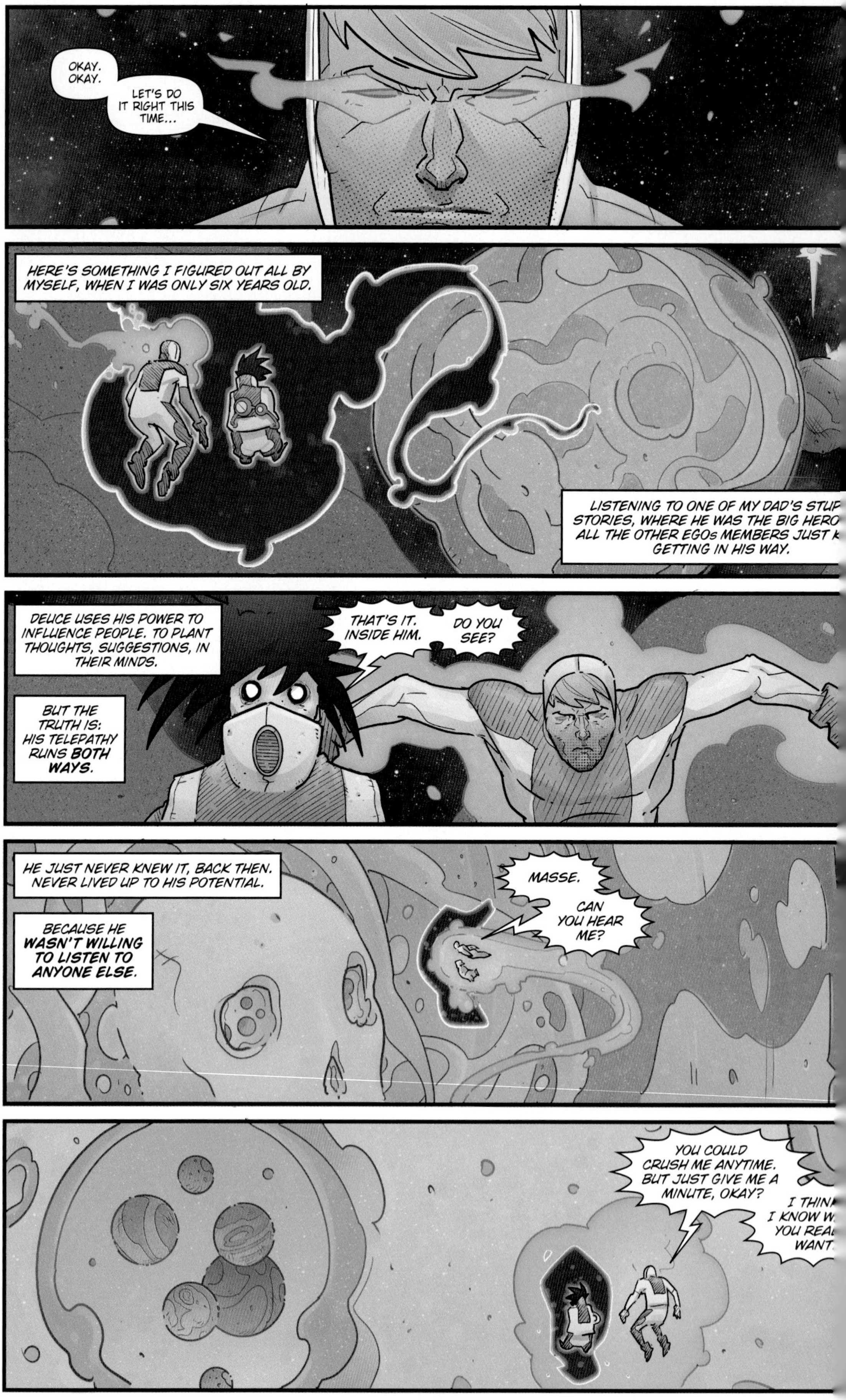
OKAY. OKAY.
LET'S DO IT RIGHT THIS TIME...
HERE'S SOMETHING I FIGURED OUT ALL BY MYSELF, WHEN I WAS ONLY SIX YEARS OLD.
LISTENING TO ONE OF MY DAD'S STUP STORIES, WHERE HE WAS THE BIG HERO ALL THE OTHER EGOs MEMBERS JUST K GETTING IN HIS WAY.
DEUCE USES HIS POWER TO INFLUENCE PEOPLE. TO PLANT THOUGHTS, SUGGESTIONS, IN THEIR MINDS.
BUT THE TRUTH IS: HIS TELEPATHY RUNS **BOTH WAYS**.
THAT'S IT. INSIDE HIM.
DO YOU SEE?
HE JUST NEVER KNEW IT, BACK THEN. NEVER LIVED UP TO HIS POTENTIAL.
BECAUSE HE **WASN'T WILLING TO LISTEN TO ANYONE ELSE**.
MASSE.
CAN YOU HEAR ME?
YOU COULD CRUSH ME ANYTIME. BUT JUST GIVE ME A MINUTE, OKAY?
I THIN I KNOW W YOU REA WANT

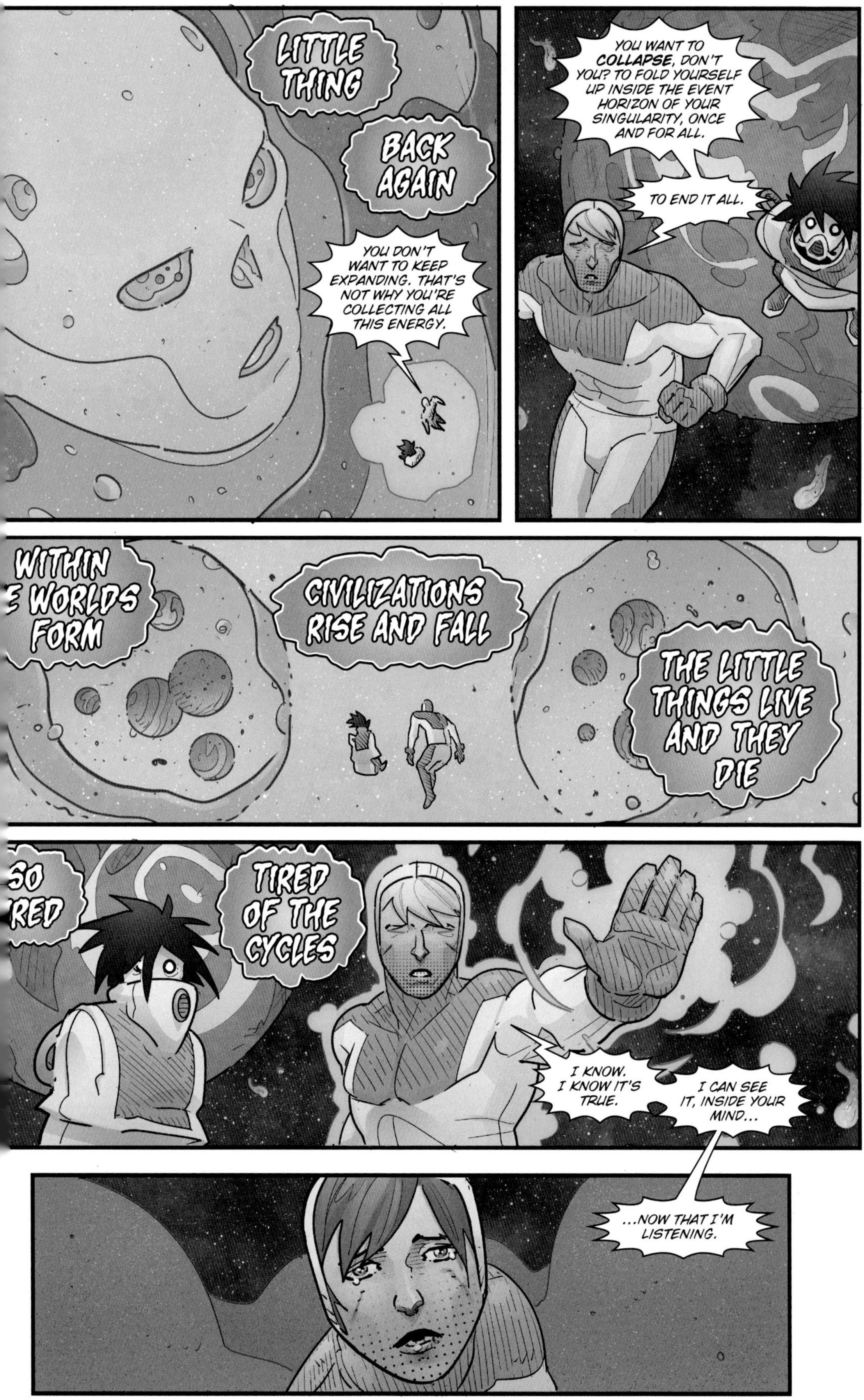

LITTLE THING
BACK AGAIN
YOU DON'T WANT TO KEEP EXPANDING. THAT'S NOT WHY YOU'RE COLLECTING ALL THIS ENERGY.
YOU WANT TO COLLAPSE, DON'T YOU? TO FOLD YOURSELF UP INSIDE THE EVENT HORIZON OF YOUR SINGULARITY, ONCE AND FOR ALL.
TO END IT ALL.
WITHIN
WORLDS FORM
CIVILIZATIONS RISE AND FALL
THE LITTLE THINGS LIVE AND THEY DIE
SO
RED
TIRED OF THE CYCLES
I KNOW. I KNOW IT'S TRUE.
I CAN SEE IT, INSIDE YOUR MIND...
...NOW THAT I'M LISTENING.

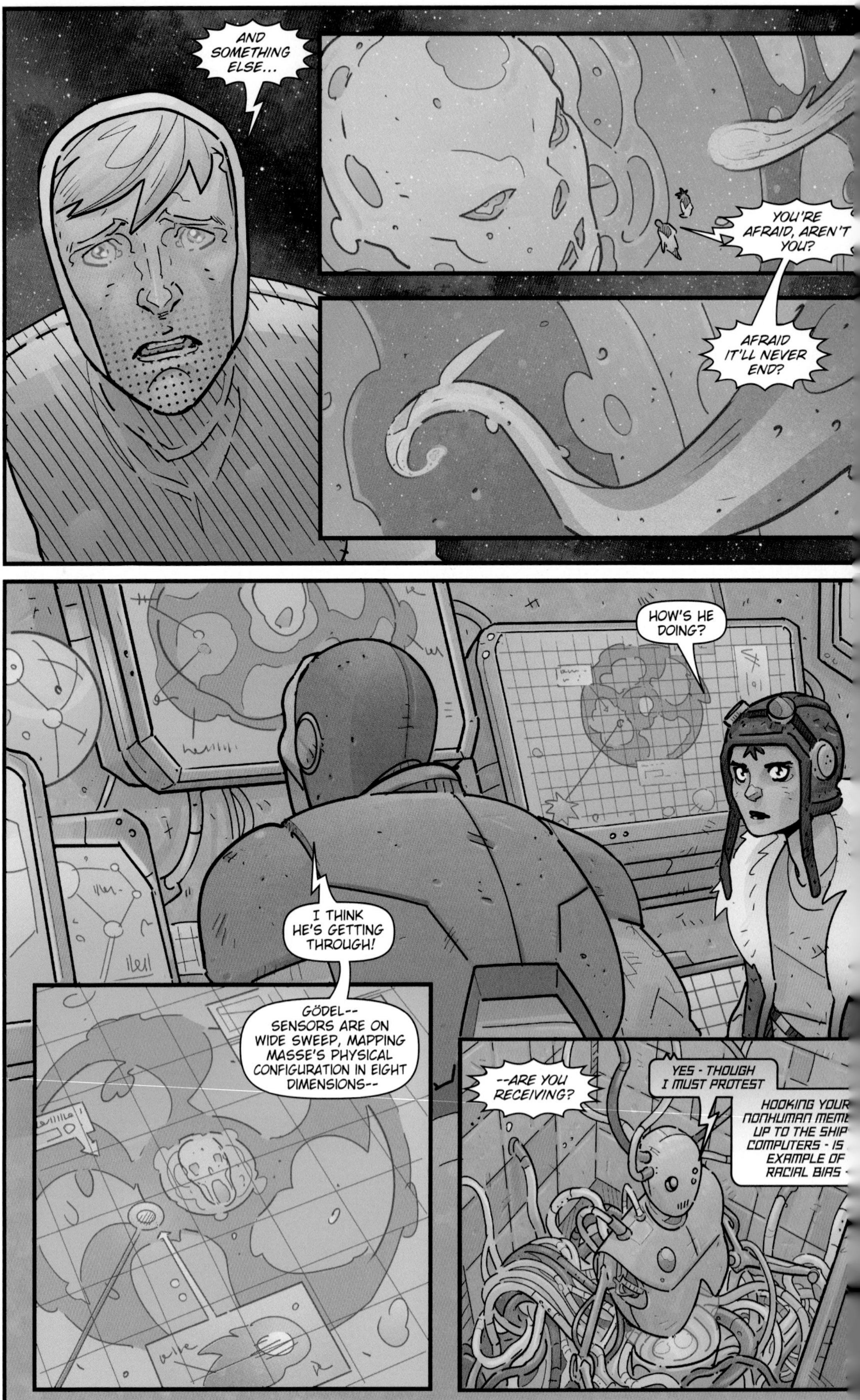
AND SOMETHING ELSE...
YOU'RE AFRAID, AREN'T YOU?
AFRAID IT'LL NEVER END?
HOW'S HE DOING?
I THINK HE'S GETTING THROUGH!
GÖDEL-- SENSORS ARE ON WIDE SWEEP, MAPPING MASSE'S PHYSICAL CONFIGURATION IN EIGHT DIMENSIONS--
--ARE YOU RECEIVING?
YES - THOUGH I MUST PROTEST

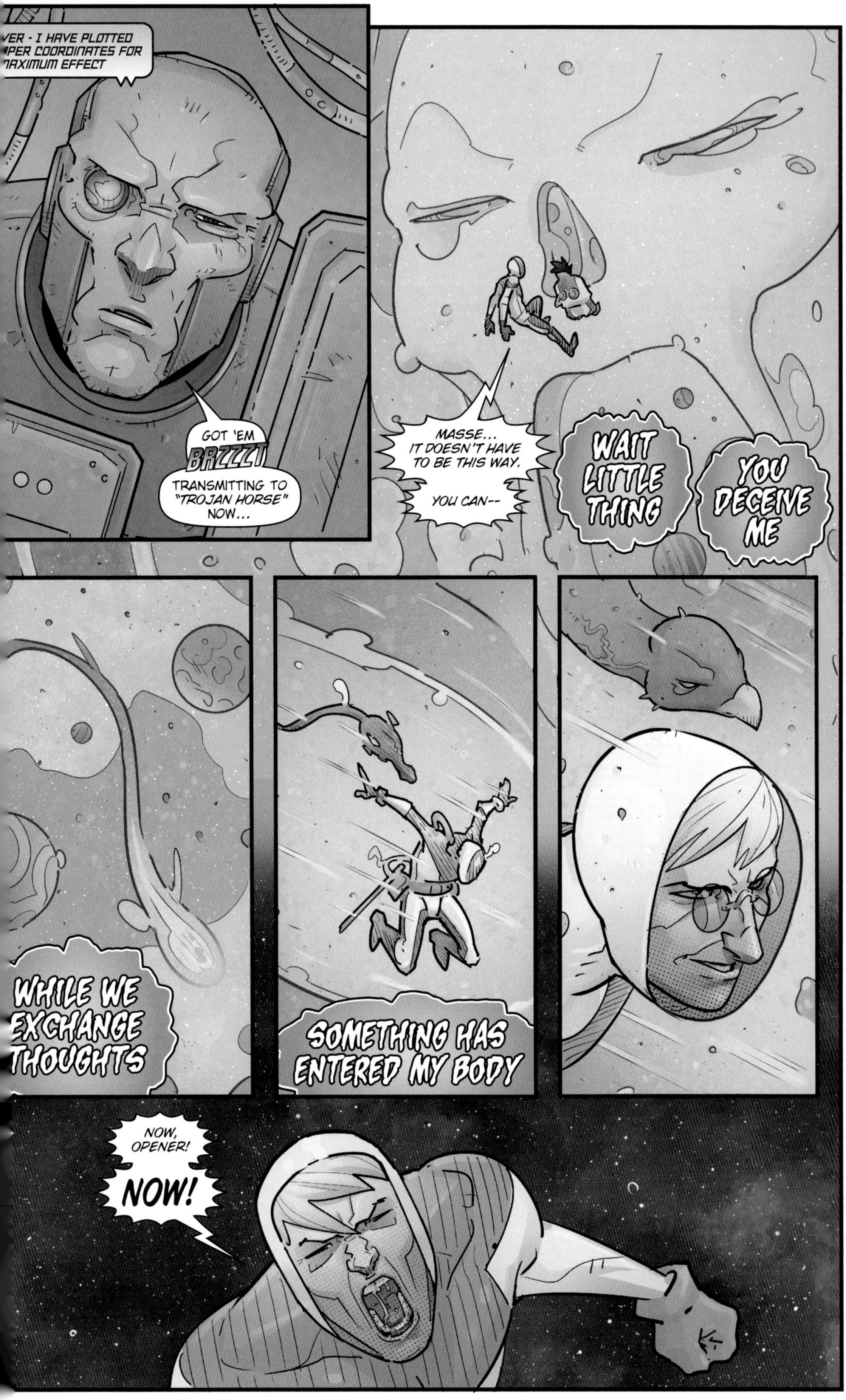
VER - I HAVE PLOTTED
PER COORDINATES FOR
MAXIMUM EFFECT
GOT 'EM
BRZZZT
TRANSMITTING TO "TROJAN HORSE" NOW...
MASSE... IT DOESN'T HAVE TO BE THIS WAY.
YOU CAN--
WAIT LITTLE THING
YOU DECEIVE ME
WHILE WE EXCHANGE THOUGHTS
SOMETHING HAS ENTERED MY BODY
NOW, OPENER!
NOW!

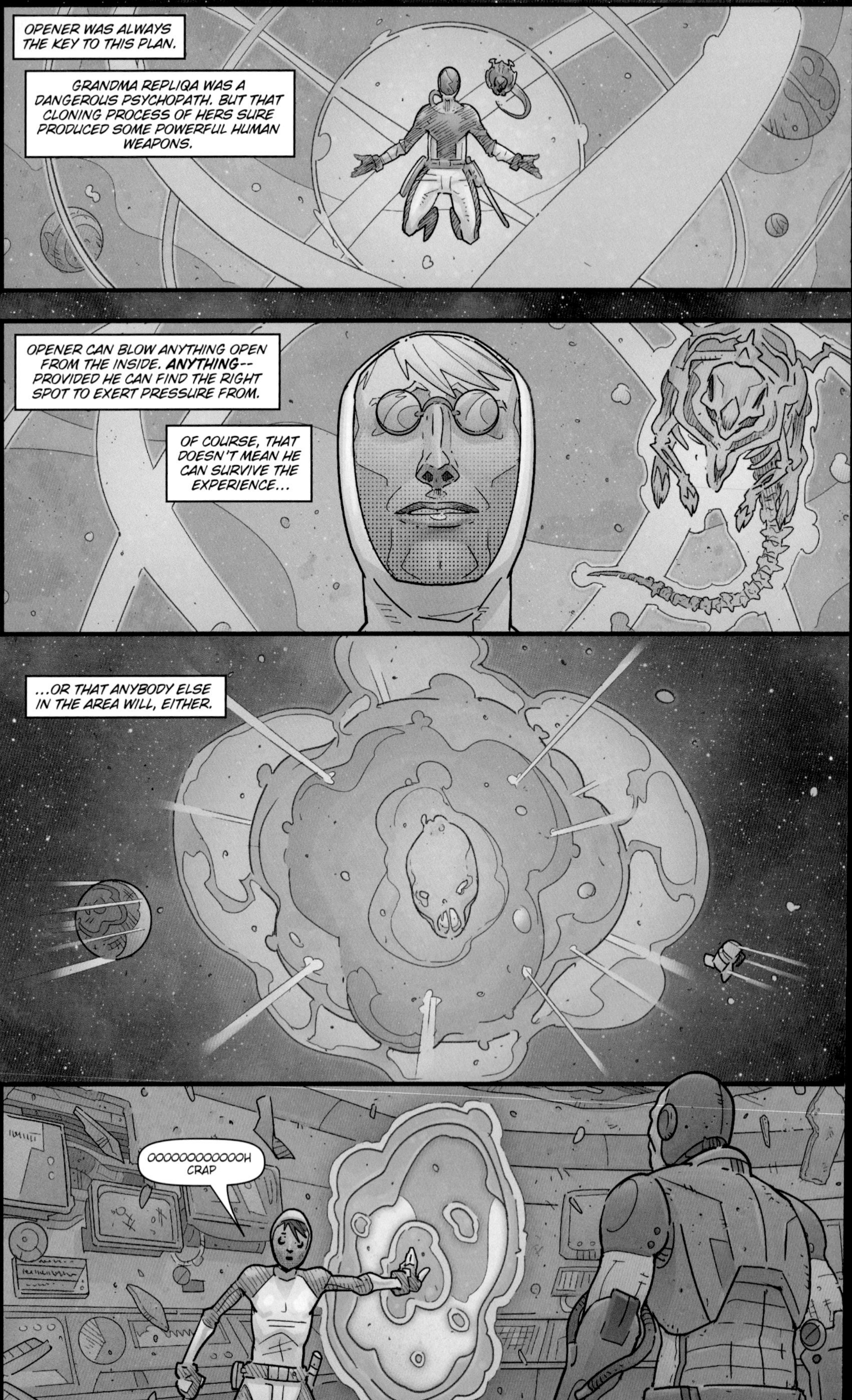
OPENER WAS ALWAYS THE KEY TO THIS PLAN.
GRANDMA REPLIQA WAS A DANGEROUS PSYCHOPATH. BUT THAT CLONING PROCESS OF HERS SURE PRODUCED SOME POWERFUL HUMAN WEAPONS.
OPENER CAN BLOW ANYTHING OPEN FROM THE INSIDE. ANYTHING-- PROVIDED HE CAN FIND THE RIGHT SPOT TO EXERT PRESSURE FROM.
OF COURSE, THAT DOESN'T MEAN HE CAN SURVIVE THE EXPERIENCE...
...OR THAT ANYBODY ELSE IN THE AREA WILL, EITHER.
OOOOOOOOOOOOH CRAP

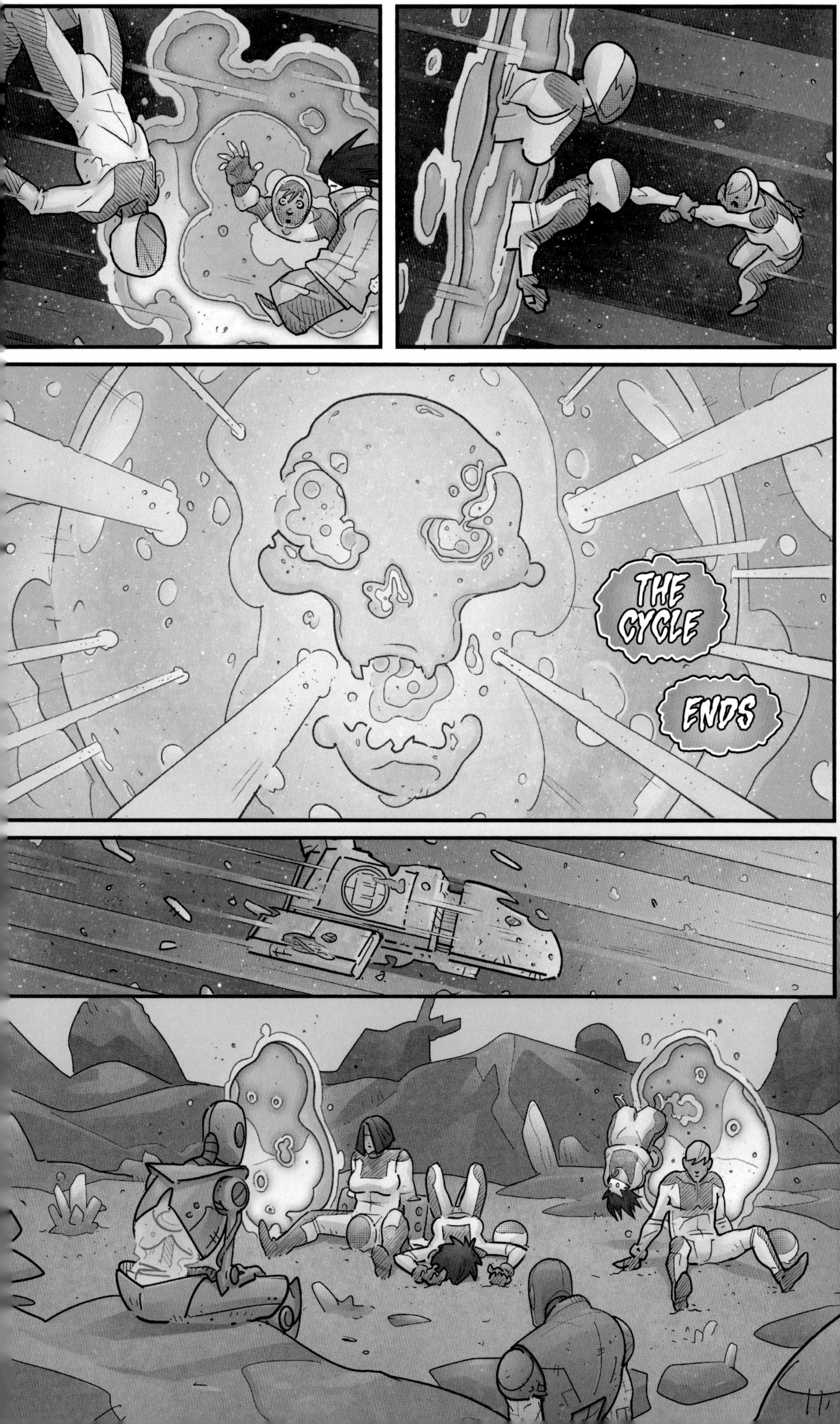
THE CYCLE
ENDS

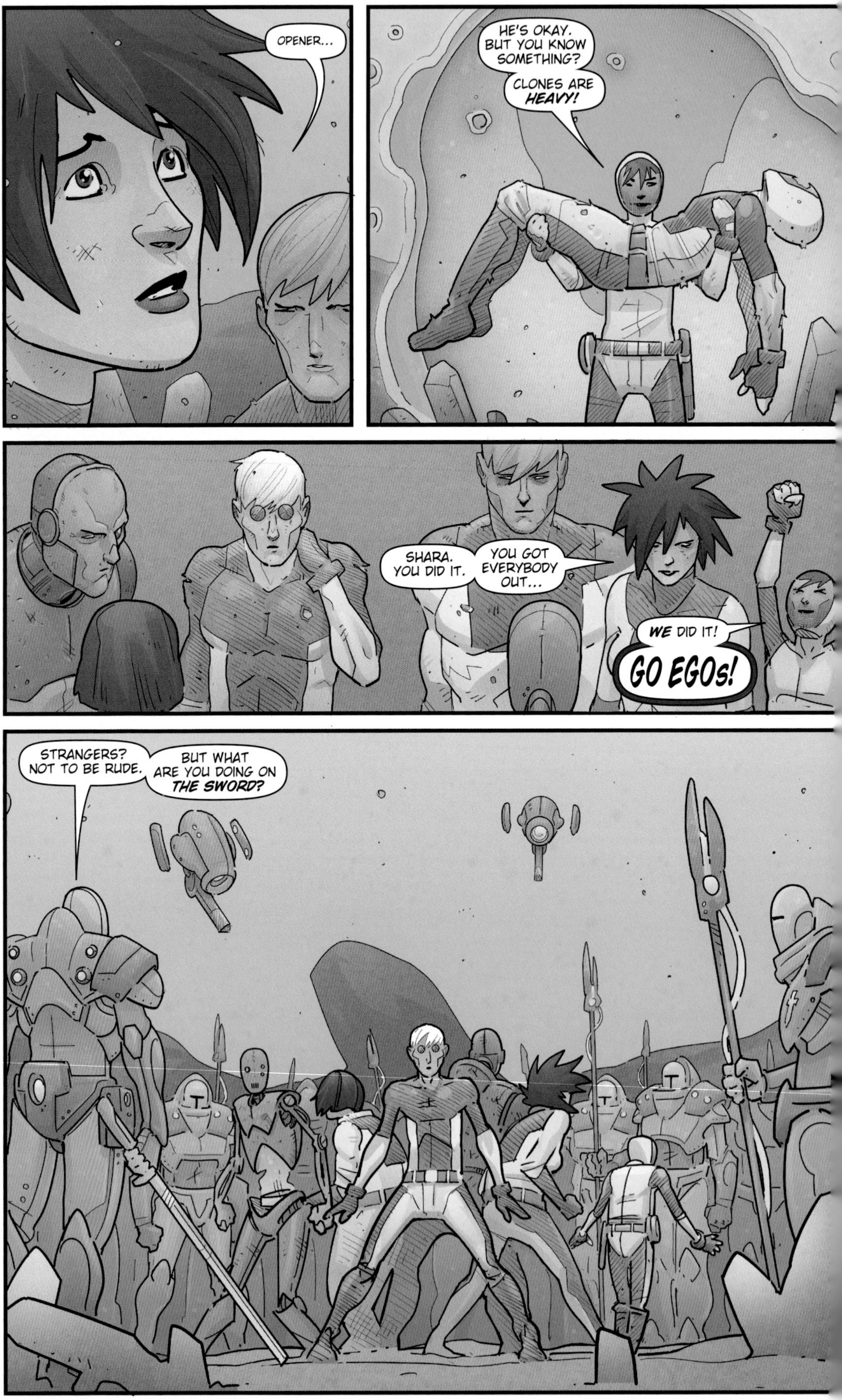
OPENER...
HE'S OKAY. BUT YOU KNOW SOMETHING?
CLONES ARE *HEAVY!*
SHARA. YOU DID IT.
YOU GOT EVERYBODY OUT...
WE DID IT!
GO EGOs!
STRANGERS? NOT TO BE RUDE.
BUT WHAT ARE YOU DOING ON *THE SWORD?*

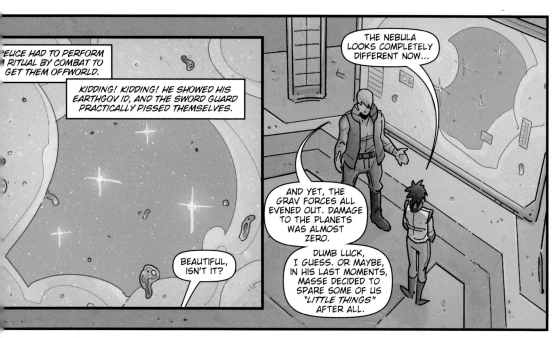

DEUCE HAD TO PERFORM A RITUAL BY COMBAT TO GET THEM OFFWORLD.

KIDDING! KIDDING! HE SHOWED HIS EARTHGOV ID, AND THE SWORD GUARD PRACTICALLY PISSED THEMSELVES.

BEAUTIFUL, ISN'T IT?

THE NEBULA LOOKS COMPLETELY DIFFERENT NOW...

AND YET, THE GRAV FORCES ALL EVENED OUT. DAMAGE TO THE PLANETS WAS ALMOST ZERO.

DUMB LUCK, I GUESS. OR MAYBE, IN HIS LAST MOMENTS, MASSE DECIDED TO SPARE SOME OF US "LITTLE THINGS" AFTER ALL.

I HOPE YOU KNOW: I HAD TO KILL HIM.

IF HE'D IMPLODED, LIKE HE PLANNED...HE WOULD HAVE TAKEN THE WHOLE NEBULA WITH HIM. BILLIONS OF LIVES--

I GOT IT.

I, I DON'T KNOW IF YOU HEARD WHAT I SAID BEFORE. THE LAST TIME WE WERE IN THIS ROOM...

I HEARD. I ALWAYS LISTEN TO YOU.

I GUESS THAT'S MY CURSE.

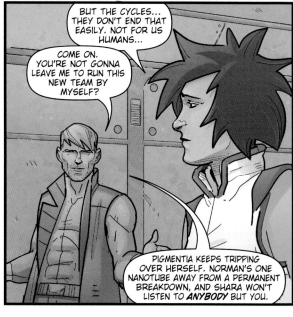

BUT THE CYCLES... THEY DON'T END THAT EASILY. NOT FOR US HUMANS...

COME ON. YOU'RE NOT GONNA LEAVE ME TO RUN THIS NEW TEAM BY MYSELF?

PIGMENTIA KEEPS TRIPPING OVER HERSELF. NORMAN'S ONE NANOTUBE AWAY FROM A PERMANENT BREAKDOWN, AND SHARA WON'T LISTEN TO ANYBODY BUT YOU.

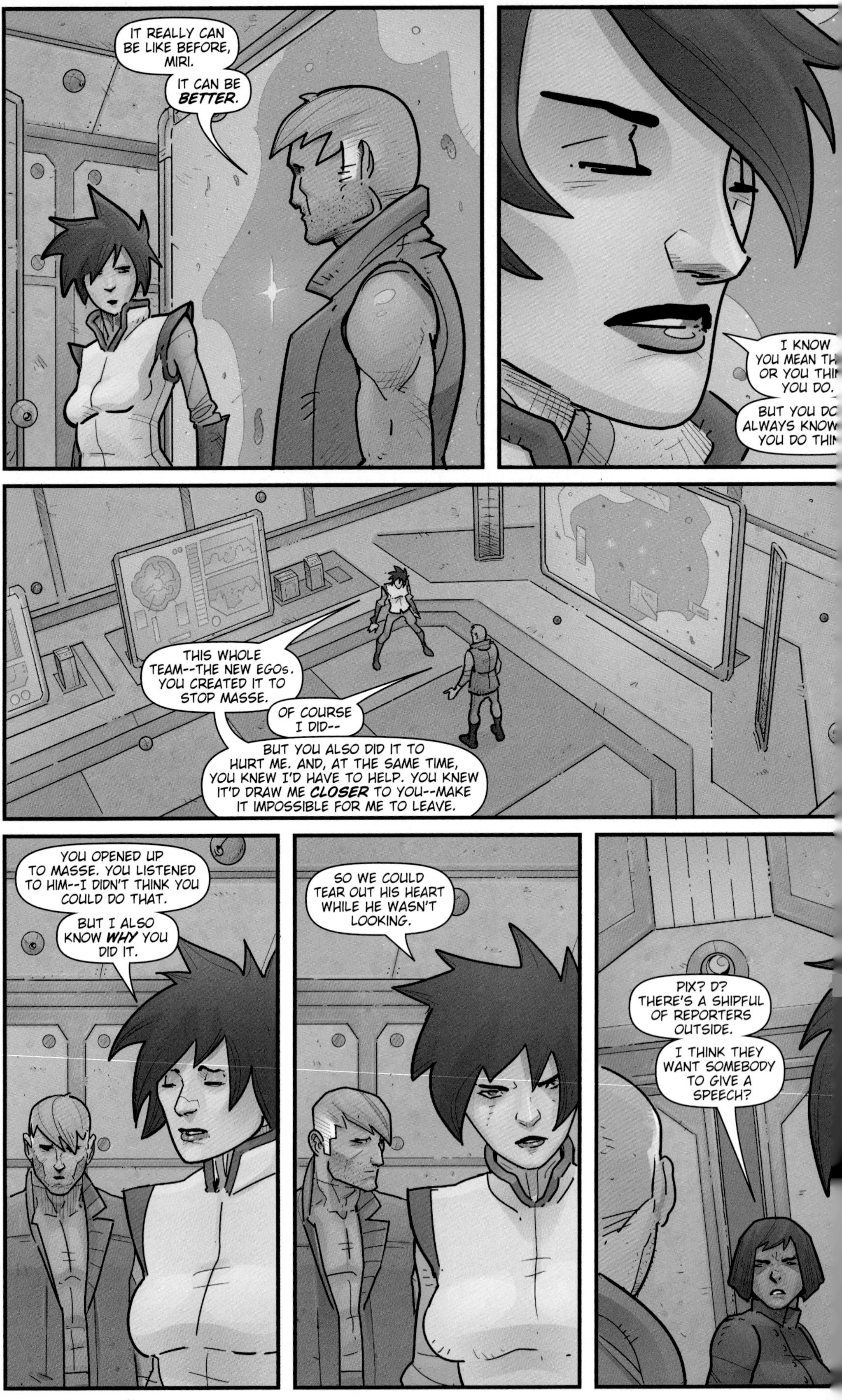
IT REALLY CAN BE LIKE BEFORE, MIRI.
IT CAN BE **BETTER**.
I KNOW YOU MEAN TH OR YOU THI YOU DO.
BUT YOU DO ALWAYS KNOW YOU DO THI
THIS WHOLE TEAM--THE NEW EGOs. YOU CREATED IT TO STOP MASSE.
OF COURSE I DID--
BUT YOU ALSO DID IT TO HURT ME. AND, AT THE SAME TIME, YOU KNEW I'D HAVE TO HELP. YOU KNEW IT'D DRAW ME ***CLOSER*** TO YOU--MAKE IT IMPOSSIBLE FOR ME TO LEAVE.
YOU OPENED UP TO MASSE. YOU LISTENED TO HIM--I DIDN'T THINK YOU COULD DO THAT.
BUT I ALSO KNOW ***WHY*** YOU DID IT.
SO WE COULD TEAR OUT HIS HEART WHILE HE WASN'T LOOKING.
PIX? D? THERE'S A SHIPFUL OF REPORTERS OUTSIDE.
I THINK THEY WANT SOMEBODY TO GIVE A SPEECH?

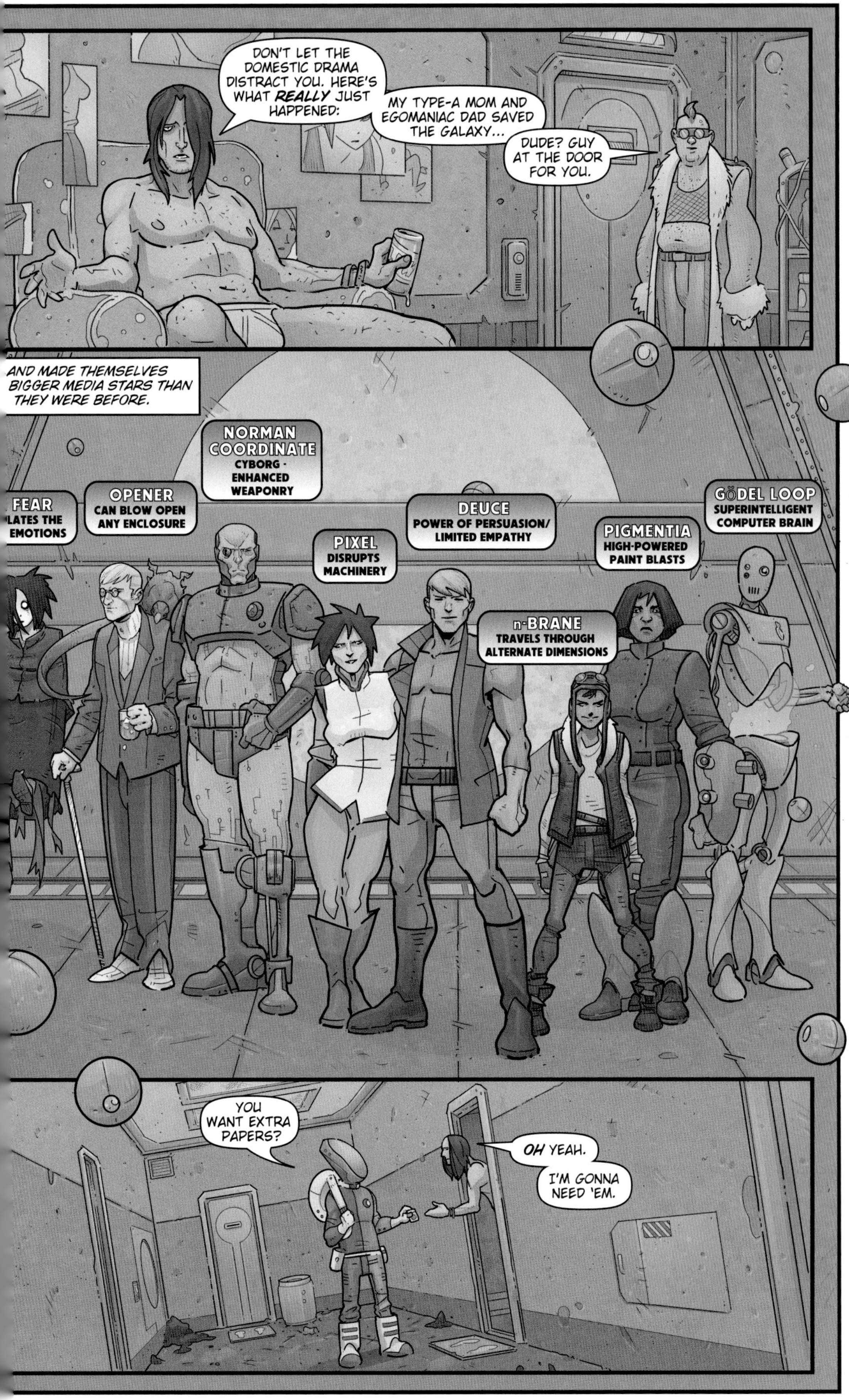
DON'T LET THE DOMESTIC DRAMA DISTRACT YOU. HERE'S WHAT *REALLY* JUST HAPPENED:
MY TYPE-A MOM AND EGOMANIAC DAD SAVED THE GALAXY...
DUDE? GUY AT THE DOOR FOR YOU.
AND MADE THEMSELVES BIGGER MEDIA STARS THAN THEY WERE BEFORE.
NORMAN COORDINATE CYBORG - ENHANCED WEAPONRY
FEAR
LATES THE EMOTIONS
OPENER CAN BLOW OPEN ANY ENCLOSURE
PIXEL DISRUPTS MACHINERY
DEUCE POWER OF PERSUASION/ LIMITED EMPATHY
PIGMENTIA HIGH-POWERED PAINT BLASTS
GÖDEL LOOP SUPERINTELLIGENT COMPUTER BRAIN
n-BRANE TRAVELS THROUGH ALTERNATE DIMENSIONS
YOU WANT EXTRA PAPERS?
OH YEAH.
I'M GONNA NEED 'EM.

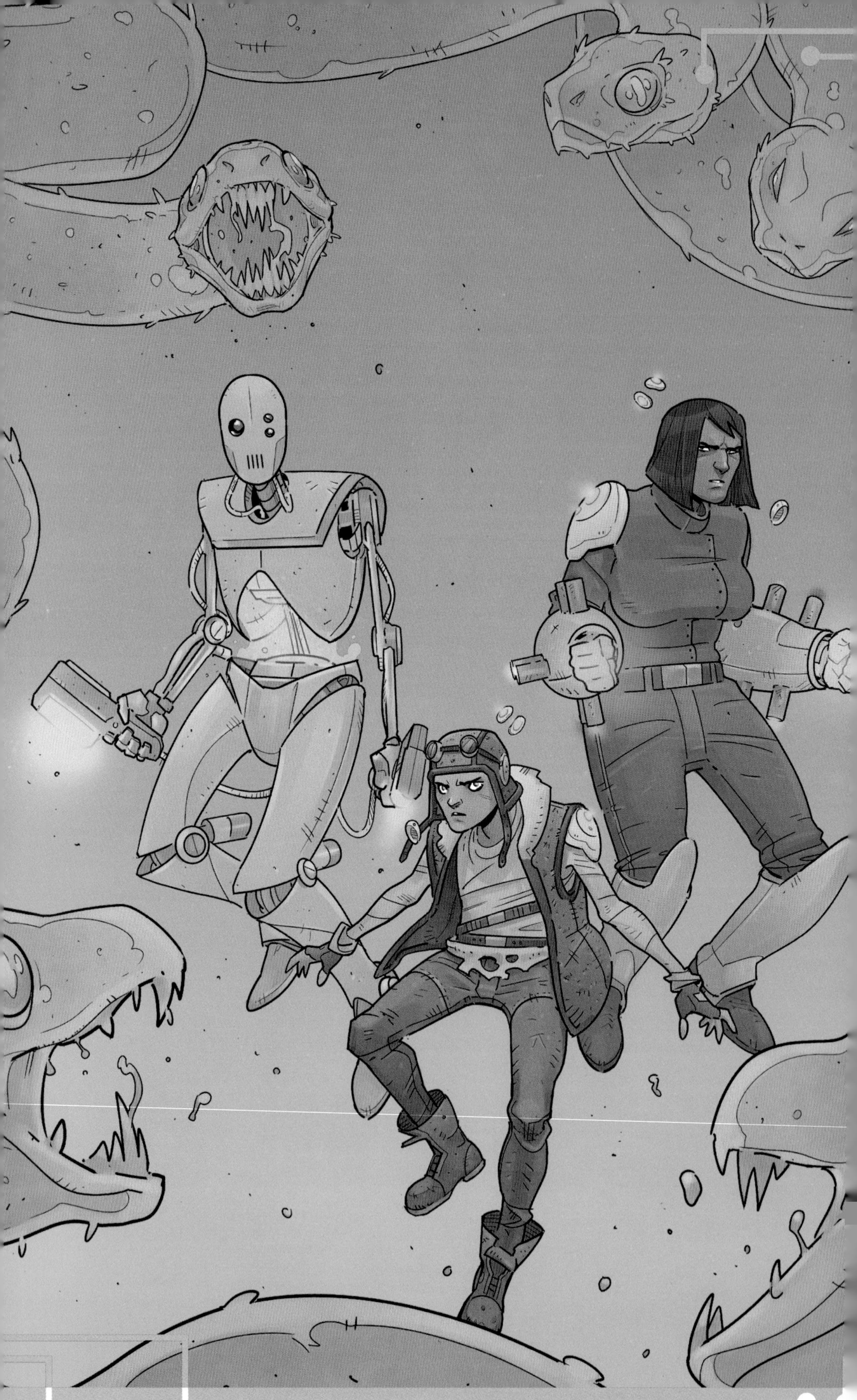

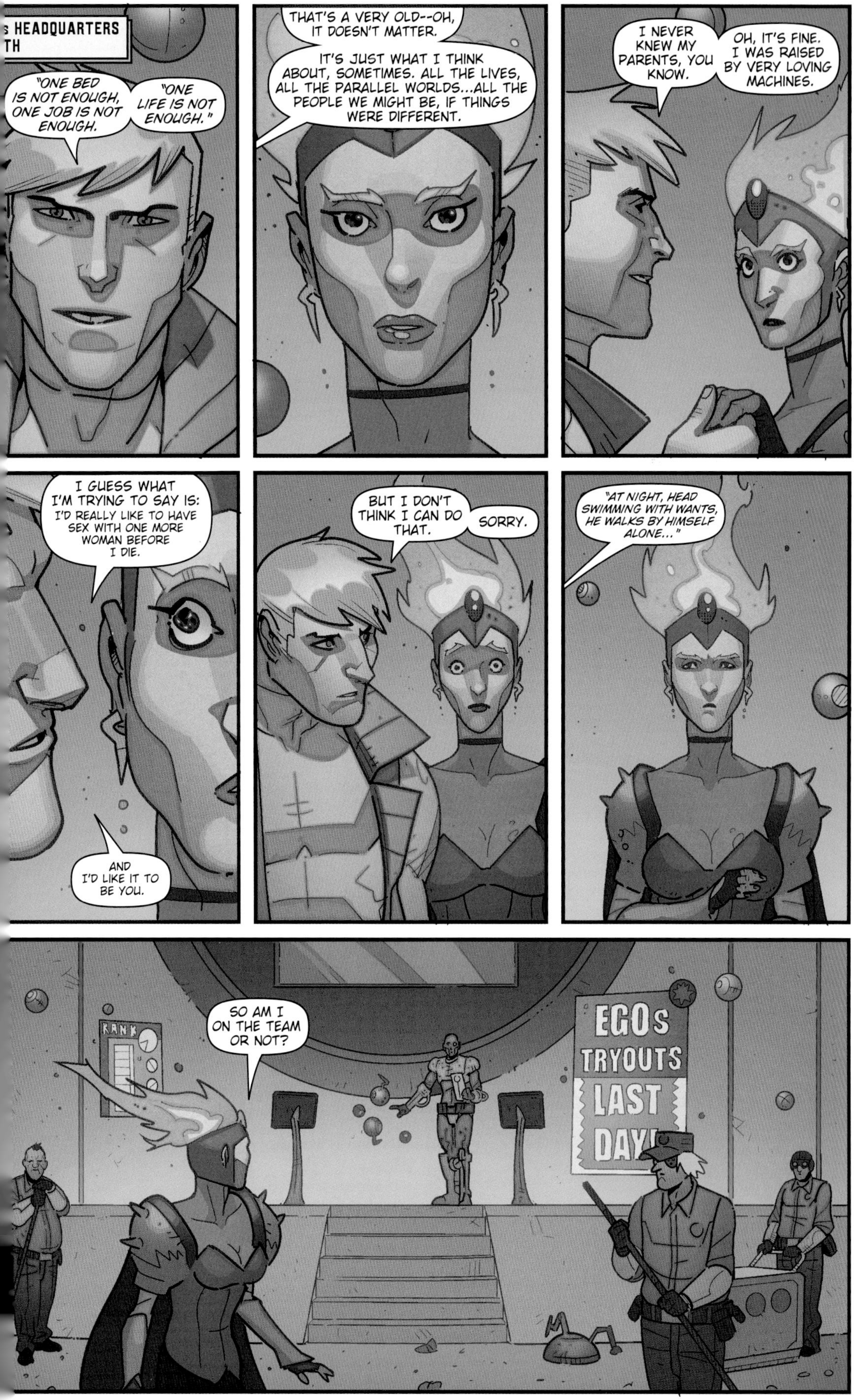
HEADQUARTERS
TH
"ONE BED IS NOT ENOUGH, ONE JOB IS NOT ENOUGH.
"ONE LIFE IS NOT ENOUGH."
THAT'S A VERY OLD--OH, IT DOESN'T MATTER.
IT'S JUST WHAT I THINK ABOUT, SOMETIMES. ALL THE LIVES, ALL THE PARALLEL WORLDS...ALL THE PEOPLE WE MIGHT BE, IF THINGS WERE DIFFERENT.
I NEVER KNEW MY PARENTS, YOU KNOW.
OH, IT'S FINE. I WAS RAISED BY VERY LOVING MACHINES.
I GUESS WHAT I'M TRYING TO SAY IS: I'D REALLY LIKE TO HAVE SEX WITH ONE MORE WOMAN BEFORE I DIE.
AND I'D LIKE IT TO BE YOU.
BUT I DON'T THINK I CAN DO THAT.
SORRY.
"AT NIGHT, HEAD SWIMMING WITH WANTS, HE WALKS BY HIMSELF ALONE..."
SO AM I ON THE TEAM OR NOT?
RANK
EGOs TRYOUTS LAST DAY!

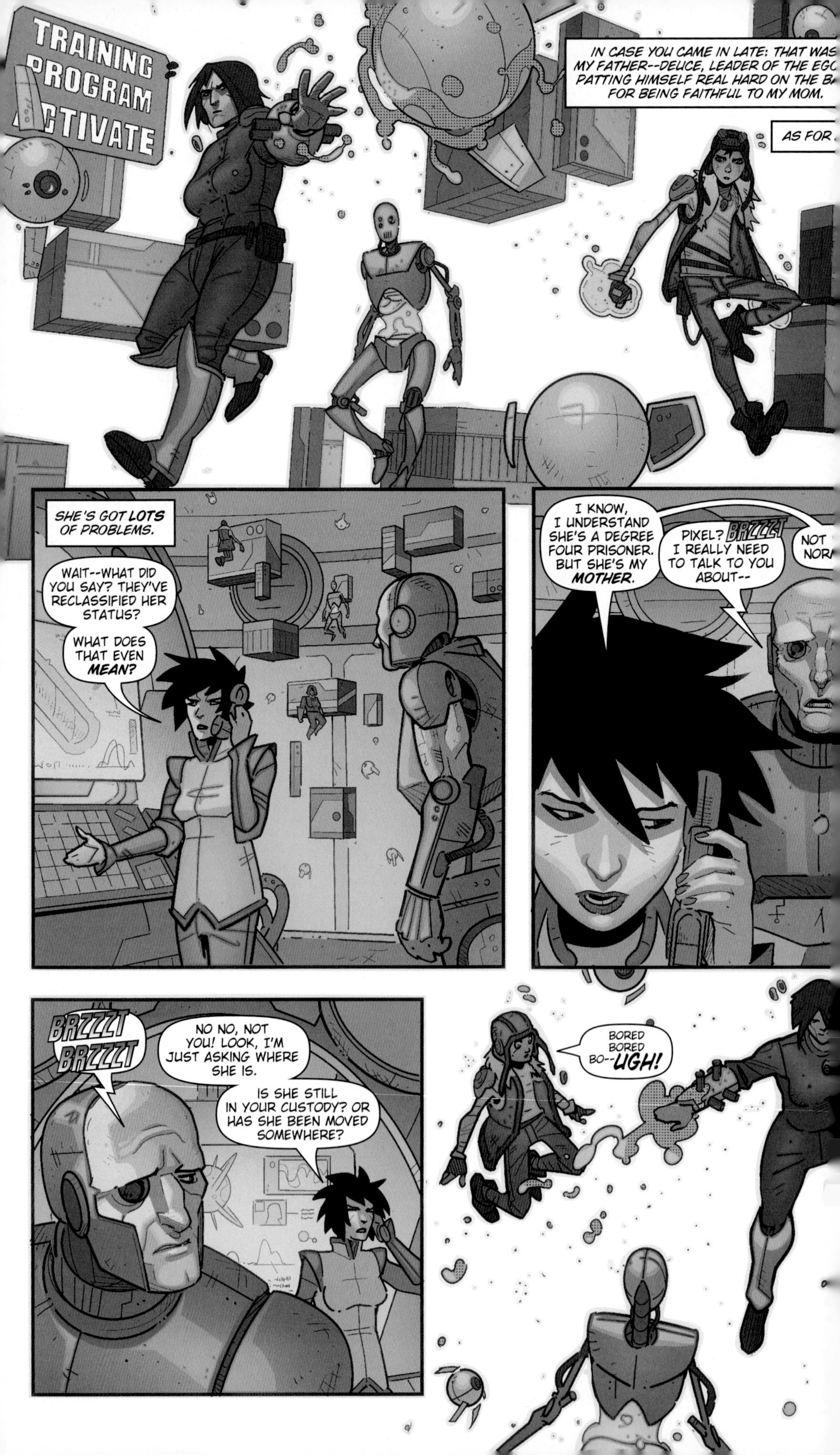
TRAINING PROGRAM ACTIVATE
IN CASE YOU CAME IN LATE: THAT WAS MY FATHER--DEUCE, LEADER OF THE EGO PATTING HIMSELF REAL HARD ON THE BA FOR BEING FAITHFUL TO MY MOM.
AS FOR
SHE'S GOT **LOTS** OF PROBLEMS.
WAIT--WHAT DID YOU SAY? THEY'VE RECLASSIFIED HER STATUS?
WHAT DOES THAT EVEN **MEAN?**
I KNOW, I UNDERSTAND SHE'S A DEGREE FOUR PRISONER. BUT SHE'S MY **MOTHER**.
PIXEL? BRZZZT I REALLY NEED TO TALK TO YOU ABOUT--
NOT NOR
BRZZZT BRZZZT
NO NO, NOT YOU! LOOK, I'M JUST ASKING WHERE SHE IS.
IS SHE STILL IN YOUR CUSTODY? OR HAS SHE BEEN MOVED SOMEWHERE?
BORED BORED BO--**UGH!**

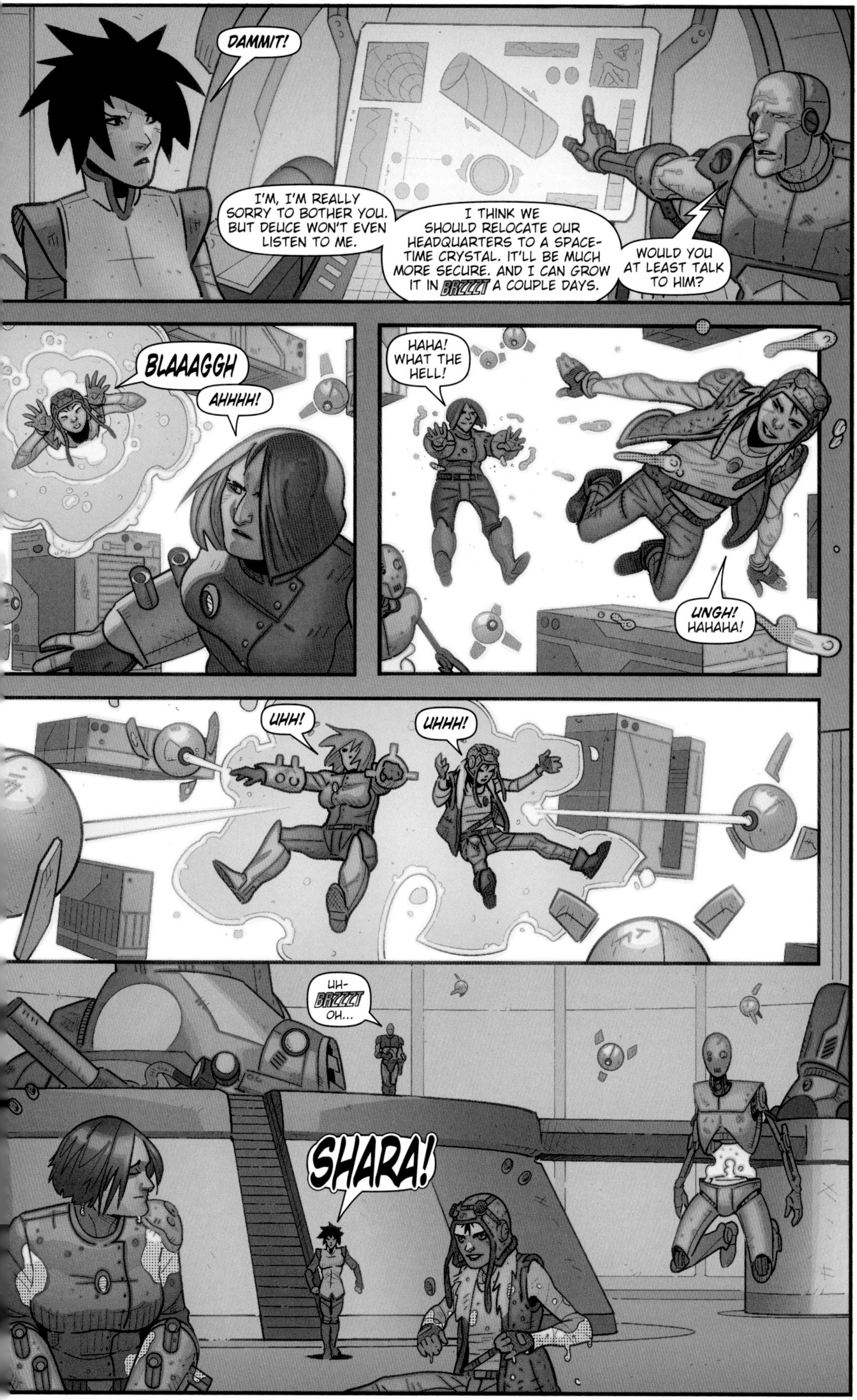
DAMMIT!
I'M, I'M REALLY SORRY TO BOTHER YOU. BUT DEUCE WON'T EVEN LISTEN TO ME.
I THINK WE SHOULD RELOCATE OUR HEADQUARTERS TO A SPACE-TIME CRYSTAL. IT'LL BE MUCH MORE SECURE. AND I CAN GROW IT IN BRZZZT A COUPLE DAYS.
WOULD YOU AT LEAST TALK TO HIM?
BLAAAGGH
AHHHH!
HAHA! WHAT THE HELL!
UNGH! HAHAHA!
UHH!
UHHH!
UH- BRZZZT OH...
SHARA!

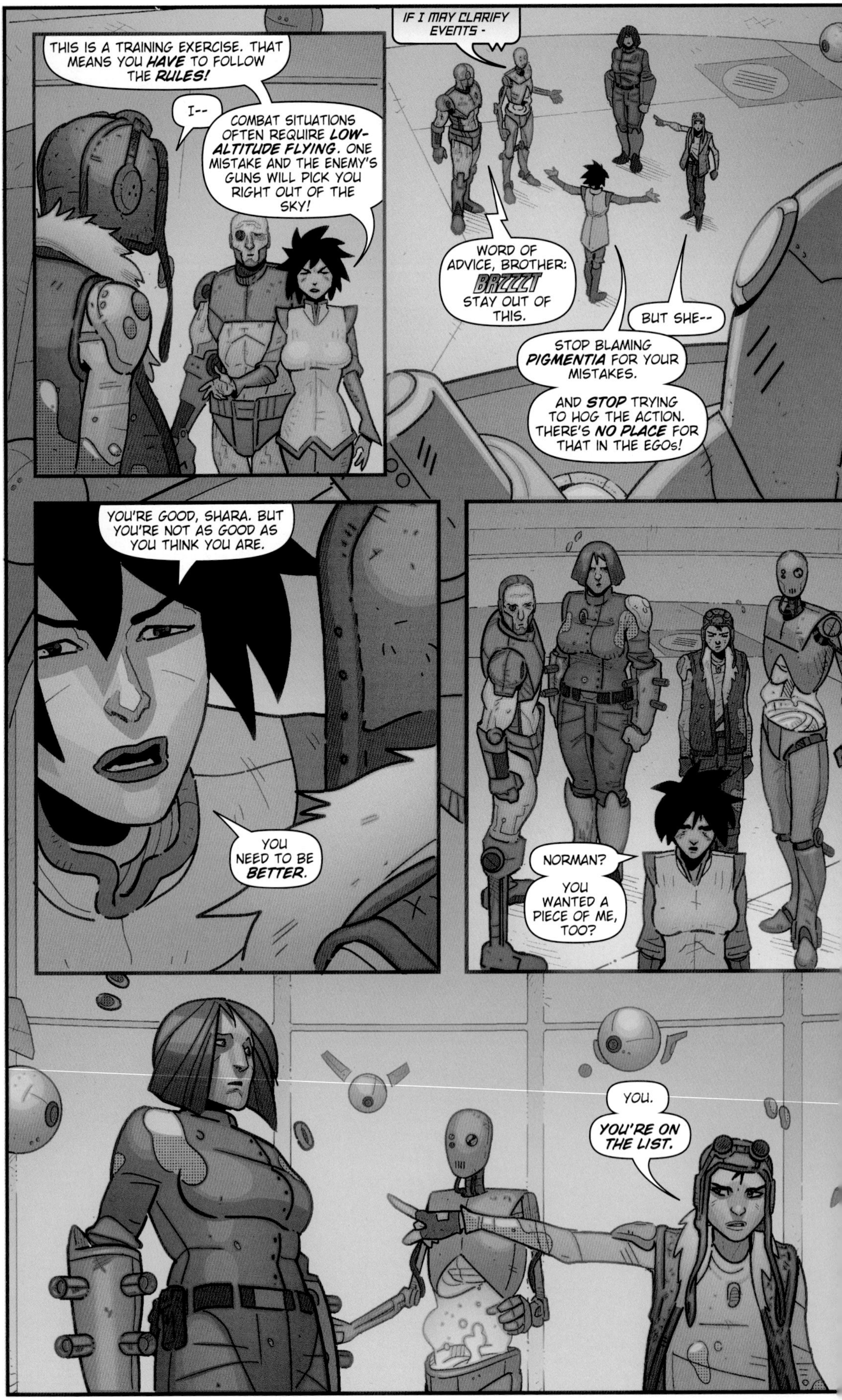

THIS IS A TRAINING EXERCISE. THAT MEANS YOU *HAVE* TO FOLLOW THE *RULES!*
I--
COMBAT SITUATIONS OFTEN REQUIRE *LOW-ALTITUDE FLYING*. ONE MISTAKE AND THE ENEMY'S GUNS WILL PICK YOU RIGHT OUT OF THE SKY!
IF I MAY CLARIFY EVENTS -
WORD OF ADVICE, BROTHER: BRZZZT STAY OUT OF THIS.
BUT SHE--
STOP BLAMING *PIGMENTIA* FOR YOUR MISTAKES.
AND *STOP* TRYING TO HOG THE ACTION. THERE'S *NO PLACE* FOR THAT IN THE EGOs!
YOU'RE GOOD, SHARA. BUT YOU'RE NOT AS GOOD AS YOU THINK YOU ARE.
YOU NEED TO BE *BETTER*.
NORMAN?
YOU WANTED A PIECE OF ME, TOO?
YOU.
YOU'RE ON THE LIST.

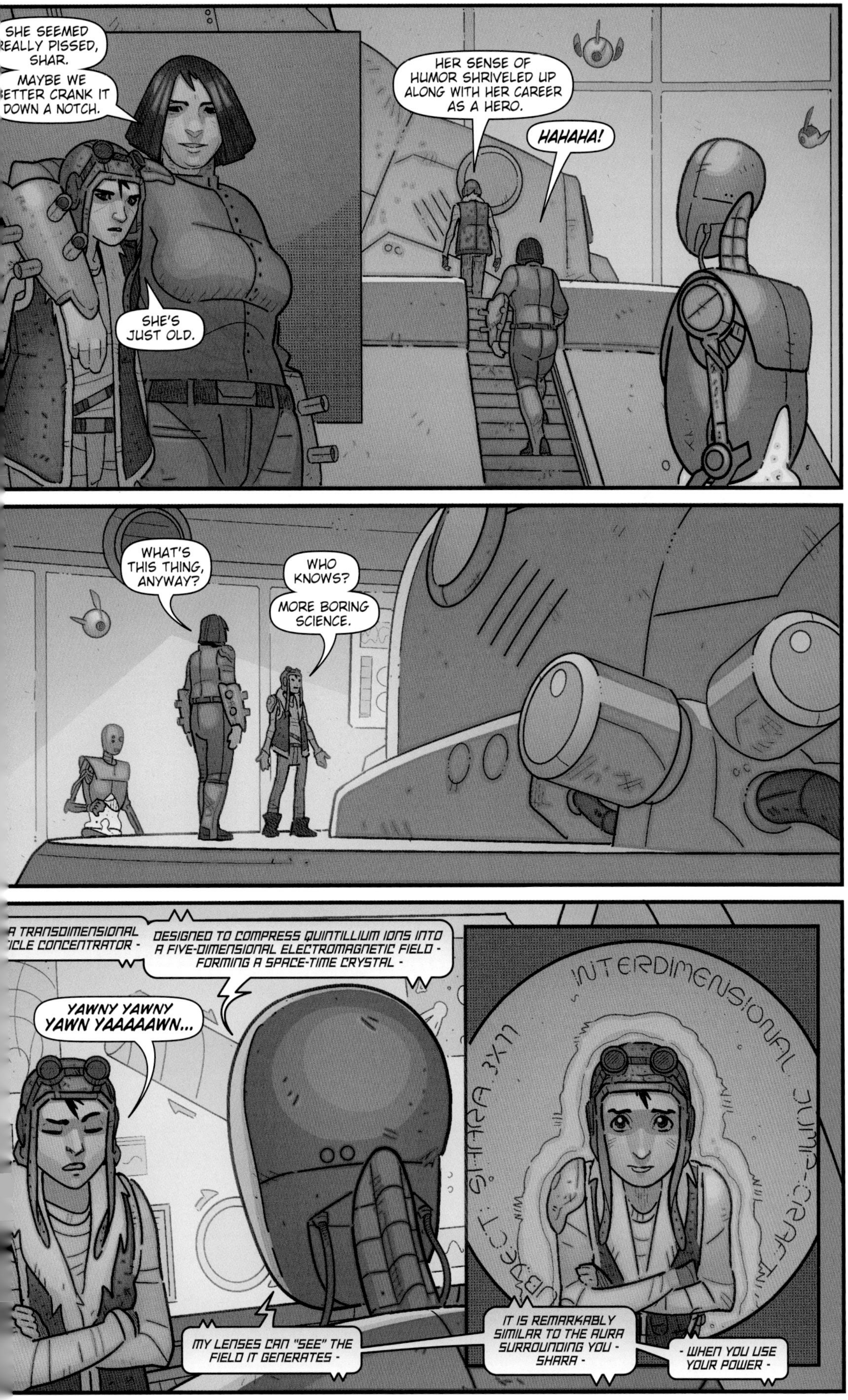

SHE SEEMED EALLY PISSED, SHAR.
MAYBE WE ETTER CRANK IT DOWN A NOTCH.
SHE'S JUST OLD.
HER SENSE OF HUMOR SHRIVELED UP ALONG WITH HER CAREER AS A HERO.
HAHAHA!
WHAT'S THIS THING, ANYWAY?
WHO KNOWS?
MORE BORING SCIENCE.
A TRANSDIMENSIONAL ICLE CONCENTRATOR -
DESIGNED TO COMPRESS QUINTILLIUM IONS INTO A FIVE-DIMENSIONAL ELECTROMAGNETIC FIELD - FORMING A SPACE-TIME CRYSTAL -
YAWNY YAWNY YAWN YAAAAAWN...
INTERDIMENSIONAL
MY LENSES CAN "SEE" THE FIELD IT GENERATES -
IT IS REMARKABLY SIMILAR TO THE AURA SURROUNDING YOU - SHARA -
- WHEN YOU USE YOUR POWER -

HEY.
WHAT IF WE--
NO. NO NO NO NO NO.
WHATEVER YOU'RE THINKIN', NO!
GÖDEL, MY POWER LETS ME TRAVEL TO ELEVEN DIFFERENT ALTERNATE CONTINUUMS.
CONTINUA
YEAH.
WHAT IF WE COMBINED MY POWER WITH THE FIELD COMING FROM THE MACHINE? WOULD I BE ABLE TO GO EVEN MORE PLACES?
I AM NOT SURE - THIS IS ADVISABLE -
C'MON, GÖDEL.
ARE YOU PART OF THIS TEAM?
OR JUST A MACHINE?
WHAT THE - HELL -
ALL RIGHT!
THIS IS A MISTAKE...
I WILL ACTIVATE THE MACHINE - YOU STAND OVER THERE -
- AND FORM A PORTAL -

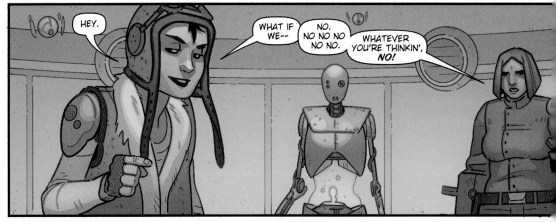

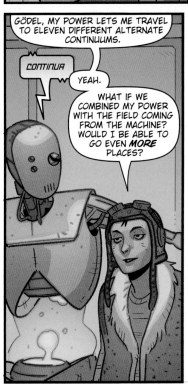

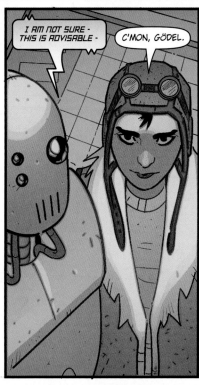

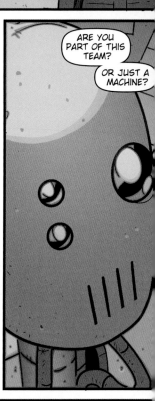

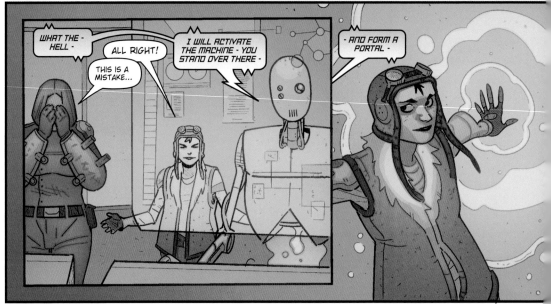

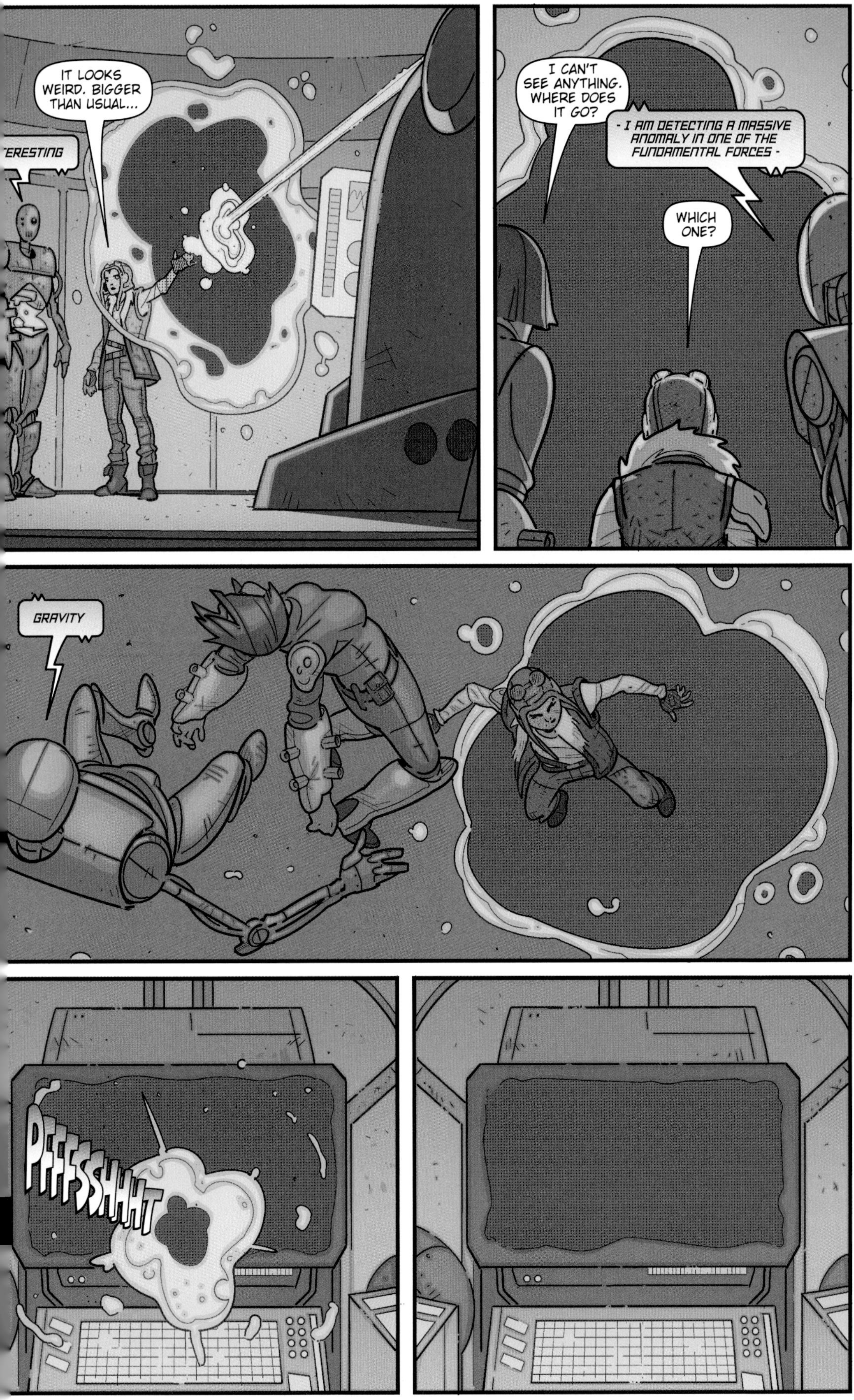
IT LOOKS WEIRD. BIGGER THAN USUAL...
ERESTING
I CAN'T SEE ANYTHING. WHERE DOES IT GO?
- I AM DETECTING A MASSIVE ANOMALY IN ONE OF THE FUNDAMENTAL FORCES -
WHICH ONE?
GRAVITY
PFFFSSHHHT

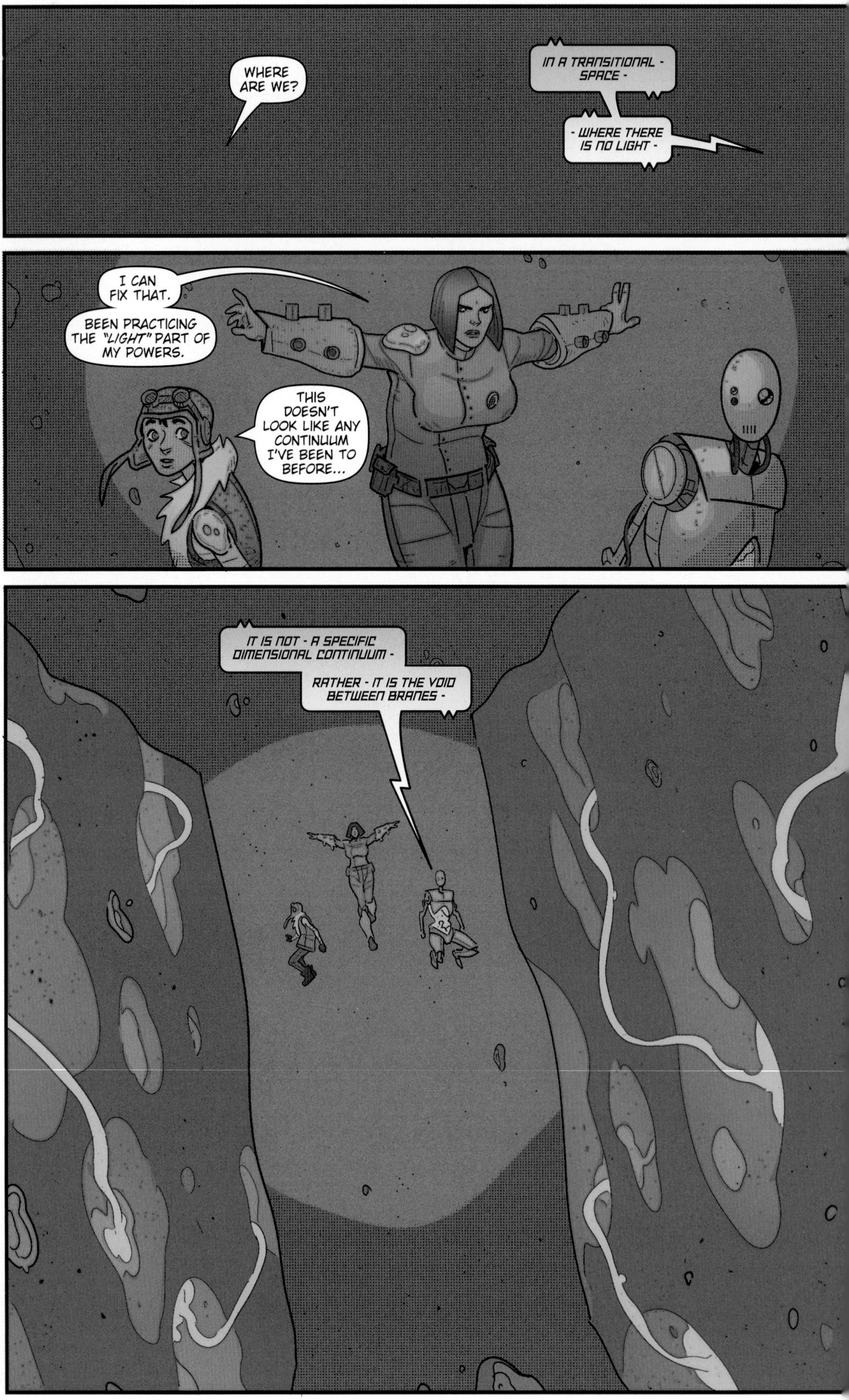
WHERE ARE WE?
IN A TRANSITIONAL - SPACE -
- WHERE THERE IS NO LIGHT -
I CAN FIX THAT.
BEEN PRACTICING THE "LIGHT" PART OF MY POWERS.
THIS DOESN'T LOOK LIKE ANY CONTINUUM I'VE BEEN TO BEFORE...
IT IS NOT - A SPECIFIC DIMENSIONAL CONTINUUM -
RATHER - IT IS THE VOID BETWEEN BRANES -

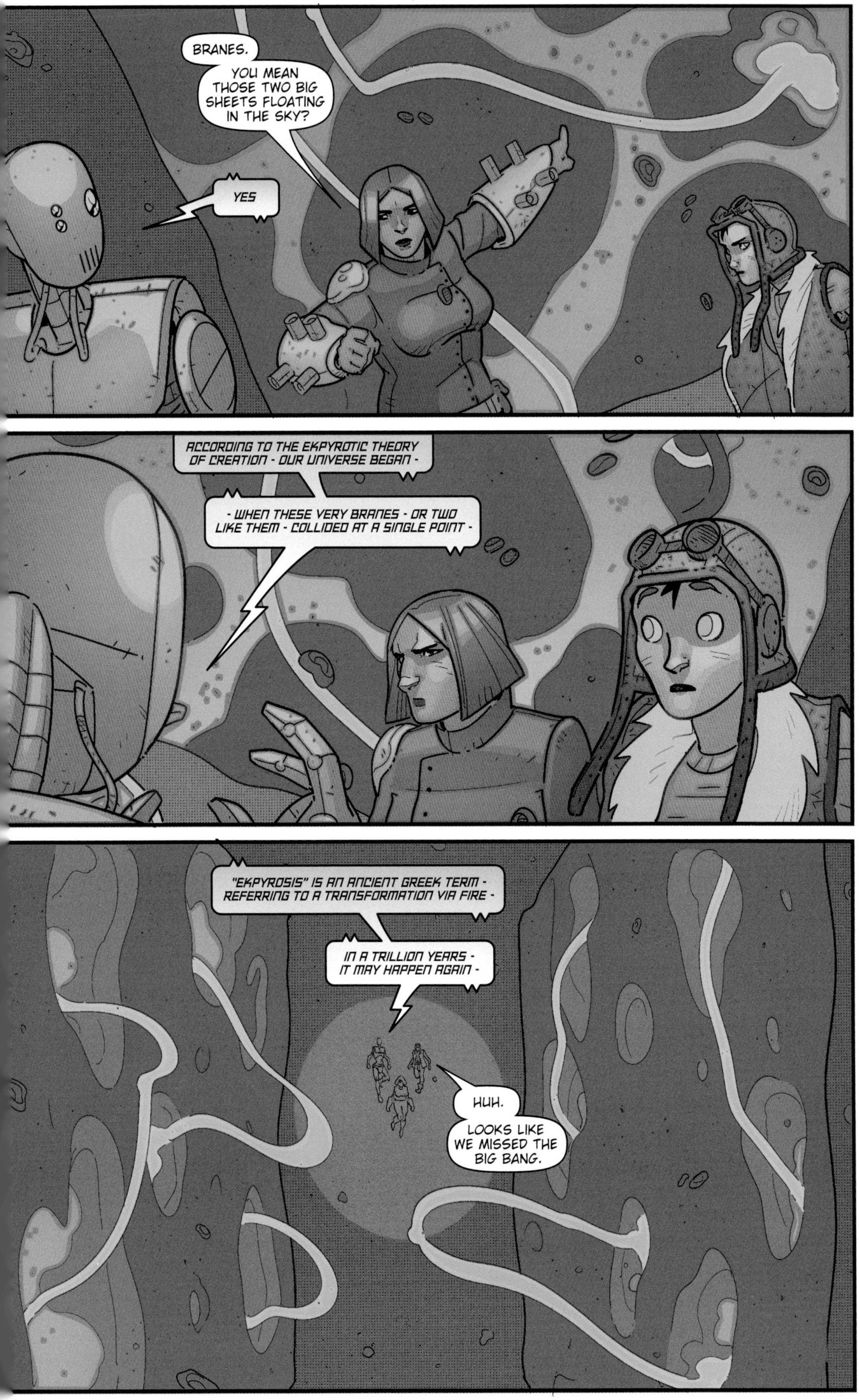
BRANES.
YOU MEAN THOSE TWO BIG SHEETS FLOATING IN THE SKY?
YES
ACCORDING TO THE EKPYROTIC THEORY OF CREATION - OUR UNIVERSE BEGAN -
- WHEN THESE VERY BRANES - OR TWO LIKE THEM - COLLIDED AT A SINGLE POINT -
"EKPYROSIS" IS AN ANCIENT GREEK TERM - REFERRING TO A TRANSFORMATION VIA FIRE -
IN A TRILLION YEARS - IT MAY HAPPEN AGAIN -
HUH.
LOOKS LIKE WE MISSED THE BIG BANG.

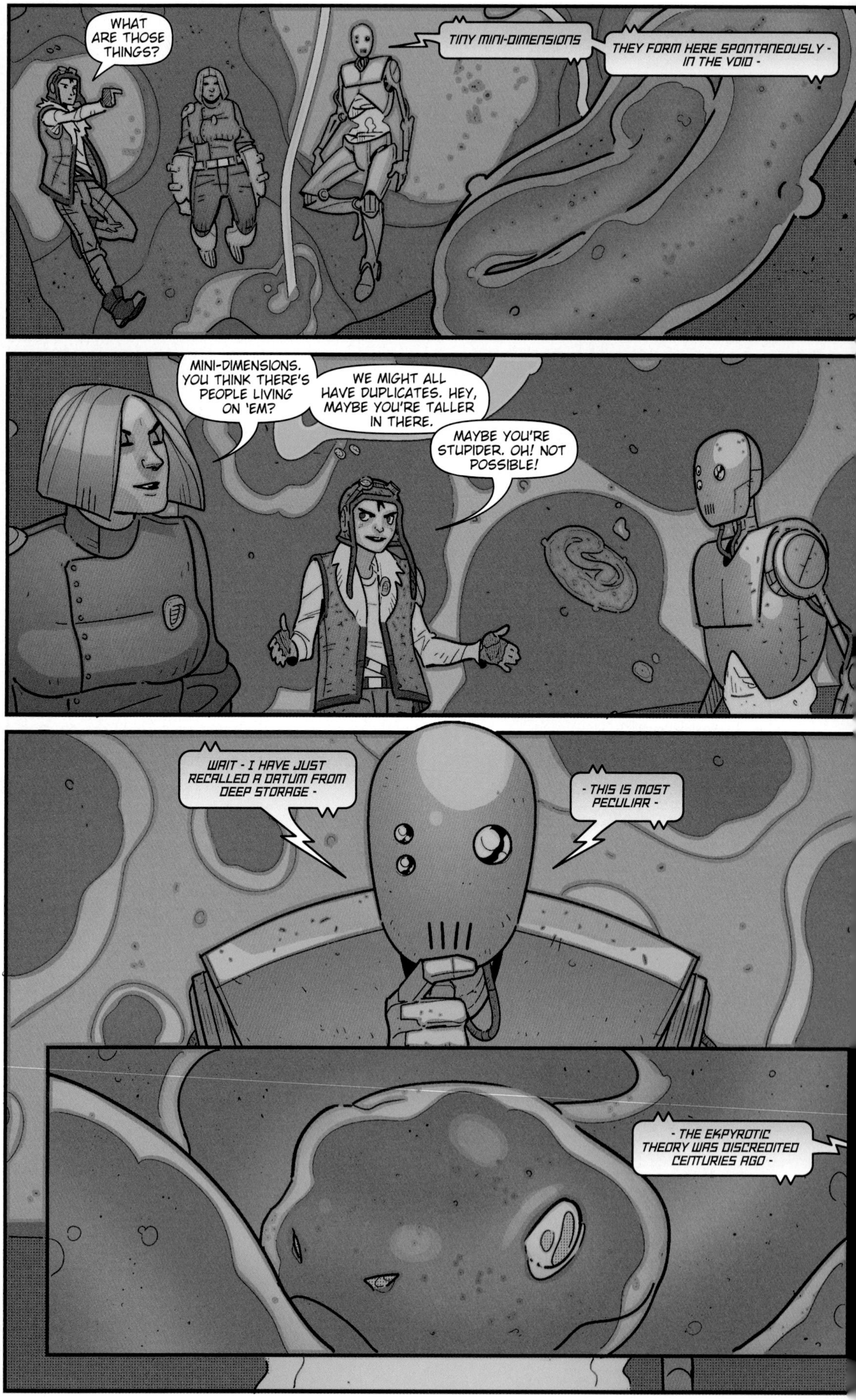
WHAT ARE THOSE THINGS?
TINY MINI-DIMENSIONS
THEY FORM HERE SPONTANEOUSLY - IN THE VOID -
MINI-DIMENSIONS. YOU THINK THERE'S PEOPLE LIVING ON 'EM?
WE MIGHT ALL HAVE DUPLICATES. HEY, MAYBE YOU'RE TALLER IN THERE.
MAYBE YOU'RE STUPIDER. OH! NOT POSSIBLE!
WAIT - I HAVE JUST RECALLED A DATUM FROM DEEP STORAGE -
- THIS IS MOST PECULIAR -
- THE EKPYROTIC THEORY WAS DISCREDITED CENTURIES AGO -

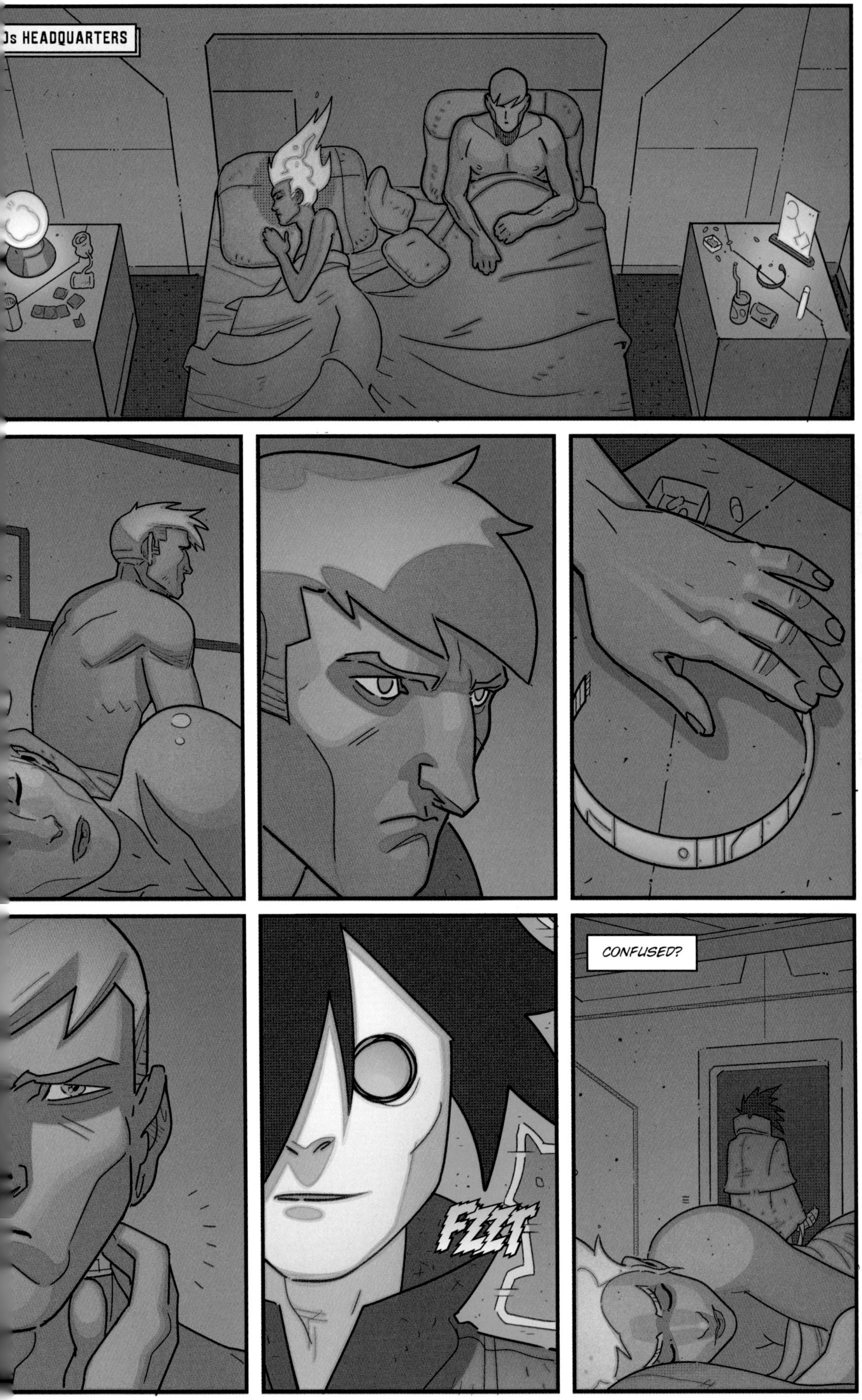

Os HEADQUARTERS
FZZT
CONFUSED?

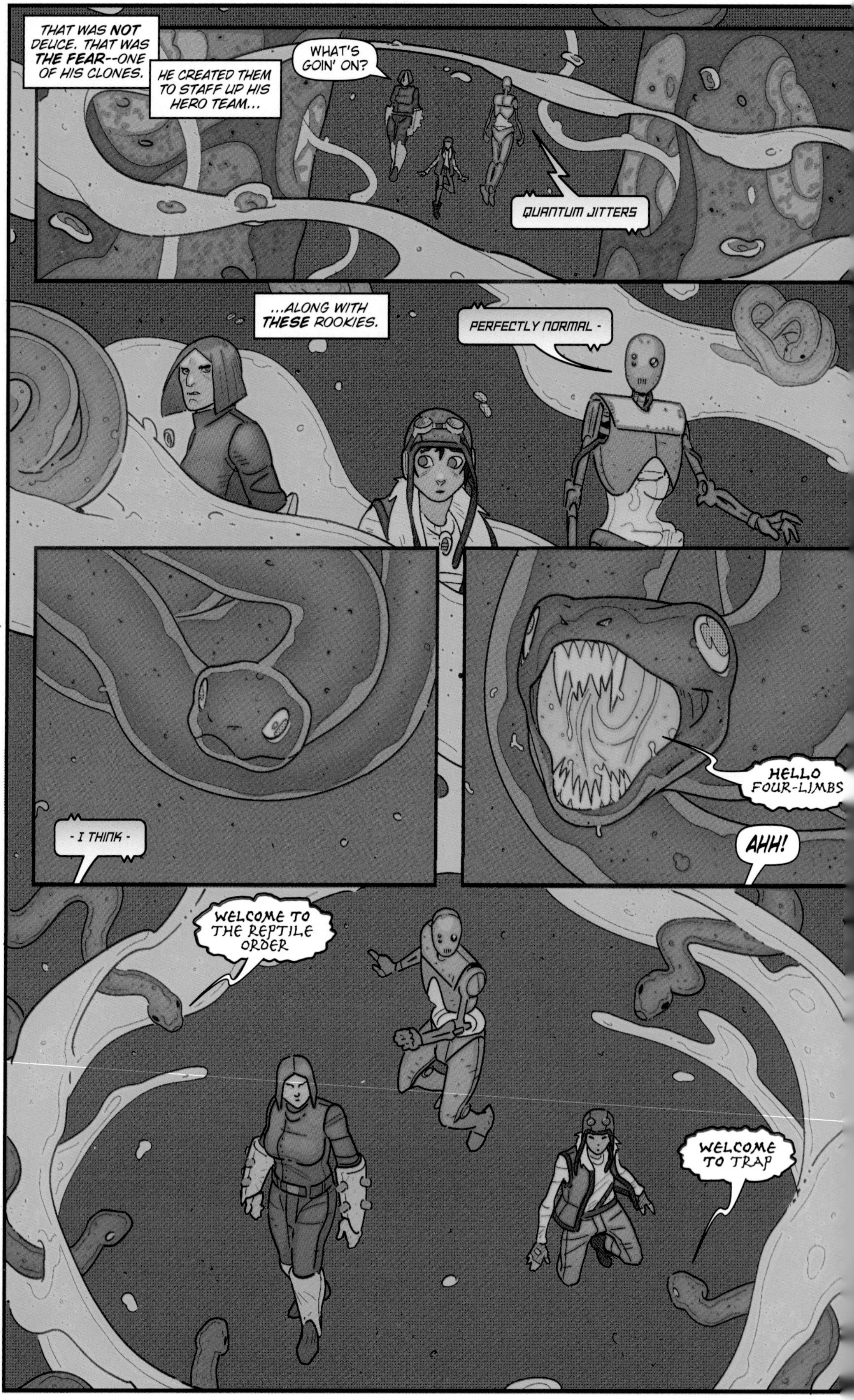

THAT WAS NOT DEUCE. THAT WAS THE FEAR--ONE OF HIS CLONES.
HE CREATED THEM TO STAFF UP HIS HERO TEAM...
WHAT'S GOIN' ON?
QUANTUM JITTERS
...ALONG WITH THESE ROOKIES.
PERFECTLY NORMAL -
- I THINK -
HELLO FOUR-LIMBS
AHH!
WELCOME TO THE REPTILE ORDER
WELCOME TO TRAP

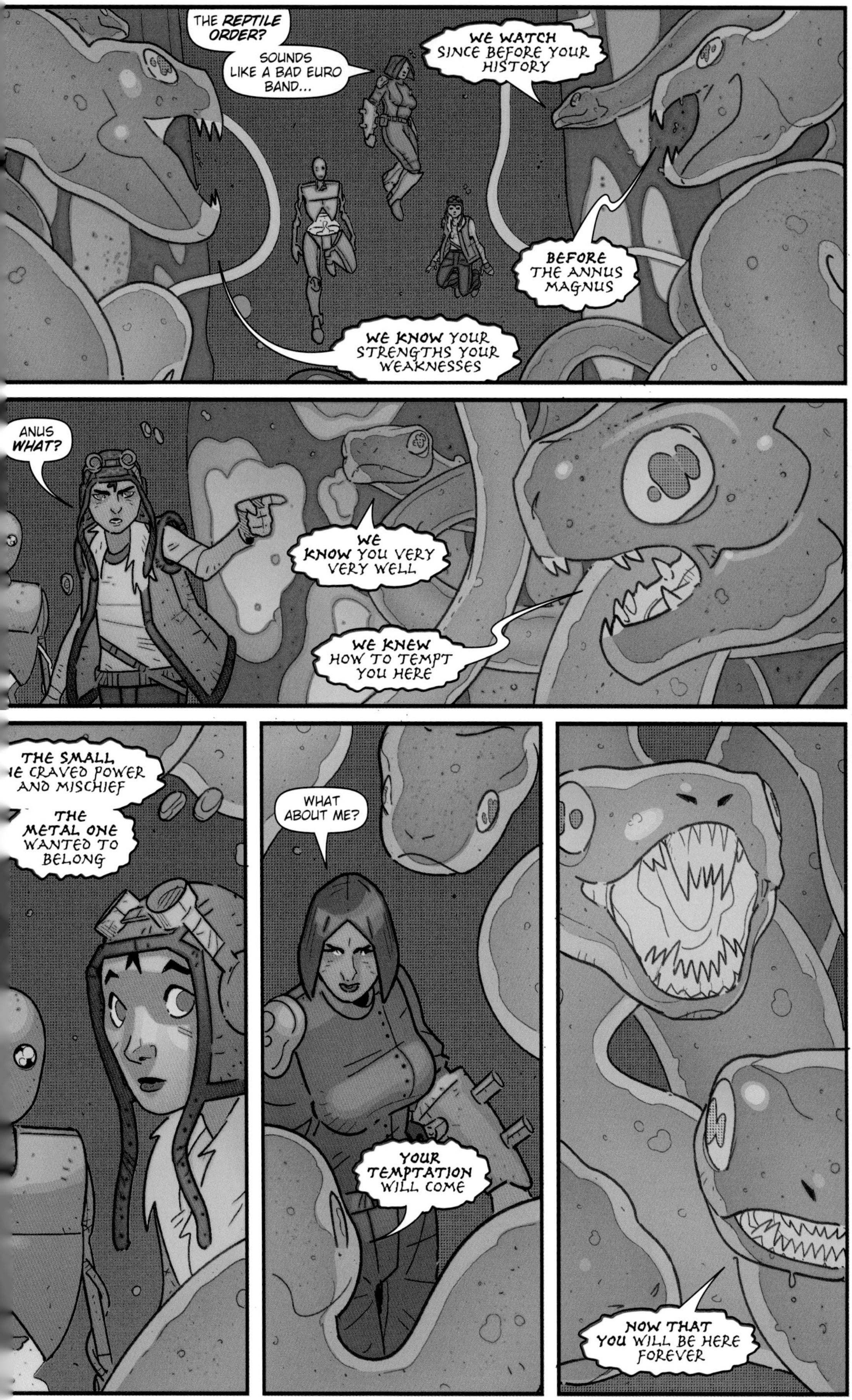
THE REPTILE ORDER?
SOUNDS LIKE A BAD EURO BAND...
WE WATCH SINCE BEFORE YOUR HISTORY
BEFORE THE ANNUS MAGNUS
WE KNOW YOUR STRENGTHS YOUR WEAKNESSES
ANUS WHAT?
WE KNOW YOU VERY VERY WELL
WE KNEW HOW TO TEMPT YOU HERE
THE SMALL ONE CRAVED POWER AND MISCHIEF
THE METAL ONE WANTED TO BELONG
WHAT ABOUT ME?
YOUR TEMPTATION WILL COME
NOW THAT YOU WILL BE HERE FOREVER

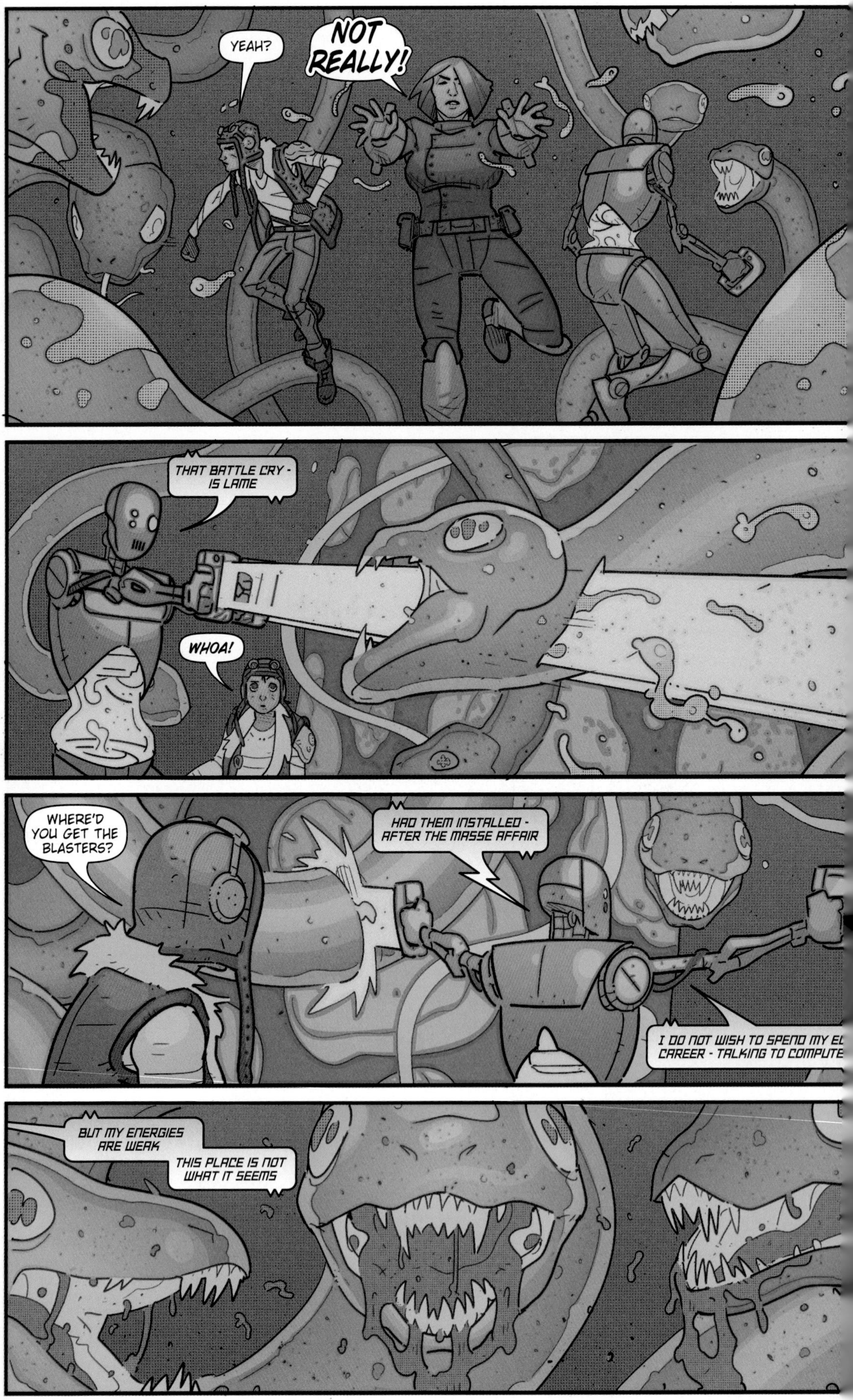
YEAH?
NOT REALLY!
THAT BATTLE CRY - IS LAME
WHOA!
WHERE'D YOU GET THE BLASTERS?
HAD THEM INSTALLED - AFTER THE MASSE AFFAIR
BUT MY ENERGIES ARE WEAK
THIS PLACE IS NOT WHAT IT SEEMS

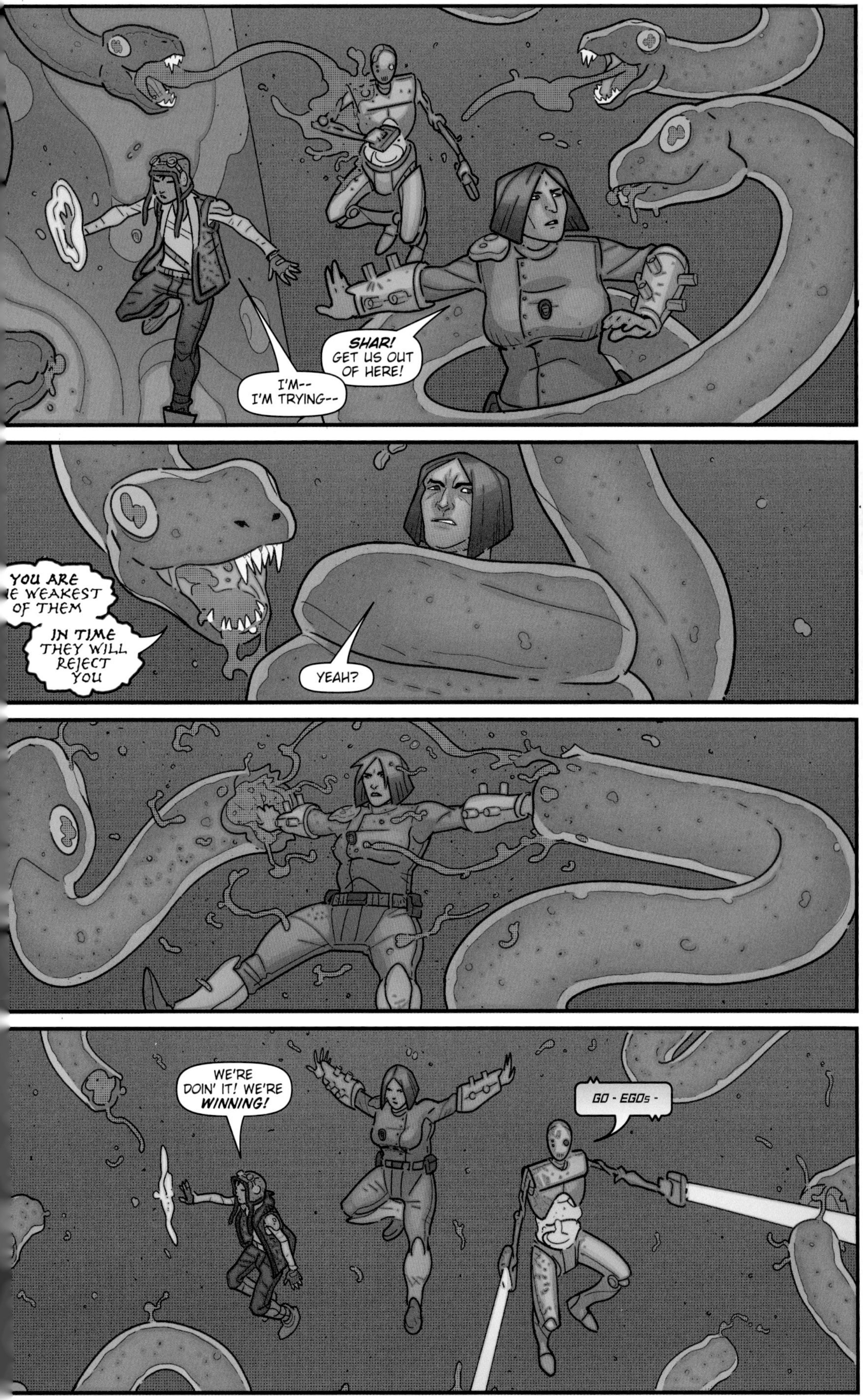
SHAR! GET US OUT OF HERE!
I'M-- I'M TRYING--
YOU ARE E WEAKEST OF THEM
IN TIME THEY WILL REJECT YOU
YEAH?
WE'RE DOIN' IT! WE'RE WINNING!
GO - EGOs -

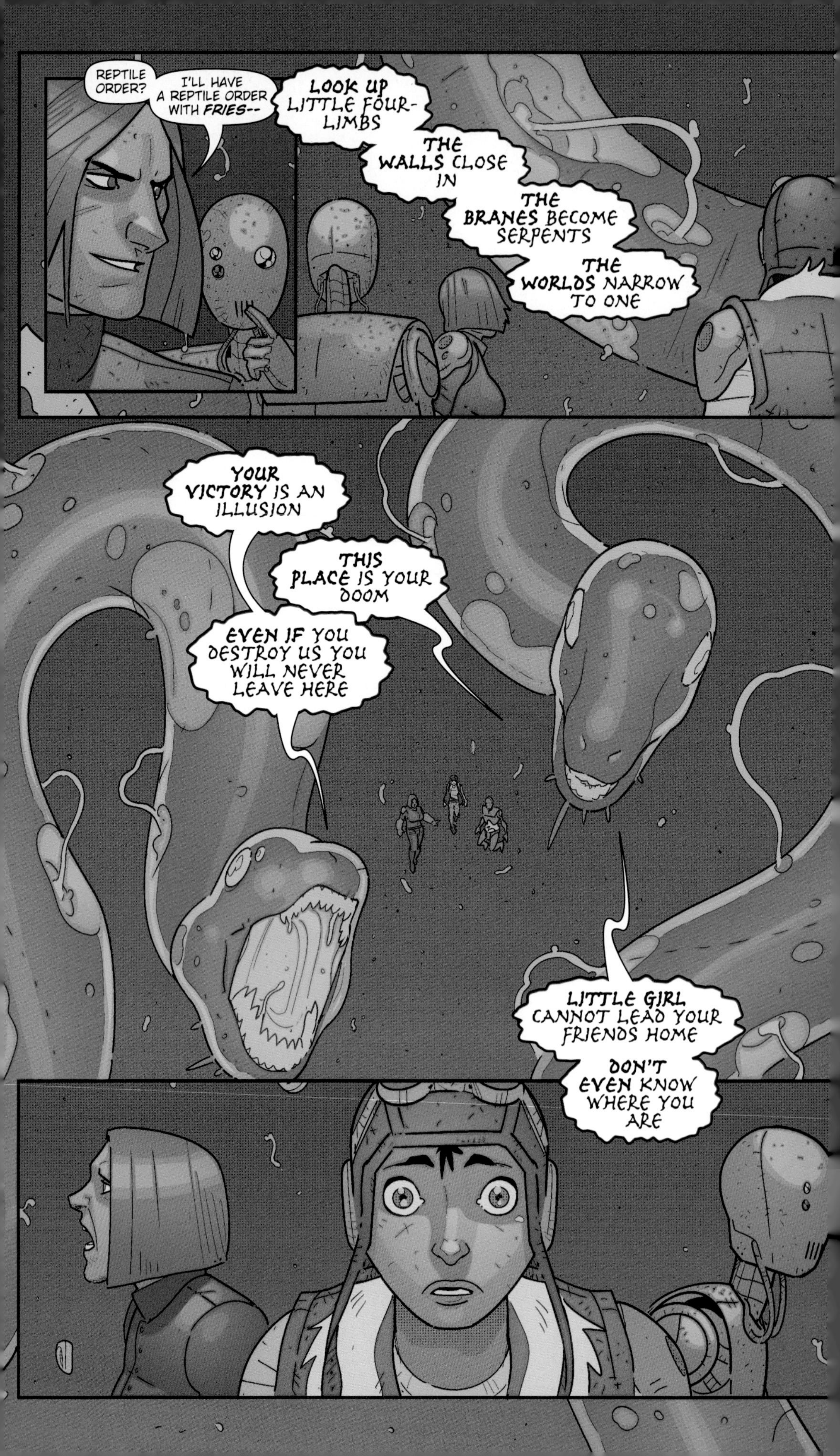
REPTILE ORDER?
I'LL HAVE A REPTILE ORDER WITH FRIES--
LOOK UP LITTLE FOUR-LIMBS
THE WALLS CLOSE IN
THE BRANES BECOME SERPENTS
THE WORLDS NARROW TO ONE
YOUR VICTORY IS AN ILLUSION
THIS PLACE IS YOUR DOOM
EVEN IF YOU DESTROY US YOU WILL NEVER LEAVE HERE
LITTLE GIRL CANNOT LEAD YOUR FRIENDS HOME
DON'T EVEN KNOW WHERE YOU ARE

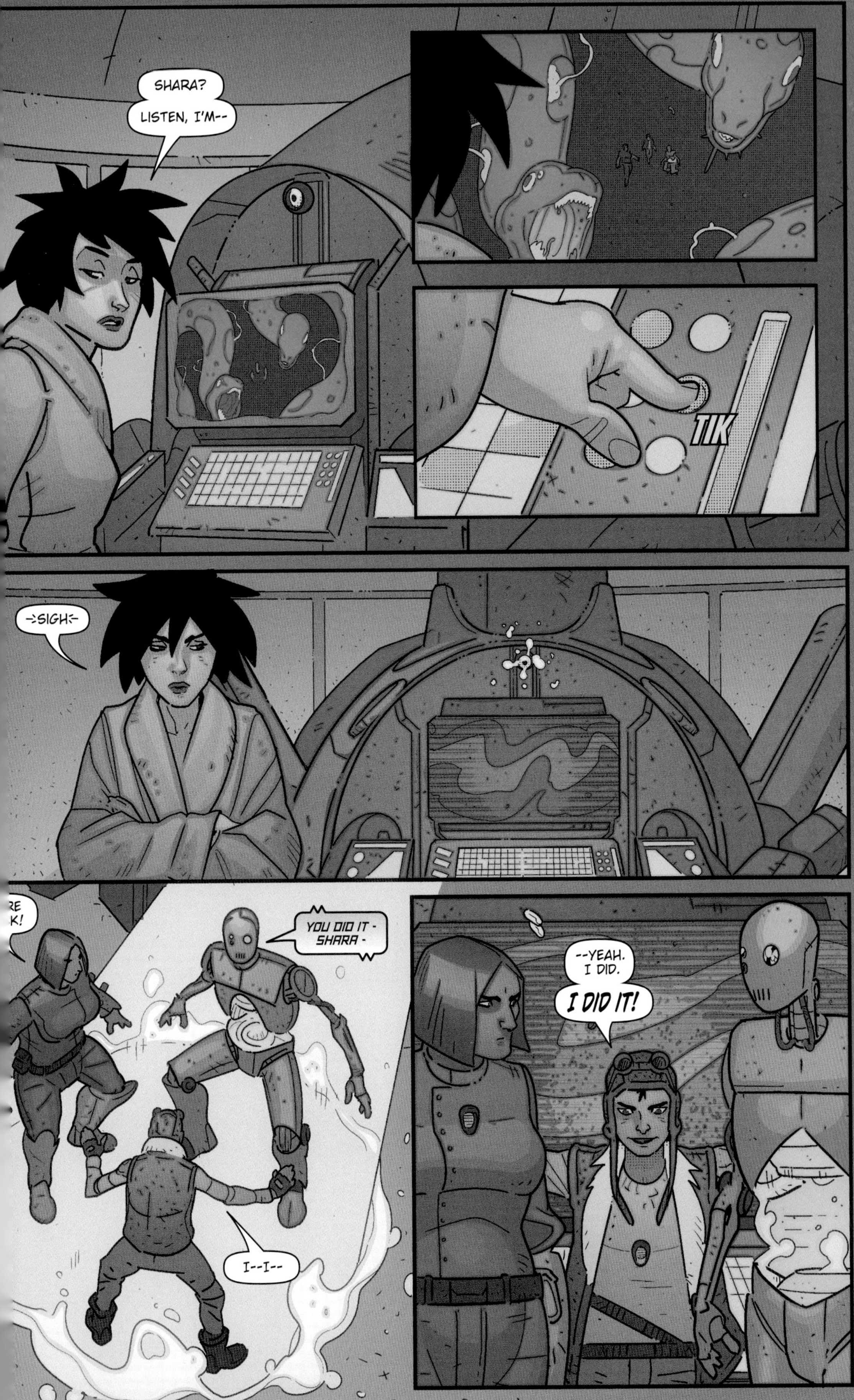
SHARA?
LISTEN, I'M--
TIK
-SIGH-
YOU DID IT - SHARA -
I--I--
--YEAH. I DID.
I DID IT!

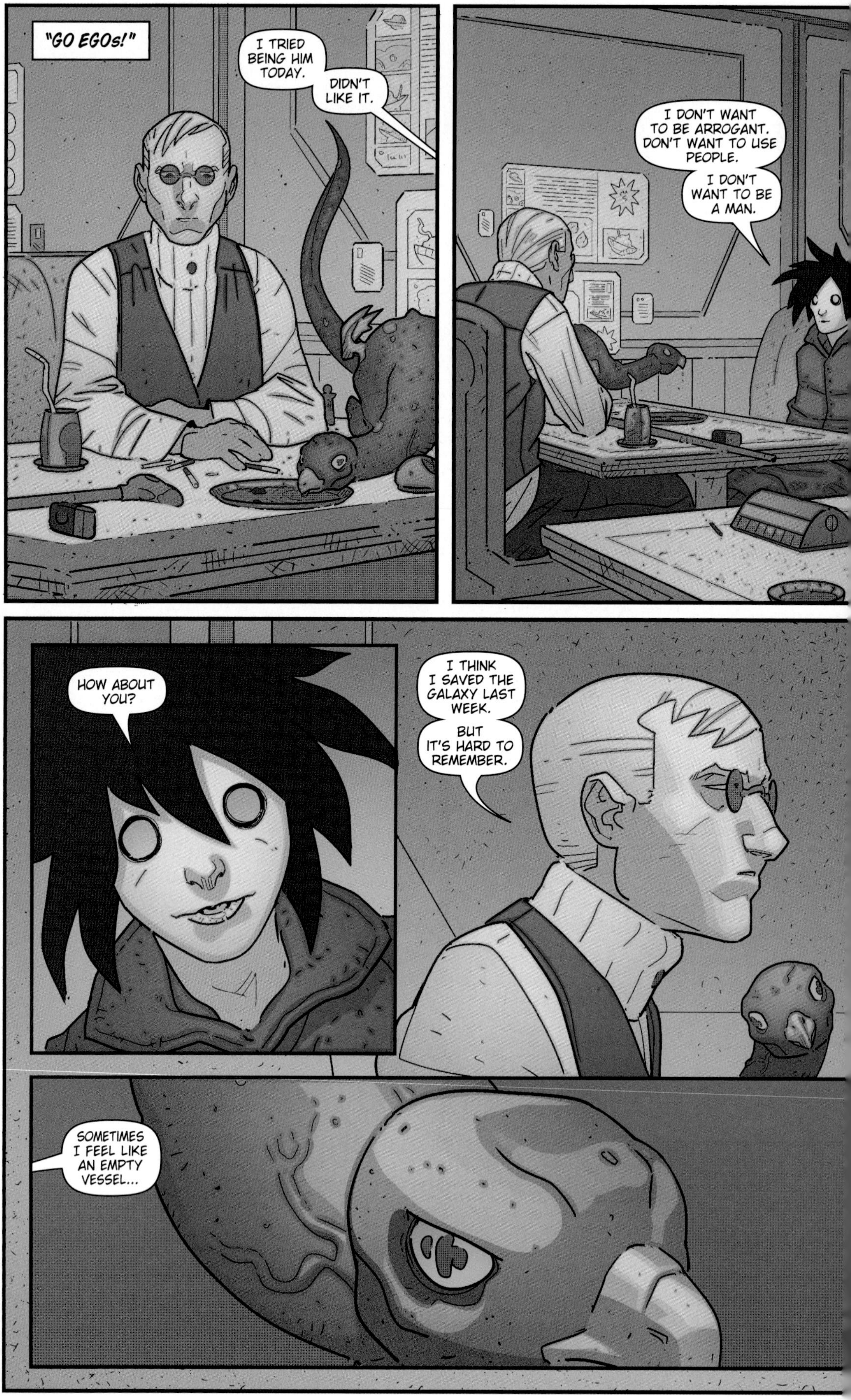
"GO EGOs!"
I TRIED BEING HIM TODAY.
DIDN'T LIKE IT.
I DON'T WANT TO BE ARROGANT. DON'T WANT TO USE PEOPLE.
I DON'T WANT TO BE A MAN.
HOW ABOUT YOU?
I THINK I SAVED THE GALAXY LAST WEEK.
BUT IT'S HARD TO REMEMBER.
SOMETIMES I FEEL LIKE AN EMPTY VESSEL...

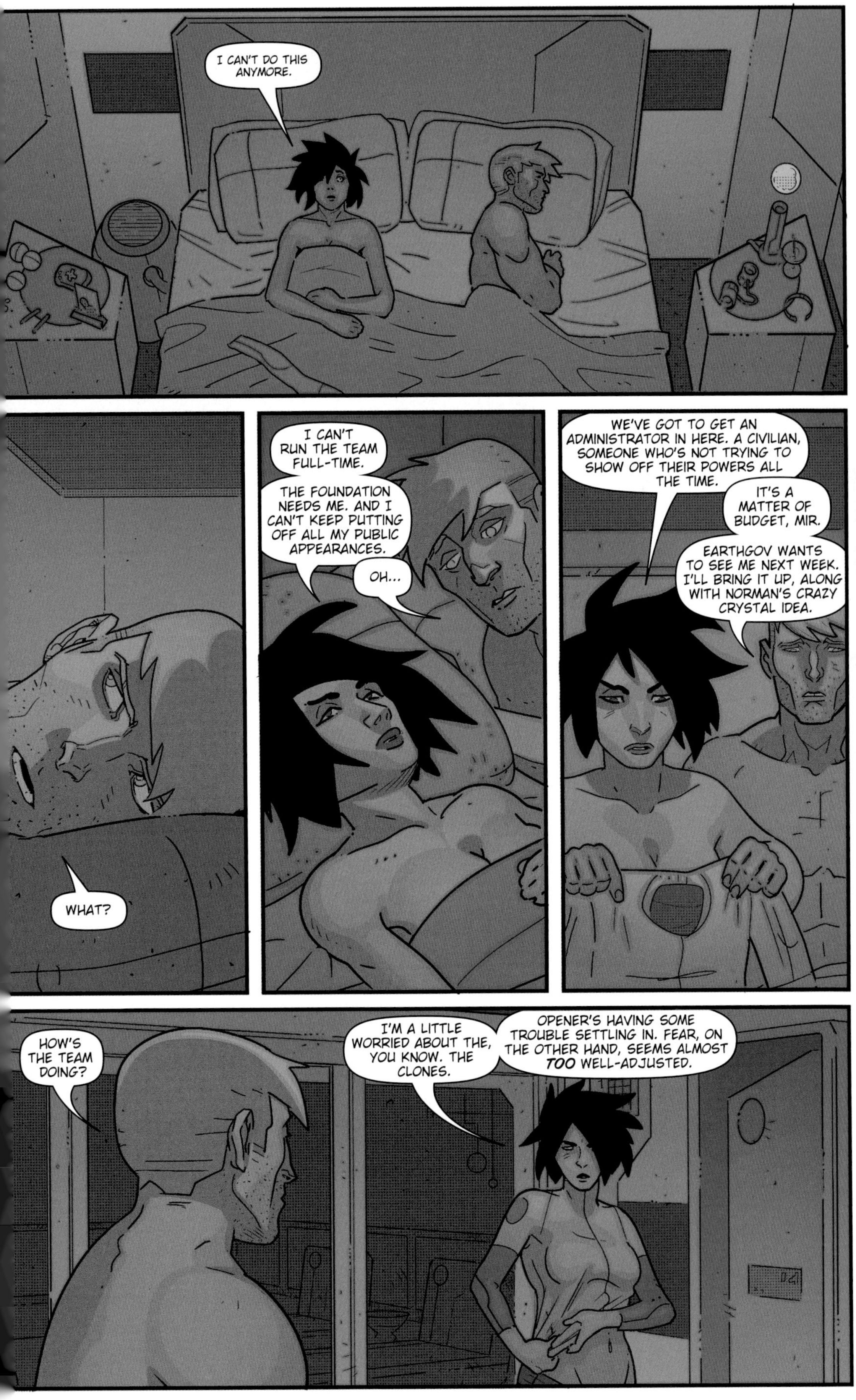
I CAN'T DO THIS ANYMORE.
WHAT?
I CAN'T RUN THE TEAM FULL-TIME.
THE FOUNDATION NEEDS ME. AND I CAN'T KEEP PUTTING OFF ALL MY PUBLIC APPEARANCES.
OH...
WE'VE GOT TO GET AN ADMINISTRATOR IN HERE. A CIVILIAN, SOMEONE WHO'S NOT TRYING TO SHOW OFF THEIR POWERS ALL THE TIME.
IT'S A MATTER OF BUDGET, MIR.
EARTHGOV WANTS TO SEE ME NEXT WEEK. I'LL BRING IT UP, ALONG WITH NORMAN'S CRAZY CRYSTAL IDEA.
HOW'S THE TEAM DOING?
I'M A LITTLE WORRIED ABOUT THE, YOU KNOW. THE CLONES.
OPENER'S HAVING SOME TROUBLE SETTLING IN. FEAR, ON THE OTHER HAND, SEEMS ALMOST ***TOO*** WELL-ADJUSTED.

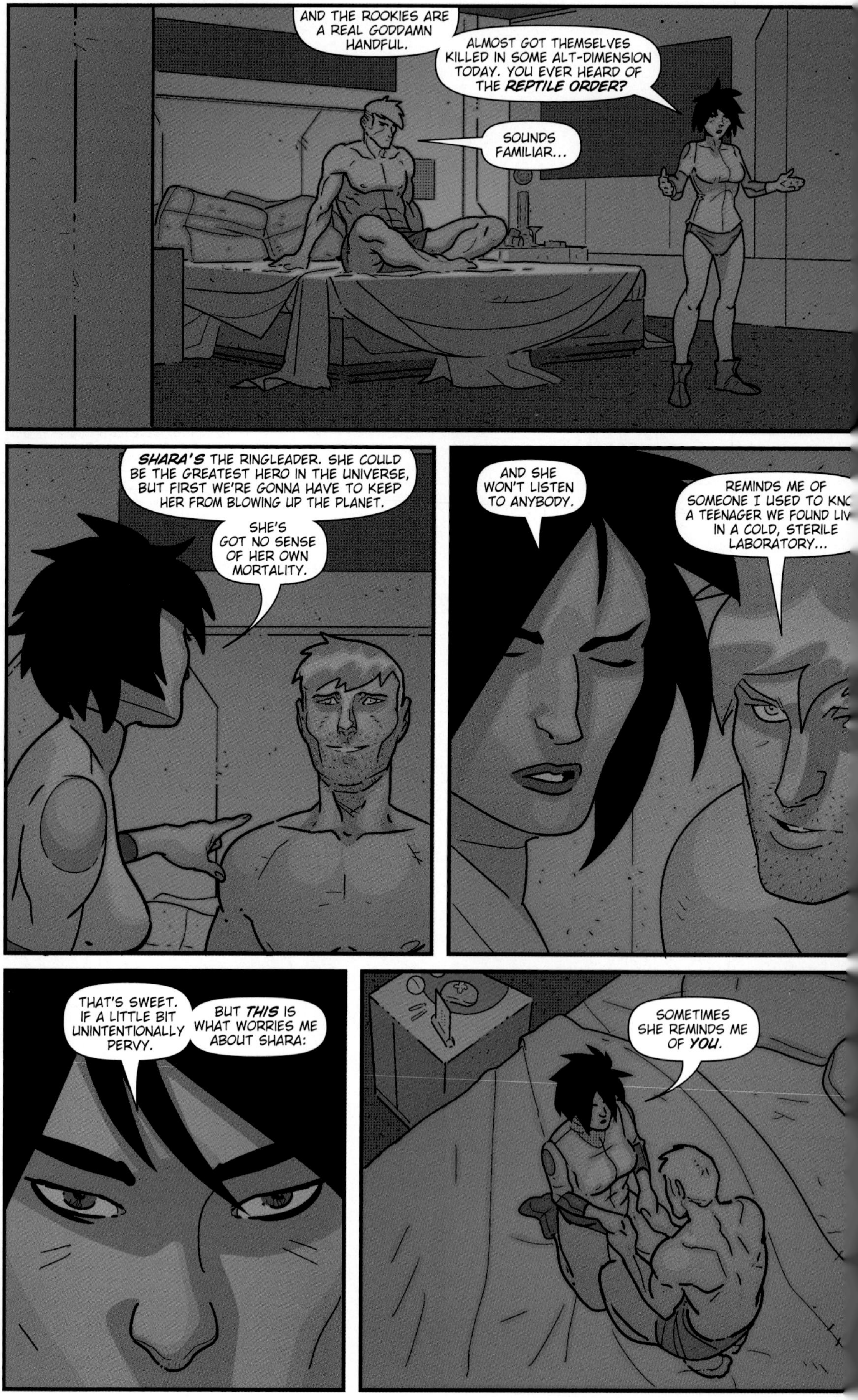
AND THE ROOKIES ARE A REAL GODDAMN HANDFUL.
ALMOST GOT THEMSELVES KILLED IN SOME ALT-DIMENSION TODAY. YOU EVER HEARD OF THE ***REPTILE ORDER?***
SOUNDS FAMILIAR...
SHARA'S THE RINGLEADER. SHE COULD BE THE GREATEST HERO IN THE UNIVERSE, BUT FIRST WE'RE GONNA HAVE TO KEEP HER FROM BLOWING UP THE PLANET.
SHE'S GOT NO SENSE OF HER OWN MORTALITY.
AND SHE WON'T LISTEN TO ANYBODY.
REMINDS ME OF SOMEONE I USED TO KNO A TEENAGER WE FOUND LIV IN A COLD, STERILE LABORATORY...
THAT'S SWEET. IF A LITTLE BIT UNINTENTIONALLY PERVY.
BUT ***THIS*** IS WHAT WORRIES ME ABOUT SHARA:
SOMETIMES SHE REMINDS ME OF ***YOU.***

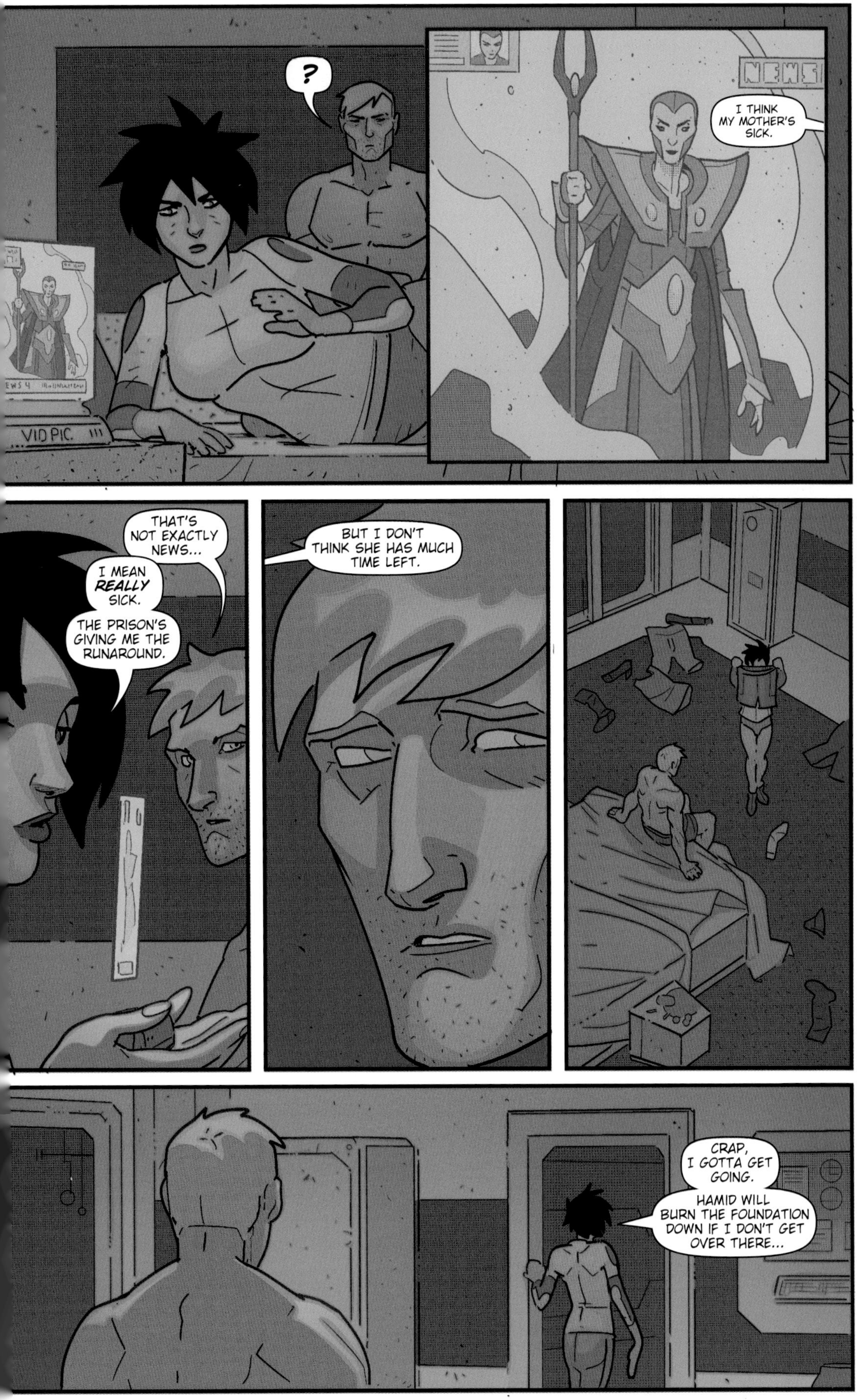

VID PIC.
?
I THINK MY MOTHER'S SICK.
THAT'S NOT EXACTLY NEWS...
I MEAN ***REALLY*** SICK.
THE PRISON'S GIVING ME THE RUNAROUND.
BUT I DON'T THINK SHE HAS MUCH TIME LEFT.
CRAP, I GOTTA GET GOING.
HAMID WILL BURN THE FOUNDATION DOWN IF I DON'T GET OVER THERE...

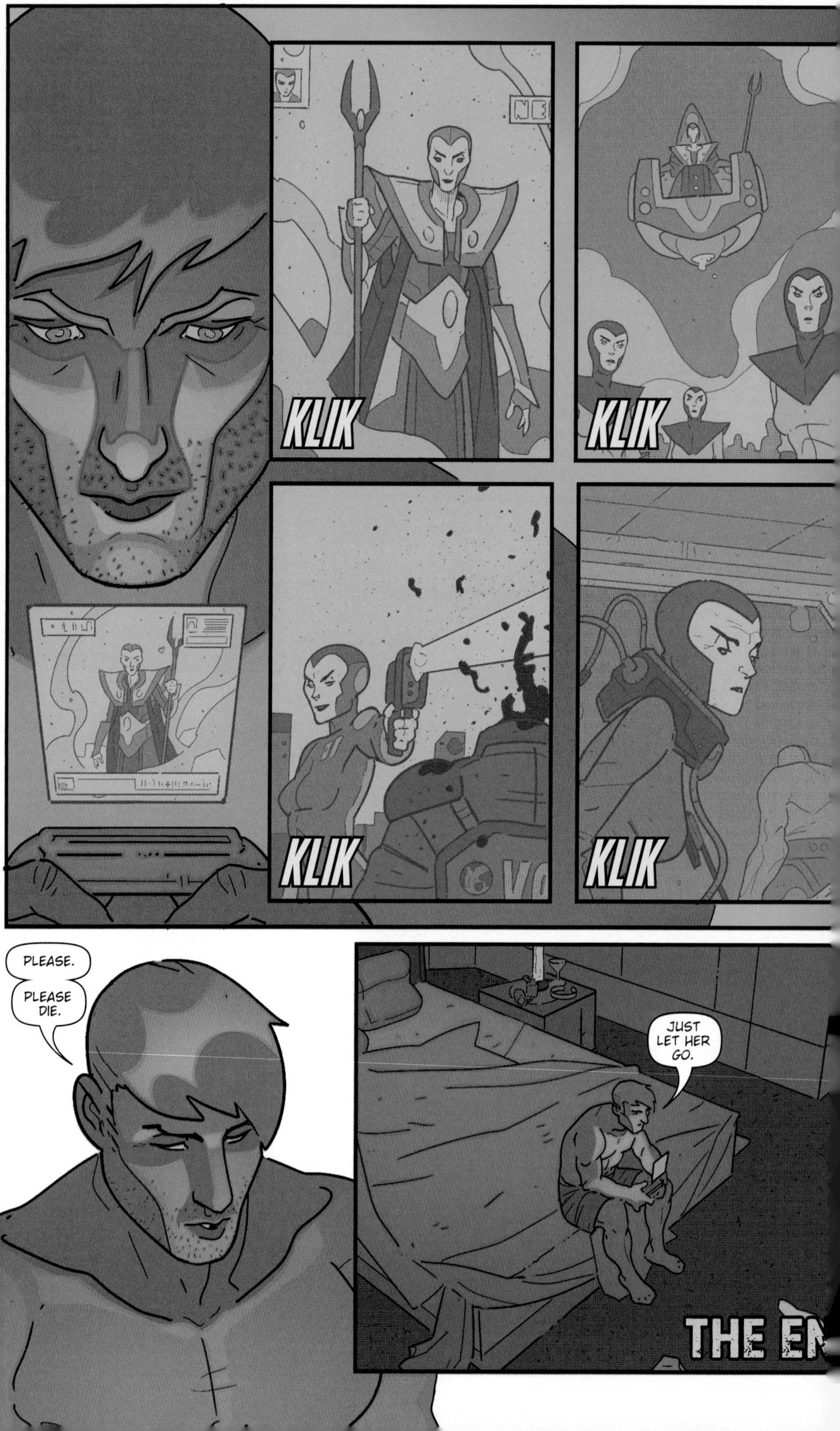
KLIK
KLIK
KLIK
KLIK
PLEASE.
PLEASE DIE.
JUST LET HER GO.
THE EN

EARTH · GALACTIC · OPERATIVES

Issue #0: EXPOSED

Written by **STUART MOORE**
Art by **GUS STORMS**

(originally presented via Twitter,
in slightly different form)

This story takes place three weeks before EGOs #1.

y the time the original EGOs split up, nobody was surprised. It
as inevitable as an artificial sunrise. Give you an example why:

euce, the EGOs' leader, and the Planetarian once had a drunken
ght over a woman. Deuce used his power of persuasion to close
e deal.

anetarian didn't like that at all. He cracked Deuce over the head
ith a bottle and tried to shove him out an airlock.

d I mention they were both married at the time?

hat was 23 years ago. Since then, the Planetarian—real name,
ggo Rasch—had always worked alone.

e was a crime-scene profiler on a cosmic scale. If a world or
moon or a space station had been destroyed, he could figure
ut why.

, today: The Planetarian floated before the wreckage of Energy
oncepts Research Station 718 Beta.

e cast his eyes across the half-mile of torn, burned metal. Every
ch was exposed to vacuum.

urniture floated in the void. Holo-projectors, too, still sparking
mpotently. Couple frozen bodies, barely recognizable.

anetarian pulled himself forward, toward the center of the
ation. His hyper-senses reached out, taking in every detail:

e pattern of blast-marks. The texture of the doorways,
umbling at his touch. Fading electrical currents surging through
e walls.

e reached the exact center of the dead station, a
evastated chem lab. Gravity was out, chairs and test tubes
ated all around.

e Planetarian closed his eyes and adopted a lotus position.
shed a floating beaker away and tried to clear his mind.

s spacesuit made the lotus position difficult. He hated
acesuits. Bulky, itchy things that should have been retired
nturies ago.

e was a large man, which made the problem worse. Trouble was,
competing technology was as foolproof as a spacesuit.

Force fields could short out, thinskins got punctured. So the
spacesuit had outlived all its competition. Until now, maybe.

Energy Concepts had been working on a new method of life-
support protection. For the past year, that had been this station's
sole mission.

But it seemed like somebody really didn't want them to succeed.

The Planetarian's consciousness reached out. He pictured the lab
as it would have been when whole: clean, gleaming, full of activity.

In his mind, scientists worked on their prototype. He knew very
little about that—only that it was small and portable.

Something intruded on his awareness. A floating energy source,
faint but persistent. He reached up and grabbed it out of the air.

Planetarian frowned. The object was smaller than his hand,
roughly the shape of a warped plastic cup lid. Just slightly burned.

His eyes went wide. This was the prototype. Or part of it, anyway.

A light winked red on its surface. He pressed it, and air began to
hiss out of the device, forming a small, floating bubble.

Slowly the Planetarian reached out his gloved hand, penetrating
the air bubble. Then, grimacing, he reached out and twisted off
his glove.

This was risky. The device was supposed to create a stable
atmosphere around its user. If it failed, his hand would be exposed
to vacuum.

But this was what the Planetarian did: absorb all possible sensory
input related to a crime scene. It was his job.

The air bubble held. Planetarian exhaled in relief and reached
forward to touch the device itself.

The second his finger grazed the singe-mark on the device, a very
strange sense-memory ran through him.

The Planetarian remembered a rash he'd had as a child. A
persistent red irritation on his palms, arms, and ankles.

It had taken him years to discover the source. His grandfather,
a very old German man, had given him shoes hand-made
of goatskin.

Allergies were rare these days. Most of them had been genetically
removed, centuries ago.

But somehow, the child-Planetarian had inherited an allergic
reaction to goatskin.

Now, floating in the station, he peered at the prototype device.
Was there *goatskin* inside it...?

Then, abruptly, he found his thoughts wrenched in a different
direction. Back into his past, again; but an even less pleasant part
of it.

Almost from the day he'd joined the EGOs, Planetarian had longed
to quit. First off, he was a loner to the core.

But more than that: The more members who joined the group, the
worse the internal bickering became.

Espero, the original leader, had been a reasonably benevolent
dictator. But after Deuce joined, every second became a
power struggle.

The Planetarian shook his head. *We were all so young,* he thought. *Today, I couldn't put up with that for...*

...for...

He whipped his head around in alarm. Someone else was here. Some foreign element—maybe even the person who'd—

"Yo yo Planet! Just like old times, huh?"

The Planetarian groaned. He didn't need to turn around: He could already picture the cut jaw, the greying blond hair, the ubiquitous smirk.

Deuce was here.

 ii

As the Planetarian turned, some instinct made him slap his glove back on and stash the prototype in his spacesuit pocket.

Deuce floated in the ripped-open lab chamber, fully spacesuited and—sure enough—grinning like he owned the whole damn galaxy.

Deuce held out his arms. "Hug, Planet? For old times?"

"Don't call me that." Planetarian glared at him. "What. On all the known worlds. Are you *doing* here?"

"Helping out an old bud." Deuce didn't seem fazed at all. Planetarian wanted to paste him one. "Per Earthgov orders."

The Planetarian frowned. "Earthgov knows I work alone," he said. "It's in my contract."

"Ah, you got me." Deuce shrugged. "I kind of convinced them to let me tag along on this one."

"Did you also convince them not to tell me in advance?"

"Didn't want to spoil the surprise," Deuce said.

What you really didn't want, the Planetarian thought, *was for me to find out you were coming and quash the idea.*

"Anyway, I'm here now," Deuce continued. "Sorry if I startled you. Miri's been real busy lately...I just wanted a little guy time."

Planetarian gritted his teeth. "Are you under the delusion that we were at one time, let's say, friends?"

"Don't be like that." Deuce pivoted off a wall, swiveling his body further into the chamber. "I'm here to help."

"By interrupting my routine? Interfering with my powers? Creating psychic chaos, the way you did years ago?"

"It wasn't that bad." Deuce looked around, studying the wreckage. "And to be honest, I've got another reason for coming."

Planetarian waited. This was the moment, he knew, when Deuce wanted him to ask what that reason was. He stayed silent.

"This life-support research that EC was doing," Deuce continued. "I thought it might be useful for the new team."

The Planetarian frowned again. "What new team?"

"Ah!" Deuce smiled wide. "Now you're interested, huh, Planet?"

"Do *not* call me that."

"Whatever you say. Peanut."

"Wait a minute." Planetarian felt rage rising inside him. "Were you messing with my mind before? Using your power?"

Deuce gave him a Who-Me look.

"My brain is a delicate instrument," the Planetarian continued. "It's my *livelihood*. If you *ever* go screwing around in there again—"

A sudden movement caught their eyes. Deuce and the Planetarian turned in unison. For just a brief moment, they were teammates again.

A spacesuited figure swung in through the wreckage. She moved swiftly, using both her arms and legs with a weird, unsettling sort of grace.

Before the Planetarian could speak, the woman pulled out a blaster and aimed it straight at him.

"Not one move," she said. "Oxana Martine, field investigator for Energy Concepts Inc. You two are trespassing on private property."

Deuce held out a hand. "Ms. Martine? Pleased to meet you. I think there's been a mixup."

Deuce's eyes were glowing slightly. *That means he's using his persuasion power,* the Planetarian remembered.

Martine turned the blaster toward Deuce. "I'm wearing a psi-screen, bro."

"I love a challenge, ma'am." Deuce smiled. "Besides, we're here on orders from Earthgov."

"Earthgov has no jurisdiction here," Martine replied.

Planetarian cleared his throat. "I cannot speak for my, uh, this man," he said, "but Earthgov has coordinated my mission with EC, Inc."

Martine frowned. "I wasn't told about this."

"Typical corporate crap," Deuce said. "Need to know, right hand/left hand. Keep the underlings in the dark."

Martine lowered the blaster, shaking her head. "I swear I quit this job," she said. "Soon as I file this report."

Deuce moved closer to her, smiling sympathetically. "You got a next step planned? Some dream you want to follow, maybe?"

She shrugged. "I make films. Pretty experimental stuff, though. Nothing the mainstream 'ceiver networks appreciate."

Deuce nodded. "That's awesome." His eyes were glowing again.

If my power were death-rays, the Planetarian thought, *Deuce would be a pile of ash.*

Planetarian peered closer at Martine. She was fortyish, her hair pulled back. Eyes looked a little wild, distracted.

"You know about the research, then?" Martine asked. They nodded. "Well, this was definitely sabotage."

"Has someone claimed credit?" the Planetarian asked.

"No. But all backup datastreams have been erased or corrupted. was sent to see if the on-site computers are salvageable."

Deuce moved in toward her. "Since we're all here, maybe we could work together." A leer crossed his face. "Pool our resources."

"NO!" the Planetarian screamed. Deuce and Martine both turned to look, startled.

"We are *not* going to work together," he said, jabbing a finger at Deuce's chest. "I don't work with anyone, and certainly not with you."

Deuce smiled, but now the smile seemed strained. "You don't mean that," he said.

"You had the right idea 23 years ago," Planetarian continued. "G away from me. Get out of my head, get out of my life. Let. Me. Work."

"Peanut," Deuce said, "you're not still mad about the girl, are yo Back at the solar conference? That was years ago."

Planetarian clenched his fists. "She only slept with you," he said "because I turned her down."

That wasn't true. He'd slept with the girl, and *then* she'd gone o with Deuce, later the same night. Which was much worse.

artine kicked off of a wall. "I'll go check the computers," she
id, "while you two take care of your imaginary girlfriend issues."

he's feisty," Deuce said, watching Martine go. "Little old for you
ough, huh? Even though you've got ten years on her."

anetarian turned to face Deuce head-on. He positioned himself
bove" Deuce in the zero-g room, hovering over him.

Ve are not teammates," Planetarian said, "and we are not
ends. Stay away from me or I swear I will hurt you."

euce just stared back, his expression blank now.

here is no EGOs anymore," the Planetarian continued. "And
ere never will be again."

l at once, Deuce's face became a mask of sadness. Planetarian
hirled away, hating himself for the pang of sympathy he felt.

 iii

e Planetarian had learned long ago not to rely solely on his
wers. A good investigator used every tool at his disposal.

ne of the earliest lessons he'd learned was: To solve the
traordinary, first examine the ordinary.

 he sought out a mostly intact stateroom. A place where an
dinary scientist had lived and, possibly, died.

ke the rest of the station it was in vacuum, but all four walls
ere intact. He cast his eyes across the floating bureau and
y chair.

mething about the unmade bed reminded him of his second
fe. Or maybe his third? It was hard to remember, these days.

flickering on the far wall caught his eye. A holo-board, a
writable bulletin-board-slash-wall-poster. It wasn't
orking right.

 walked over and peered at the holo. Jabbed it, hard, with his
bow. Dark brown letters faded up, in jagged handwriting:

NG LIVE THE PRIMATE ORDER

e Planetarian frowned. He'd never heard of the Primate Order.
other clue to the station's destruction?

 cleared his throat and shook out his limbs, best he could in the
acesuit. Closed his eyes and allowed himself to float, rigid.

e solution to this mystery was right in front of him. But he
uldn't solve it, he knew, because his mind was too clouded
th anger.

hy did Deuce have to butt his nose into everything? And what
.s all that crap about a new EGOs team? Planetarian shivered
the idea.

d then there was Martine. Deuce was right—she wasn't
anetarian's type at all. And there was something off about her.

t that didn't mean the Planetarian wanted to watch Deuce drool
over her. He'd had enough of that crap for one lifetime.

uce tended to think of women as either conquest-worthy or
pendable. Disgusting, the Planetarian thought.

 knew he had a lot of the same problems as Deuce. He'd been
rking on it, but…old habits.

p it! he told himself. Concentrate on the job. The research…the
rk that was being done here. The life-support prototype…

th a sinking feeling, he reached into his pocket. The prototype
is gone. His eyes snapped open—

to see Martine floating right before him. She wore no spacesuit,
t a simple blue jumper.

e breathing-prototype floated before her chin, and a second
mponent hovered next to her shoulder, generating a full-body
ce field.

Planetarian flailed in zero-g for a moment. Damn spacesuit!
Before he could gain control, Martine kicked him in the face.

He spun backward, crashing against the bureau. Looked up to see
Martine leaping off the corners of the room like a rubber ball.

"What—" he began. But she caromed off the wall, grinning, and
slammed a chair into his stomach.

He shook his head, dazed. Whatever she was up to, he couldn't
beat her with speed. With no spacesuit, she was much faster than
he was.

So this time, he just let her come. Then he held up both bulky
arms and let her bounce off.

She cried out in surprise, the voice traveling through his 'ceiver.
She tumbled backward, dropping a handheld tracking device.

The device tumbled up past him. Planetarian caught sight of a
single word on its screen: GOATSKIN.

Too late, he realized he'd let the tracker distract him for a crucial
second. Stupid, he thought. Too used to solving mysteries!

Martine aimed a blaster at him and fired. Planetarian twisted
away, but the tight beam punched a hole through his suit
and shoulder.

He cried out in pain. And then, even worse, he heard a telltale hiss.
His air was seeping away.

"Wh—" he gasped. "Why?" The suit's temp was already dropping.
His air would be gone, he knew, in minutes.

Martine smiled again. When she spoke now, there was something
strange about her words. Something not quite human.

"It's a shame," she said. "Two old men who used to be
friends. Now they can't stand each other. When one got in the
other's way…"

She gestured at Planetarian as he clutched his leaking shoulder-
joint. "…the consequences were tragic."

Now he understood. Martine planned to frame them for each
other's murder.

It wouldn't quite ring true to investigators, he knew. But there
would be no better explanation. So the case would be closed.

Only one chance, the Planetarian thought, hating the idea. Deuce.
He reached for his old EGOs omniceiver.

He winced at the pain in his shoulder, trying to keep his
movements quiet. But Martine just laughed.

"I already took care of him," she said. She made a mock-kissing
motion. "He's even more of a little man-child than you."

The suit was growing cold now. "You still haven't…told me," he
gasped. "Why did you do this?"

Martine held out a long arm and spun around. Then she gestured,
dramatically, at the wall-holo: LONG LIVE THE PRIMATE ORDER.

"Your age is long past," she said, her voice gravelly now. "There
are forces out there in the Galaxy that you can't even imagine.

"Forces that have evolved a complex structure, yet are very
simple too. Threats that could crush your old EGOs with barely
a thought.

"Of course, that isn't even necessary. Everyone knows your team
couldn't stand each other by the end."

Martine gestured at the wincing, writhing Planetarian. "Soon the
EGOs will just be a sad, sad memory."

She smiled, indicating the floating life-support prototypes. "And
we will have a device that could revolutionize space travel."

An alarm sounded in Planetarian's ear. His air was down to 15%.
Damn, he thought. Damn spacesuit!

Keep her talking, he thought. "G...goatskin?" he asked.

She laughed. "Yeah, would you believe it?" She gestured at the floating prototypes. "They used it to solve certain conductivity probl—"

Suddenly she stopped speaking. Shivering, Planetarian looked up to see:

Deuce had Martine in a headlock. They struggled and grunted, tumbling in the free space of the damaged stateroom.

Another alarm chimed in Planetarian's ear: Air down to 10%. The suit felt cold, like an open grave.

It would have to be now. "Hold her," he said, and launched himself toward Deuce and Martine.

Deuce twisted around, turning Martine to face the Planetarian's charge. She tried to raise her blaster.

Planetarian reached out with his big hands, and Martine flinched. But he wasn't reaching for her.

He grabbed hold of the life-support prototypes, one with each hand, and wrenched them away from her body.

Martine's force field winked off. The air-bubble around her dissolved. She screamed and spasmed, ice crystals already forming on her mouth.

As the Planetarian hurled her body away, a disturbing phrase recurred in his mind: *conquest-worthy or expendable*.

Deuce grabbed his shoulder. "Start it up!" Deuce said. "Quick!"

Planetarian nodded. He pressed the chin-prototype's red light and an air bubble started to form around him.

Deuce activated the second prototype. Immediately Planetarian felt a warm, blanketing force field reach out to engulf him.

He shrugged out of his damaged spacesuit, tossing it away. A final alarm rang out: Air at 0%.

Planetarian looked around, amazed. The prototype was working. He was encased in a fully protective life-support field.

"Peanut," Deuce said, his voice shaking. "Look at that!" Planetarian turned, irritated at the nickname—

—then stopped at the sight confronting him.

LONG LIVE THE
PRIMATE ORDER

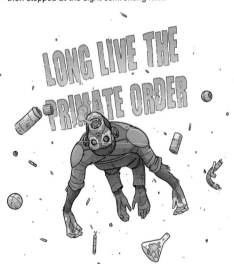

Martine's body was frozen. She still wore the jumpsuit, and ice had formed on her eyes and nostrils.

But she was no longer human. Her jaw had elongated, her face was covered with fur. She looked like an ape.

As the Planetarian watched, the Martine-ape's body floated past the words on the wall: LONG LIVE THE PRIMATE ORDER.

Deuce stared at her for a long moment. Finally he said, "Her films sounded pretentious."

Planetarian gestured at the words PRIMATE ORDER. "You ever hear of that?" he asked. Deuce just shrugged.

"Someday maybe we'll know." The Planetarian frowned. "She sa she'd killed you."

Deuce smiled again, that cocky smile that made you want to hit him. "Almost. But I planted a suggestion in her mind. Distracted her."

Despite himself, Planetarian was impressed. "You've been practicing."

"I've grown, I guess. A little, anyway." Deuce turned away, as if t hide some emotion on his face.

"Well." Planetarian grimaced and held out a remarkably non-spacesuited hand. "Thanks. For saving my life, I mean."

Deuce clasped his hand. Then held onto it for too long. Planetaria felt a sinking feeling inside.

"I'm not using my power," Deuce said, leaning in intensely. "But want you to listen to me for a minute."

Deuce gestured at the PRIMATE ORDER holo again. "Martine, whoever-whatever she was, was right about one thing:

"There *are* dangerous forces out there. Forces that have to be stopped. The galaxy needs the EGOs, Viggo. Now more than ever.

The Planetarian stared into his erstwhile companion's eyes and took a deep breath. Then he chose his words with care.

"Deuce," he said, "I'm grateful to you. Without you, that frozen corpse floating around this room might be me.

"But you and I were together for less than an hour and look wha happened. *Before* the attack of the ape-lady, I mean.

"All the old conflicts got dredged up. The stress, the competition. All the crap that broke up the team in the first place.

"The EGOs are in the past, man. Leave 'em there. That's where they belong."

When the Planetarian looked up, Deuce was staring at him. Slowly, gravely, Deuce nodded.

Planetarian clapped him on the back. "Take care, man. Best to Miri." He turned and started to leave.

Deuce's voice came over his 'ceiver, strong but sad. "You too. Peanut."

As he climbed inside the hatch of his one-man spacer, Planetari was overcome by a brief, strong sensation of regret.

As if he'd failed some final test. Missed his final chance to connect…with *something*, though he couldn't say what.

Then he felt a strange itching on his face. He reached up to scratch it, and noticed the breathing device still floating before him.

"No way," he said aloud, scratching the red bumps sprouting on his chin. "This thing *really* has goatskin in it?"

It was going to be a long, itchy trip back to Earth.

THE END

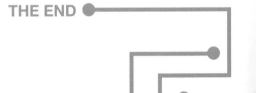

BURRITOS, DYSTOPIA, AND THE UNBROKEN CONTINUITY

A Conversation with the EGOs Creators

Originally Presented in EGOs #1-2

ello dear friends, and thank you for purchasing this fine picto-fiction book! My name is Stuart Moore, writer and o-creator of EGOs, and for this page I thought it would be a good idea to invite Gus Storms, artist and co-cre-tor, out to my local bar (Abilene, in Carroll Gardens, Brooklyn) and record the results. Will we discuss weighty atters of science, fiction, and culture, or just spill Sixpoint Bengali Tiger on ourselves? Let's find out!

GM: Okay, we're gonna start by introducing ourselves. ve been a writer and editor in the comics field and the ook industry for quite a while. My recent works are ostly prose: I've done a couple of stories for the launch Amazon's Kindle Worlds, set in the Valiant Entertainment niverse. I've also written the Marvel novel version of *Civil Var*, their big event project from a few years ago, and I o-wrote *The Art of Iron Man 3* and *The Art of Thor: The ark World*. I've recently finished up a comic book series alled *THE 99*, an international super hero team, and I've one a lot of comics for Marvel and DC, most recently *Web f Spider-Man*. I'm currently editing the Marvel novels n a freelance basis, I have a graphic novel coming from ark Horse called *Mandala*, and I'm working on a big new oject called *The Zodiac Legacy* with Disney and none ther than Stan Lee.

o what about you, Gus? Where did you come from? hat's your story?

S: I have no considerable pedigree. I haven't done uch. I'm moderately untested. I am fresh out of the gate. raduated from SVA, the School of Visual Arts, in fabulous ew York City about a year ago, and was graciously picked by Stuart to work on the project we're talking about day. Other than that, I have my own baby, my own series, lled Space Creep, that I'm also invested in. And then I'm orking on a—thank you.

aiter: Decent? Good?

S: Excellent.

GM: That was a burrito review.

S: Yeah. Burrito review. I'm working on a series for the u Tang Clan, or Ghostface Killah more specifically, that is companying his new concept album, *Twelve Reasons to e*. That's a six-issue miniseries.

GM: That sounds pretty wild.

S: Yeah. It's a surreal gangsta/gangster epic of betrayal d someone fused into twelve magical records. So what's t to like?

GM: And I should mention: The way we met was, you ere taking a class from my friend Marie Javins who's o my business partner—

S: Yeah! The great, charismatic Marie Javins.

GM: —and she's handling production work on this ok as well. She said to me, You've got to see this guy's rk. And she's usually right.

GS: She's a generous, sparkling human being. I'm infinitely full of gratitude to her.

SGM: She's currently down in Mexico City having stomach problems, so –t hope you feel better by the time this seesprint, Marie.

GS: Don't drink the water, Marie!

SGM: Don't do that.

Okay. Hopefully if you're reading this, you're at the end of the book and you've probably read it. If you haven't read it, there may be

SPOILERS

But we want to talk just a little bit about where this project started because it's very close to my heart. I've done creator-owned books before; I've had various projects that have come out and others that have languished in development. This one came about last year when I decided I wanted to just write something, something fresh, and figure out what to do with it later. I kept the initial storyline short, because I wanted something that could feasibly be drawn in a reasonable amount of time and for a reasonable amount of money. I took pieces from various notebooks and ideas I'd had before, but once I got into it I basically had three goals.

One of them was to write a big, colorful comic book with lots of characters, like the ones I enjoyed as a kid—but with real, complex human characters at the heart of it. And the way that developed, as hopefully you've seen, is that it's really all about a marriage—a longtime marriage between two characters who both have severe personal character flaws, but who love each other nonetheless. That means they have a bond that'll never go away, but it doesn't necessarily mean that they'll stay together.

The second thing I wanted to do was, in the writing, to see how many concepts—science fiction concepts in particular—and characters I could throw out, as quickly as possible, without making the book seem crowded, without risking losing the reader. And that's where having you on board, Gus, has really helped, because your storytelling is very precise and clear. I think in the wrong hands this could have turned into a bit of a muddle.

GS: Well, storytelling-wise, I prize clarity above experimentation. I envy my comrades-in-arms who are a little more esoteric in their storytelling, but I like the classical mode of just making everything clear, walking people through it, holding them by the hand as much as possible.

SGM: Well, it *is* clear, but it's also dynamic. And the third thing I wanted to do was to craft a first issue in particular, the very first chapter of the book that you hopefully have in your sweaty hands or you can page back through it on your iPad –

Some early character sketches, starting with The Planetarian.

GS: – in your grimy little mitts.

SGM: Grimy little mitts! I wanted a first issue with a real twist at the end. Something that threw the main character into full focus, and hopefully made the reader step back and rethink what she'd just read. And in that, I was somewhat inspired by the first issue of the Vertigo title *Scalped*, written by Jason Aarons. *Scalped* introduces you to a character and walks you through a day in his life, and he seems to be one thing but at the end of the first issue you learn he's something different. The twist in EGOs is of a completely different type, but structurally that was what I was trying for.

So then I handed the whole mess over to you, and you had to suddenly do a zillion character designs and figure out what an entire future universe was going to look like. How

did you approach that?

GS: Well, my general inclination is dystopia—just nasty, disgusting putrescent Western stuff. This project I wanted to be a little more streamlined: It's the corruption behind the scenes that's more important, but everything should b glistening and shiny. And I made it as glistening and shiny as I'm capable of. So that was the general conceit.

There are two primary teams of characters. One is just briefly referenced: the early, original team. They were a little more classic and had less frills. And then the new team is much stranger.

SGM: And that combination works really well because what I wanted was to evoke an old-fashioned, shiny future but in a more complex, textured sort of way.

GS: As one of the stylistic references, one of the old… what was it, Legion of Heroes?

SGM: *Legion of Superheroes*. Nobody reading this is going to believe you don't know that name.

GS: Well, I don't have quite the same comics reading history that a lot of more credible comics artists do. I didn't grow up reading comics or anything. I just liked the medium so much.

SGM: I didn't know that.

GS: Yeah, it's always weird to people that I decided to do this. I just like drawing and writing a lot, so it's a good fit. But other than a few of the notable '80s-'90s Vertigo titles I was unaware of it all until I got into comic book school.

But I like that, where everything is hyper-colored and they have like weird bubble-attacks and stuff. You can see it in the first-issue battle scenes, with all the clones…

SGM: The flashback scene.

GS: …where everybody has a weird zappy power and they're all flashing at each other. I would have even liked more time for that. That was fun.

SGM: That could have been a whole issue on its own, absolutely. That was part of the complexity, part of trying to make the story work in a smallish space. Which I sort of love, too, because…I think there's a trend in modern storytelling…there are several countervailing trends too, but one trend I like is to not waste time. A lot of the TV shows I really like nowadays—I'm just rewatching *Battlestar Galactica*, but even in shows like *Mad Men* or *The Sopranos*, things move along very quickly for the mo part. If there's a bit of interpersonal dynamic that you do need to see, it tends to wind up on the cutting room floor like that sort of streamlined approach to storytelling.

GS: Sure. But those are also pretty languid…they stretc out over a million seasons.

GM: They can be.

S: But yeah, I like concision. That's the name of the [ga]me, right? Trying to deliver as much product in the very [li]mited amount of time that comics have.

GM: You almost have to. No matter what, you never [ha]ve enough pages.

S: Absolutely. I know from my own endeavors in writing, [it'] s impossible. I'm the most attenuated human being…I [en]vy people who can write little short gems of stories. I [ha]ve no skill in that. I need to get better at that.

GM: I don't naturally think that way either. Yes, writing [sh]ort is harder. I think I've done enough comics work that, [wh]en I sit down to write something, I now have almost a [co]untdown clock in my head starting with 22 pages, or 20 [pa]ges. I've talked to writers who overwrite and cut a lot…

S: You have to.

GM: No, I very rarely do that. I have notes…I wind up [sk]ipping scenes. But once I'm into it, I pretty much write to [it]. And I revise after that, of course, I make changes. I'm a [ve]ry structurally inclined writer. I use a pretty tight outline [for] the most part, and I work things out very carefully. [Th]at's good in some ways…it keeps me from going [as]tray, especially when you're dealing with a very confined [am]ount of space. But I'm trying to loosen up a bit. I'd [lik]e to get a little more spontaneous with some of [the] characters…I'd like the characters to lead me a [littl]e more.

[I tr]ied to do that with Deuce and Pixel, in this story. I didn't [wo]rk out very rigorously where we were going to leave [the]m at the end of the first storyline, in chapter 3.

S: And it did remold itself a little bit. Particularly, I think [the] third episode was a little more up in the air, and we did some back and forth on that.

SGM: I just threw a lot of characters into the story and some of them—in fact, a lot of them—were intended to be real throwaways. If you look at the end of the first issue, you can kind of see where that was going. But once you started doing character designs—and you sent me quite a few, in a small period of time—there were some of them I just loved. I couldn't treat them as expendable.

You said there were two teams, but actually there are more than that, the way it evolved. And I sort of moved some characters—let's just say obliquely that I moved some of them from a team with a small chance of survival to a team with a slightly greater chance of survival. Or I had some of them survive where they wouldn't have, before. And that's completely down to the designs and what you did with them.

I suck at powers. I'm terrible at super powers. I think if you really look at the original team too closely, like half of them have telepathic powers.

GS: Non-drawable powers, yeah. You like objects that are fundamentally impossible to draw. (laughter) I meet up with some comics artists and draw every two weeks, telling them about…Masse, for instance, is the primary villain. That was Stuart's brilliant idea, but I collaborated on that guy more than most of the characters. And he's a really compelling villain: He's a sentient galaxy, which is a logistical nightmare. How do you have people fighting a galaxy? Comics is full of concessions.

SGM: Yes!

GS: It always is, so he has to be this small galaxy… and he has some notable size shifts. He has to be fighting people who are nothing near planet-sized.

SGM: Yeah, I knew the scale would have to be fudged.

The many possible looks of the evil Repliqa.

GS: And nobody cares.

SGM: And to me, that's part of the fun of comics. You do have elements in there that are just big and implausible, actually impossible in a lot of ways, but you go along with it because it's fun and it's visual. It's a good medium for that because the reader can interpret things like scale a little more freely than he can in film, I think. In film you're a little more locked into the way objects actually interrelate.

GS: Yeah. Part of it is the unbroken continuity: In film, you're always seeing the same image. In comics, you're jumping from page to page—the frames are all different. And the reader is much more generous with concessions about draftsmanship—artists have different styles and a lot of people are way more idiosyncratic than me in their artwork. And you accept everything, because it's all of a piece.

SGM: As long as it all hangs together, which your work does. Your buildings look constructed, your people look like they can move…that sounds like faint praise, but it's not.

GS: I'll take what I can get. (laughter)

SGM: I shouldn't admit this, but I didn't plan out very well what shape the EGOs team would take once it sifted out, once it settled down, which basically happens toward the end of the second chapter and into the third. And through serendipity, or happenstance I guess, we wound up with a pretty good team.

GS: I love the team, yeah.

SGM: It's all part of a universe. I'm obviously a science fiction buff, and a lot of my original comics projects have been science fiction. When you're writing a project like this, which involves people shooting force bolts out of their hands, there's a balance between plausibility and spectacle. But I did try to make it as plausible as possible. I wanted it to feel like it could be taking place within a real science fiction universe. And I know you approached it the same way. You had some ideas about Masse pretty early on, about how he would function and how that played into his motivations.

GS: Yeah, the conceit of Masse—I always thought that he's a galaxy and what functions as his neurons are stars, in the same complexity and density as our neurological makeup. He has planetary systems, solar systems, within himself. But he's ancient, he's utterly alien, and **[SPOILER CENSORED]**. I'm a fan of the old Vampire the Masquerade role-playing game…in that world, there are the antediluvians who have just lived so long that they're completely alien and their ennui is unimaginable. You always wonder what any sort of sentient will look like after…whenever we think about human longevity, we think maybe 200 years in the future, right? And even that, I don't know what that would do to a human brain. In some of my own stuff, I'm very interested in this idea: When longevity becomes a reality, what happens to the brain? How does the brain cope with that unnaturality? I like the thought of these ancient minds that are alien and insane.

SGM: I'm also reading now *Physics of the Future*, the latest book by Michio Kaku. He wrote a book called *Hyperspace*—

GS: Very familiar with Michio Kaku, yes.

SGM: This latest book is just basically about scientific advances in all different fields. Where we stand now, where we're going to stand by mid-century, and where we're gonna stand by the end of the century. And he talks a lot about artificial intelligence, which has been a bit of a dead end. It's been the big promise ever since the early '80s at least. And the problem is that the human brain is *so* complex—

GS: And relatively unknown.

SGM: It is unknown, but a lot of the problem is just the sheer number of synapses and neurons and the multiple ways in which they interconnect. He also talks about life extension, and it sounds like we're gonna get *that* sooner—

GS: Oh yeah. That's way more quotidian. I love watching formal debates between Kurzweil and whoever. Although Kurzweil is arguably a hack—

SGM: He is over the top.

GS: I have some friends in the longevity scene, and maybe he's not totally loved in there.

SGM: Oh, the singularity stuff is…it's like sleight of hand. I don't quite believe in it.

GS: But that argument is…artificial intelligence…just thinking of the epistemology of knowing what a chair is and all the interrelations of knowing the symbology of, like the semiotics of "chair," a throne vs. a toilet, all of these things. I don't know how they're ever going to be able to place the ontological perception of a "chair" in a computer.

SGM: In a way, it's the same problem as the concept of teleportation, where you would have to disassemble something and reassemble it in such precise detail. And fact, I don't know if I did this on purpose, but I think I left teleportation out of EGOs completely.

GS: It's tough.

SGM: And I tend to do that. First of all, it's an odd device. It was used well in *Star Trek*, and they had very strict rules on it: It could only be short-range, and you had to be in contact. But as a concept, it's one of those odd ones and I think mostly because of Star Trek, people assume it's plausible. But it's—

GS: It's crazy.

GM: It's crazy. It's way off. Hyperspace you have accept…

S: I've been meaning to ask you. I'm sure we're off pic here—

GM: That's fine. We can be off topic.

S: I'm also a science fiction buff, always, forever. And hink in creating a world, which I've been dealing with tely, the first question one has to ask oneself is: Are you ing to do a plausible model, which is done more and ore often with some of the hard-science-fiction/space-era authors? Is it going to be colony ships?

GM: You mean slower than light?

S: Yeah, yeah. Or almost faster than light travel, but nerations to get to a habitable planet. And then that's e using Mars as a refueling station, and you colonize anets on your way, and grow fuel there. So that's an tremely important question, which we haven't really ked about with EGOs. Oh, sorry, there is! There is like an tra-space that people go through…

GM: Yes, there is. There's a hyperspace. And in fact, ara, the one character who we haven't talked about—e might be my favorite. I love the goggles outfit you gave r. She's like a little junior aviator.

S: Sure, that's the steampunk thing.

GM: And she's a bit of our identification character, sort She plays a smallish role in the first storyline, but she's Peggy Olsen from *Mad Men*, she's the newcomer just ning the group. But she has access to more other-acial dimensions than the others do. And that, again—r code name eventually will be n-Brane, which is a smological concept that I barely understand. It's related string theory and has to do with different continua.

S: It's nonsense.

GM: Well, I don't think it's nonsense, I just think I'm too pid to understand it. (laughter)

S: But it's also like essentially poetry.

GM: Yeah, that's what I like about it. Warren Ellis said nething like that once, he said he was attracted to ence largely when it sounded like poetry.

S: Yeah.

GM: But to get back to what you were saying ore: Conceptually, with EGOs, I started from a fairly nventional colonized-galaxy, galactic empire or galactic eration type of backdrop. Which requires you to make kinds of assumptions, some of which are plausible d some of which aren't. There's no particular reason to ieve that a galactic confederation, even one that has ter than light travel, would behave very much like the Roman Empire or anything like that. But we start from that point, we play with it, we work out the implications as well as we can, and we tell the kinds of stories we want to tell.

GS: And of all the things that are implausible about science fiction, I feel like the probability of our government continuing…we haven't developed that much new stuff. We haven't developed many systems of government, really.

SGM: That's true.

GS: There's a lot of little names, but they all boil down to maybe three precepts, and generally two parties no matter what system you're in. There's always the optimists and the populists, the populari.

SGM: We could use a few more populari in this country, right now.

GS: Sure, well, you could always use more populari. The question is the genuity of the populari. They're very rarely doing it for anything but their own political gain. So I would be interested to see what the next…we haven't had a new [political system] since Communism. So what the next one would be, if there was another one, I can't imagine.

SGM: I have another project I'm developing, where the starting point was a ruthlessly libertarian future imposed by outside forces, and where that would go. What kind of rebellions that would lead to further on. That's very different from this project, because in that case I started with an idea—well, I started with an image, but then I added a political framework to the backdrop. In *this* case, with EGOs, I wasn't trying to break the mold in terms of the setup. What I wanted was a good backdrop, where we could tell the kind of character stories and adventure stories we wanted to tell.

GS: And it's more of a romp.

SGM: Yeah. I hope it's a romp that makes people cringe once in a while, because that's kind of what I was going for.

Freestyle
Espero
Receptra
The original team

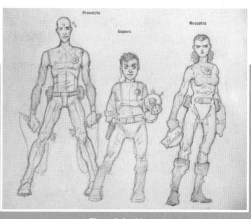

GS: Can we talk about the future of EGOs…just kind of… spitball? Is that a thing?

SGM: Yeah. We're gonna "spitball."

GS: So the first storyline is a three-issue series. It's modest in its actual amount of issues, although not in its scope. But then we've been talking…it's sort of loose right now, but about the continuation. The big question is which characters…I want to see more history. There's a lot of rich characters. I want to see characters from the old team, but I also want to see what the Opener does in his everyday life. You can get a little more banal…what is that character about? What does he go home and do?

SGM: That's funny, I think I made a note about that just the other day. I have an idea in mind for a second storyline, which would probably run about five issues. but before that I think we might do a single issue, just sort of catching up on these characters, focusing on them, giving us a little more insight into what they're about, as you say. [UPDATE: THAT FOURTH ISSUE IS CHAPTER 4 OF THIS VERY BOOK, AND THERE WILL INDEED BE A SECOND, FIVE-PART STORYLINE.]

We're doing some stuff with the Fear in issues #2 and 3 that could continue. The Deuce and Pixel relationship will remain central.

There's a mention in the first issue of something called the Crunch War, which was basically that generation's World War II—it was the big thing that almost tore the galaxy apart. It had a lot of different implications—it had cosmological implications, it had character implications. In the second big storyline, we'll see a planet that's still suffering from fallout from the War.

GS: That's a good idea.

SGM: And that will involve another member of the original team.

GS: Maybe just cameos.

SGM: Well, there are cameos. If you look very carefully at issue #1, there's one page where everyone's watching the announcement of the new team on video, and one of those panels has two members of the original team that we don't identify by name.

GS: Oh yeah. I love that couple.

SGM: I love them too! I want to see more of them. I don't have plans for them yet, because as far as I'm concerned, they're just a couple sitting at home being slightly bitter about their younger years. But that could turn into something.

GS: We can talk about more…basic day in the life stuff, toned-down action, not on a huge galactic scope.

SGM: Well one thing I hope is, if the project is successful—and this tends to be the way books go if they're planned to run for a while—the initial story tends to be a little more packed because you're trying o draw people in, you're trying to show them what you're about. And then after that you get a little more chance to spread out.

GS: It's sort of like the extrapolation from the first issue. the first issue has to be all of these things, super-dense. The first issue is the most complicated thing in the world where you have to pull someone in, there has to be the right amount of action. There needs to be somewhat of a cold open, but you want all the right characters, and you pack in history and world-building.

SGM: Yeah. And obviously, readers will have to judge fo themselves, but I was encouraged by the fact that, when I sat down to write this book, the first issue script flowed out pretty fast. That's usually a good sign for me.

GS: Oh yeah. Ditto. That is the apotheosis. Why else are you doing it if not for that time when everything is movin through you, as opposed to you struggling?

SGM: Well, that's probably enough self-congratulation for now.

GS: See you in the pages!

opener

The Opener